The life of Beethoven

Musical lives

The books in this series will each provide an account of the life of a major composer, considering both the private and the public figure. The main thread will be biographical, and discussion of the music will be integral to the narrative. Each book thus presents an organic view of the composer, the music, and the circumstances in which the music was written.

Published titles

The life of Bellini JOHN ROSSELLI
The life of Beethoven DAVID WYN JONES
The life of Berlioz PETER BLOOM
The life of Debussy ROGER NICHOLS
The life of Mahler PETER FRANKLIN
The life of Mozart JOHN ROSSELLI
The life of Webern KATHRYN BAILEY

The life of Beethoven

DAVID WYN JONES

PUBLISHED BY THE PRESS SYNDICATE OF THE UNIVERSITY OF CAMBRIDGE
The Pitt Building, Trumpington Street, Cambridge CB2 1RP, United Kingdom

CAMBRIDGE UNIVERSITY PRESS
The Edinburgh Building, Cambridge, CB2 2RU, United Kingdom
40 West 20th Street, New York, NY 10011-4211, USA
10 Stamford Road, Oakleigh, Melbourne 3166, Australia

First published 1998

Printed in the United Kingdom at the University Press, Cambridge

Typeset in FF Quadraat 9.75/14 pt, in QuarkXPress™ [SE]

A catalogue record for this book is available from the British Library

Library of Congress cataloguing in publication data

Wyn Jones, David.
    The life of Beethoven / by David Wyn Jones.
        p.   cm. – (Musical lives)
    Includes bibliographical references and index.
    ISBN 0 521 56019 5 (hardback). – ISBN 0 521 56878 1 (paperback)
    1. Beethoven, Ludwig van, 1770–1827. 2. Composers – Austria –
Biography. I. Title. II. Series.
    ML410.B4W97   1998
    780'.92–dc21   98–3638   CIP
    [b]

ISBN 0 521 56019 5 hardback
ISBN 0 521 56878 1 paperback

To my daughter, Yolande

CONTENTS

List of illustrations x

Preface xi

1 The young courtier 1

2 A new career in Vienna 28

3 Cursing his creator and his existence 55

4 Drama and symphony 74

5 Patrons and patriotism 102

6 Empires of the mind 125

7 Towards a public comeback 144

8 Facing death 171

Notes 184

Annotated bibliography 191

Index 194

ILLUSTRATIONS

1 Christian Gottlob Neefe 9
2 Elector Maximilian Franz 15
3 First page of piano part of op. 1 no. 1 (1795) 43
4 Draft of aborted symphony in C major (1795–6); from 'Kafka' sketchbook 52
5 Engraving of Beethoven (c. 1801) (Johann Joseph Neidl) 53
6 Part of the Heiligenstadt Testament (1802) 66
7 The Theater an der Wien 71
8 Prince Lobkowitz 81
9 The Malfatti family 113
10 Engraving of Beethoven (1814) (Höfel) 121
11 Steiner's music shop in the Paternostergassel 134
12 Archduke Rudolph 145
13 Opening bars of Missa Solemnis from the autograph score (1821–4) 154
14 Drawing of Beethoven by Stephan Decker (1824) 163
15 Invitation card to Beethoven's funeral (1827) 182

Illustrations are taken from the following sources: Beethoven-Haus, Bonn (1 and 7); British Library, London (4); Gesellschaft der Musikfreunde, Vienna (3); Historisches Museum der Stadt Wien, Vienna (11, 12 and 14); Österreichische Nationalbibliothek, Vienna (5); Staats- und Universitätsbibliothek, Hamburg (6); Staatsbibliothek zu Berlin-Preussischer Kulturbesitz, Berlin (13); private possession (2, 8, 9, 10 and 15).

Beethoven has always been celebrated as one of the major creative figures in Western civilization. Even in his own lifetime he was regarded as someone who stood apart from the norm, while the nineteenth and twentieth centuries were to nurture this individuality to the point of deification. Artistic deification can so easily lead to petrifaction, and Beethoven is an instance of someone who has become detached from his original surroundings. While it is readily acknowledged that composers such as Handel, Verdi and Mahler engaged creatively with the musical environment of their time, there is an unchallenged reluctance to accept that Beethoven's career was conditioned in a similar way. Perhaps to a greater extent than is the case with any other composer, his life and output have been considered in isolation. The circumstances in which he lived, the influence of musical practices of the time, and his relationship with other musicians have tended to be undervalued or ignored in order to perpetuate the image of the composer as a single-minded artist.

This biography appears as part of a series entitled 'Musical lives', and it attempts to do just that: trace Beethoven's life as a working musician in Bonn and Vienna at the end of the eighteenth and the beginning of the nineteenth century. Accordingly this account places less reliance on the rich anecdotal heritage associated with the composer in favour of primary and contemporary documentation. With this emphasis on the context in which the composer lived and worked it is hoped that Beethoven emerges as a more varied musical personality than posterity has often allowed him to be and with his individuality enhanced rather than circumscribed.

Many people have helped in the preparation of this volume and it is a pleasure to acknowledge them: Malcolm Boyd for his careful reading of the proofs; Gill Jones and her colleagues in the Music Library of the University of Wales, Cardiff for being unfailingly helpful in tracking down material and only slightly less amenable when I failed to return it on time; Angela Lester, who helped me disentangle some of the more tortuous passages of early nineteenth-century German prose; and Else Radant Landon for reading the manuscript and correcting many facts and misapprehensions about Vienna in Beethoven's time. Above all my wife, Ann, and daughter, Yolande, must be thanked for their understanding and support.

1 The young courtier

For thirty-four years, from the age of twenty-two until his death in 1827, Beethoven lived and worked in Vienna, a city that determined his artistic development. But he had been born in Bonn and maintained a real affection for the Rhineland, its people and his upbringing there. Letters to old friends and acquaintances from the Bonn period, such as Nicolaus Simrock the music publisher and Franz Gerhard Wegeler the physician, are unfailingly warm, occasionally nostalgic, even sentimental. In June 1801 he wrote to Wegeler:

> you are still the faithful, kind and loyal friend – But you must never think that I could ever forget yourself and all of you who were once so dear and precious to me. There are moments when I myself long for you and, what is more, would like to spend some time with you. For my fatherland, the beautiful country where I first opened my eyes to the light, still seems to me as lovely and as clearly before my eyes as it was when I left you. In short, the day on which I can meet you again and greet our Father Rhine I shall regard as one of the happiest of my life.[1]

That day was never to come, an unrealized desire that served only to intensify Beethoven's attachment: the more he grumbled about life in Vienna, the more sentimental he became about Bonn. Yet, this was not mere escapism, for it was founded on a memory of a musical world that had virtually disappeared, one that Beethoven would have been entirely happy to have joined.

Bonn was the capital of the electorate of Cologne and the seat of its archbishop. Along with a dozen or so other ecclesiastical principalities in the Holy Roman Empire, such as Bamberg, Basel, Mainz, Salzburg, Trier and Würzburg, Cologne exercised firm governmental control over its territory, though continuity and development were compromised because its ruling power was not hereditary. Each ruler had to be elected by an ecclesiastical chapter. While the Pope had some influence, elections were usually highly political with competing German states, even the foreign governments of Britain, France and Holland, taking an active interest. The geographical position of the electorate of Cologne made it especially susceptible to outside influence. The main part of the principality stretched along the west bank of the Rhine for some forty miles north of Cologne and twenty miles south of the city; there was a further parcel of land fifty miles to the east, running north of the town of Siegen towards the Rothaar mountains. Much of the revenue of the principality derived from its position on the ancient trading route along the Rhine, the gateway to Holland and the sea. A hundred miles to the south-west lay France, and sandwiched between the two was the Austrian Netherlands, part of the Habsburg monarchy. Increasingly during the course of the eighteenth century Cologne attracted the interest of Prussia which, as always, was anxious to limit the influence of the Habsburg dynasty.

For these reasons the political allegiances of the electorate of Cologne changed frequently in the seventeenth and eighteenth centuries. At the end of the seventeenth century Louis XIV's France exerted control and influence, and in the early decades of the eighteenth century members of the Bavarian ruling family were successively elected to the archbishopric. When the most munificent of these Bavarian rulers, Clemens August, died in 1761 the archbishopric passed, unusually, to a local person, the dean of Cologne cathedral, Maximilian Friedrich.

It was in the interest of none of these various competing powers that the social and economic life of the electorate be allowed to decay. As a result Bonn, together with Augsburg and Salzburg, emerged as one of the leading small cities in the Holy Roman Empire. There was no real division between the city and the court; without the court there would have been no town. By 1790 the population of Bonn was to reach nearly 11,000, many of whom were connected in some way with the court, as architects, administrators, bodyguards, chaplains, clerks, cooks, hunting masters, maids, musicians, painters, servants and so on. The town had a weekly newspaper, the *Bonner Intelligenzblatter*, dominated by court news, and its citizens had the chance of winning the electoral lottery.

Music played an important part in court life. The typical eighteenth-century division of music into three areas, church, theatre and chamber (that is, instrumental), was found here, and each was well represented. The private church was contained within the palace walls, as was a concert room and a theatre that seated 100 guests. The court musicians worked in all three venues, their number supplemented in church services and concerts by local people, and in the theatre by visiting troupes of actors and musicians. In 1773 the regular musical personnel of the Bonn court consisted of a Kapellmeister (Beethoven's grandfather, also Ludwig van Beethoven), seven singers (including Beethoven's father, Johann van Beethoven), two organists, seven violinists, two violists, two cellists, a double bass player and an organ blower. Grandfather Ludwig died on Christmas Eve 1773 at the age of sixty-one. Over the next decade the musical forces of the court were rejuvenated and expanded in number, from twenty-five to forty-one, a substantial complement of musicians, equal to all but the most extravagant of German courts, such as Mannheim and Stuttgart, and larger than many, including Haydn's Esterházy court and Mozart's Salzburg court. Ludwig van Beethoven's successor was Andreas Lucchesi, born in the Venetian territories and noted as an organist; at Bonn his composing interests shifted from opera to church music.

Of the two generations of the Beethoven family that had served the electoral court, Ludwig van Beethoven (1712–73) and his son Johann van Beethoven (1739/4–92), the former had the more distinguished career. He joined the court in 1733 as a singer, before working himself up to be a worthy and conscientious Kapellmeister. It is likely that he composed church music for the court, though nothing has survived. Johann was his third child and joined the court at the age of twelve as a treble, later alto; after his voice broke he sang tenor, a post he held for over thirty years, albeit with more resignation than enthusiasm, supplementing his income with private teaching and some violin playing. Successive generations of musicians who devoted their lives to one court were not uncommon in the period and Ludwig and Johann naturally expected that a third-generation Beethoven, if musical, would continue the family tradition.

Johann van Beethoven had married Magdalena Keverich in 1767; it was her second marriage. Between 1769 and 1786 she gave birth to seven children (five boys and two girls), three of whom survived childhood, Ludwig van Beethoven, Caspar Anton Carl van Beethoven (1774–1815) and Nicolaus Johann van Beethoven (1776–1848).

Beethoven's precise birthdate is unclear. He was baptized on 17 December 1770 and since it was the custom to baptize children as soon as practicable after birth, typically the same day or the day afterwards, his birthdate was either 16 December or 17 December. In the baptism records the formal Latin 'Ludovicus' is used but there is ample evidence that the French form, Louis, was used in his childhood and youth, a habit that surfaces from time to time in his adult years too. French was a living second language in Bonn and Beethoven maintained a fluency throughout his life, if sometimes of a gear-crashing kind. His formal schooling probably began at the age of six or seven when he entered the town's Tirocinium where the basic curriculum seems to have consisted of reading, writing but no arithmetic. At the age of eleven boys had the options of entering the Gymnasium but Beethoven's formal education ended at the primary level. It is assumed that his father taught him the rudiments of music, the piano and perhaps a little violin, but Johann seems to have been relatively unambitious on behalf of his son. The contrast with the father–son relationship in the Mozart family could not be more striking. While Leopold Mozart devoted much of his adult life to raising the phenomenally gifted Mozart, acquainting him with the full range of musical styles in Europe through many journeys, Johann was contentedly parochial, accepting the fact that Bonn's musical life was all that his son needed for a career that was to ape his own or, if he was particularly fortunate, that of the grandfather. Apart from one journey to Holland at the age of eleven, Beethoven's musical experience as a boy was totally formed in Bonn and its environs.

On only one recorded occasion did Johann van Beethoven seek to display his son as a prodigy. On 26 March 1778 in a concert room on the Sternengasse in Cologne, he arranged a concert given by two of his pupils, 'Mademoiselle Averdonc, court alto, and his little son aged six'. Beethoven was actually just over seven in March 1778 but the mistake was probably genuine rather than deliberate. The father's confusion led to Ludwig, too, being confused about his age until 1810 when he first saw his baptism certificate.

Gradually Johann passed the musical education of his son to court colleagues, to local musicians in town and to visiting musicians. The court organist, Aegidius van den Eeden, gave him lessons in organ and figured bass, supplemented later by instruction from other Bonn organists, Willibald Koch from the Franciscan monastery, Hanzmann from the Minorite order and Zensen, the organist of the minster.

The musical repertoire at the court, in church services, concerts and opera, was a broad one. As always, church music tended to be the most conservative and traditional, in the sense that the daily repertoire was as likely to consist of music that was several decades old as it was to feature newly composed works. The court library held masses by respected Viennese composers from the first part of the century such as Antonio Caldara, Franz Tuma and Georg Reutter alongside modern compositions by Albrechtsberger, Joseph Haydn and Gassmann. In instrumental music Bonn had easy access to the torrent of publications coming from the commercial musical capital of Europe, Paris, and from the international firm of Hummel, based in Amsterdam and Berlin. Music by Mannheim composers such as

Eichner, Holzbauer and Johann Stamitz was available, as was music by Austrian composers such as Dittersdorf, Haydn and Vanhal, and by French composers such as Cambini and Gossec. This diversity of repertoire was an appropriate reflection of Bonn's geographical position on the Rhine: a major trading station with easy access to Paris and Amsterdam while still maintaining links with the old network of music distribution in southern Germany and Austria through manuscript copies.

A similar cosmopolitanism is evident in Bonn's operatic life during the composer's youth. Comic operas by leading Italian composers of the day, such as Galuppi and Piccinni, were given alongside regular performances of *opéras-comiques*. From the end of the 1770s Bonn participated in the new German trend of setting up companies devoted to German plays and opera (Singspiel). The director was Georg Friedrich Wilhelm Grossmann who assembled a company that performed at the court theatre during winter and toured elsewhere in the summer months. When it was resident at the court it used the electoral orchestra and, when necessary, the court singers too, including Johann van Beethoven. German translations of plays by Molière, Voltaire, Goldoni and Shakespeare were presented as well as the fervent plays of the new national tradition, the works of Lessing and Schiller. A similar mixture of translated and original works was evident in the operatic repertoire. German versions of Italian operas by Anfossi, Cimarosa and Salieri, and of French operas by Grétry, Monsigny and Philidor alternated with newer products of the German Singspiel movement, Holzbauer's *Günther von Schwarzburg* and, later, Mozart's *Die Entführung aus dem Serail*.

The vitality of musical life at the court spilled over into the town itself. Johann van Beethoven taught at the homes of minor aristocrats and court officials, tasks he passed over to Ludwig as the young boy became musically competent and socially assured. One of the most enthusiastic musical amateurs in the town was Johann Gottfried von Mastiaux. In his spacious house in the Fischergasse he had a music room large enough to accommodate up to two dozen performers; he and his five children played all manner of instruments, string, wind and keyboard. Mastiaux was an avid admirer of Haydn's music, amassing a virtually complete collection of the symphonies, almost certainly acquired directly from the composer.

Musical life in Bonn, therefore, was well organized, modern and vital. However, in comparison with larger centres, such as Hamburg, and certain courts such as Dresden and Mannheim, it lacked a commanding figure, a performer or composer who was of more than local significance, someone who could provoke the still dormant talent of the young Beethoven. That situation was rectified with the arrival of Christian Gottlob Neefe (1748–98).

Neefe had been born in Chemnitz in Saxony, a very different part of German-speaking Europe. He studied jurisprudence at the university in Leipzig and thrived in an intellectual society that included the musician Johann Adam Hiller, the philosopher Johann Jakob Engel, the engraver Johann Friedrich Bause and the painter Adam Friedrich Oeser. A widely read and cultured man, Neefe, like so many lawyers before and since, was increasingly drawn towards a career in music. Hiller nurtured his talents as a composer of German opera, works that were soon performed throughout the German states. In the summer of 1779 Neefe joined the theatre company in Bonn as its new music director, though still under the overall direction of Grossmann. Given that Neefe was a Protestant rather than a Catholic, a musician of national rather than local significance and a broadly educated man rather than a jobbing musician, Bonn was an unlikely place for him to settle; Leipzig or Hamburg would have been more conducive to his talents and upbringing. Two years after arriving he was offered the additional post of court organist on the death of van den Eeden. Neefe's combined income was now the same as that of Kapellmeister Lucchesi and he was rapidly establishing himself as the leading musical figure in Bonn. So what had probably been intended as a short stay turned out to be a permanent arrangement; Neefe was still in post when the electoral court was finally disbanded in 1794.

Neefe's own compositions included several German operas, such as *Adelheit von Veltheim*, performed by Grossmann's company in 1780. Dealing with an elopement from a Turkish harem, the opera was hugely successful and may have encouraged Grossmann and Neefe to stage performances of Mozart's harem opera, *Die Entführung aus dem Serail*, three years later. Neefe also composed numerous songs (including settings of twelve odes by Klopstock), keyboard sonatas and a keyboard concerto. While in Bonn he exploited his linguistic and literary talents, translating the texts of Italian and French operas into German, writing his autobiography, a biography of Grossmann's wife, some poetry and several contributions to music journals.

A generation younger than Johann van Beethoven, Neefe became Bonn's favourite teacher of keyboard instruments and music theory. It is not known when Ludwig's lessons with him began, but by 1782 the boy was acting as his assistant in church services, playing the organ, and, in the following years, began deputizing regularly as a continuo player in opera performances. In 1784 Beethoven's contribution to the musical life of the court was officially recognized when he became a salaried member of the retinue. Formal lessons and informal apprenticeship alike were unforgettably characterized by Neefe's commanding personality, and the impressionable teenager learnt as much from his teacher's general attitude to music and its role in society as he did about playing the organ and realizing figured bass. Beethoven sometimes complained that Neefe was too severe with him but a decade later he readily acknowledged his inspiring influence.

> I thank you for the advice you have very often given me about making progress in my divine art. Should I ever become a great man you too will have a share in my success.[2]

Neefe's teacher, Hiller, was a pupil, twice removed, of Johann Sebastian Bach and this pedagogic heritage made Beethoven the only member of the Viennese Classical School whose formative years were in any way influenced by the north German master. Bach's *Well-Tempered Clavier* was central to Neefe's teaching and Beethoven soon knew the music intimately: the beginning of a life-long admiration

C. G. NEEFE.

1   Christian Gottlob Neefe

for the composer. Neefe almost certainly would have encouraged Beethoven to explore the music of Bach's son Carl Philipp Emanuel. Even more important than this composer's music was his treatise on keyboard playing, *Essay on the True Art of Playing the Keyboard* (1753–62). Alongside authoritative paragraphs on the execution of ornaments and the realization of figured bass Bach provided many observations on the emotional commitment needed by a performer: 'A musician cannot move others unless he too is moved. He must of necessity feel all of the affects that he hopes to arouse in his audience, for the revealing of his own humour will stimulate a like humour in the listener', and elsewhere, 'Play from the soul, not like a trained bird.'³ Twenty years later one of Beethoven's most illustrious pupils, Carl Czerny, was reared on this volume and one can easily imagine these exhortations being reaffirmed by Beethoven. Neefe followed C. P. E. Bach in emphasizing the duty of the composer to his art, and warned of the dangers of pandering to public taste.

> A composer should not concern himself with the plebeian listener, who never knows what he wants, and understands virtually nothing … Woe betide the composer who wants to address such people. He will spoil his talent, that has been given to him, by having to compose minuets, polonaises and Turkish marches. And then – good night talent, genius and art.⁴

These are lofty views expressed with the characteristic rhetoric of late eighteenth-century German culture. Freedom of expressive intent, even if it meant intellectual exclusiveness, was to be constantly articulated by the adult Beethoven.

Neefe also had a strong sense of German identity, a new element in Beethoven's experience that contrasted with the pragmatic allegiances – Dutch, French, German and Italian – that had always been evident in Bonn. He never set foot in France or Italy, devoted his career to the development of German opera and song, and sought to displace the traditional primacy given to French and Italian music. 'You certainly know how German I think and feel' he once said. Patriotism and nationalism were to figure too in Beethoven's career, largely activated by the political upheavals that occurred during his life.

For over 200 hundred years, religion had prevented the fostering of a German national identity, but increasingly in the eighteenth century Protestant and Catholic areas of German-speaking Europe seemed willing to place such differences aside in a new nationalist quest. The Calvinist Neefe now worked in a Catholic court and, in a gesture that at least suggests a pragmatism that sought to diffuse tensions, he had his children baptized as Catholics. Beethoven's religious outlook was to be equally undogmatic. Brought up in the Catholic liturgy, he was never in the equivalent position to Neefe where he had to embrace a different Christian creed, but he was never a church-going Catholic and his eagerness, for instance, to promote the Mass in C and the Missa Solemnis throughout Europe suggests that the Catholic creed meant as much, or as little, to him as the Calvinist one did to Neefe. Faith, in the broadest sense, however, meant a great deal to Beethoven, and led him to explore oriental religions, a curiosity one suspects that Neefe would have shared.

In his autobiography Neefe wrote that he was 'no friend of ceremony and of etiquette' and that he 'detested creeps and gossips', social attitudes that his young pupil was to raise to rudeness. The imagery of Neefe's further observation that he 'hated bad princes more than bandits' recalls a similar, though not exact, juxtaposition in a line from Schiller's 'An die Freude', a line that is omitted in the 'Choral' symphony but which Beethoven certainly knew: 'Beggars shall become princes' brothers'. For Neefe and Beethoven princes and patrons had a moral duty to support the work of the artist, something that would earn them respect; if they did not offer this support they deserved, and in Beethoven's case were to receive, contempt.

The high-minded tone of Beethoven's later tribute to Neefe suggests that he was consciously appealing to Neefe's character. Educated, principled, intellectually enquiring as well as high-minded, Neefe, the court organist, was set apart from his fellow musicians, and instilled these distinctive qualities in the young Beethoven.

One of the many manifestations of the new authority that German musicians, especially those from the north, wished to accord themselves and their art was the increasing number of journals devoted to music. One of the most ambitious and widely read in the 1780s was the *Magazin der Musik*, issued in Hamburg and edited by Carl Friedrich Cramer. Appearing twice a week, the periodical featured surveys of music in various towns, localities and courts. A 'Report on the electoral court of Cologne at Bonn, also other musicians in the town' was provided in a letter written by Neefe and dated 30 March 1783. He begins with the leading figures at court, Mattioli the violinist, Lucchesi the Kapellmeister, and himself as court organist and music director of the theatre; details of their careers are given with, in the case of Mattioli and Lucchesi, an assessment of their principal qualities. As promised in the title of the account, there is a section on musicians not employed by the court. Pride of place is given to Mastiaux: 'a man who wishes and recognizes no other delight than music; it is his most favoured daily companion'. Altogether eleven town musicians are listed. The last is Neefe's pupil, Beethoven, whose abilities are outlined in an appreciation that is noticeably longer than the majority:

> Louis van Betthoven, son of the above-mentioned tenor, a boy of eleven, and with a most promising talent. He plays the piano very skilfully and with power, sight-reads very well, and to summarize; he plays mostly the Well-Tempered Clavier by Sebastian Bach, which Herr Neefe placed in his hands. Whoever knows this collection of preludes and fugues through all the keys (which one might almost refer to as the *non plus ultra*) will know what that means. As far as his usual duties allow, Herr Neefe has given him some instruction in thorough-bass. He is now training him in composition, and in order to encourage him has arranged for the publication in Mannheim of nine variations for piano on a march. This young genius deserves assistance, so that he can travel. He would certainly become a second Wolfgang Amadeus Mozart, if he were to carry on as he has begun.[5]

Although Neefe, like everybody else, thought Beethoven was a year younger than he was, his admiration is genuine rather than sensationalized. The report makes it clear that he ought to broaden his musical horizons through travel. Rich and diverse though musical life at Bonn was, it was also claustrophobic; Beethoven needed to experience music in other cities and in different circumstances so that, like Neefe, he might enhance Bonn's musical life rather than just be part of it. The parallel evoked by Neefe was that of Mozart, who between the ages of six and twenty-five had travelled throughout Europe as a pianist and composer. By the time he was twelve Mozart was known throughout Europe as a performer who also had several symphonies, concertos, sonatas, an opera and a mass to his credit. Although Beethoven at the same age was certainly no Mozart, Neefe felt that his talents should be nurtured in much the same way.

From the distance of over two hundred years it is easy to give Neefe's words a significance that they did not possess to contemporary readers. Mozart was not then the man-myth he is now; he was not even the figure that he was ten years after the report was written. He was merely the most well-known example of a prodigy who had travelled widely to form his musicianship. While Neefe's remarks are easily misconstrued by modern commentators, there is no doubt that if writer and subject had re-read this issue of the *Magazin der Musik* a few years later they would have been struck by its fortuitous prescience, for Mozart's music was about to become much more familiar in Bonn, largely through political circumstances rather than musical perception. The seeds had been sown a few years later.

By the late 1770s Elector Maximilian Friedrich was an ageing man, and the succession had already become a subject of debate amongst the competing German-speaking states of Europe. To ensure a smooth transition of power, particularly if it involved a switch of political allegiance, many ecclesiastical principalities in the Holy Roman Empire elected, during the lifetime of the reigning ruler, a successor or 'co-adjutor' who then automatically succeeded to the throne. The Austrian ambassador in Bonn was Franz Georg Metternich-Winneburg (father of the famous Metternich who shaped Austrian politics in the early nineteenth century), who, in conjunction with Baron Belderbusch, began to encourage the view that the next elector should be a member of the Habsburg family. The youngest son of Maria Theresia, Maximilian Franz, had been destined for a military career but in the War of the Bavarian Succession he had contracted a debilitating disease that affected his knee joints, which, despite several operations, left him relatively immobile and unsuited to a military career. In 1780, at the age of only twenty-four, he became an obvious candidate for the co-adjutorship. Maximilian Franz took out the necessary minor orders so that he could become a ruling archbishop; the

Pope was persuaded to agree to the plan; and Prussia was kept in the dark long enough for it to be presented as a *fait accompli*. Archduke Maximilian Franz was elected co-adjutor in August 1780; exactly four years later in a ceremony in Cologne cathedral he was anointed archbishop and elector.

Like most members of the Habsburg family, Maximilian Franz was passionately fond of music. One of his first acts as elector was to ask for a report on the members of the musical retinue at court. Thirty-six members were succinctly evaluated by a bureaucrat who, at some point, had obviously crossed swords with Neefe:

> No. 8 Johan Betthoven: his voice has virtually gone, has served for a long time, is very needy, a passable performer, and married . . .
>
> No. 13 Christian Neffe the organist: in my unbiased opinion this person could really be dismissed because he is not particularly accomplished on the organ; moreover he is an outsider of virtually no merit, and a Calvinist . . .
>
> No. 14 Ludwig van Betthoven, a son of the Betthoven mentioned in No.8, is not in receipt of payment, has played the organ during the absence of Kapellmeister Lucchesi; he is of good ability, still young, calm and collected in performance, and poor.[6]

Despite the author's observations on Johann van Beethoven and Neefe, both were retained as the musical retinue was expanded and strengthened over the next few years. By 1790 it numbered over fifty people, making it one of the largest court establishments in Europe. There were now thirteen regular singers, but an even more significant increase had occurred in the orchestral forces: fifteen violins, four violas, two cellos, three basses, two flutes, two oboes, two clarinets, three bassoons, two horns, four trumpets and timpani. Neefe and Beethoven had dual responsibilities, the former as organist and violinist, the latter as organist and viola player. Maximilian Franz maintained the traditional tripartite division of musical activity: church, theatre and concert. While operas from France and north Germany continued to be performed there was a notable trend towards the end of the decade to mirror the contemporary scene in Vienna. Many

2 Elector Maximilian Franz

operas that had had successful runs in Vienna were played in Bonn, including Dittersdorf's *Doktor und Apotheker*, Martín y Soler's *L'arbore di Diana*, Mozart's *Le nozze di Figaro* and *Don Giovanni*, Paisiello's *Il barbiere di Siviglia* and *Il rè Teodoro*, and Salieri's *La grotta di Trofonio* and *Axur*.

An increasing familiarity with instrumental music from Vienna is discernible in this period also. Nicolaus Simrock was a horn player at the court who also ran a shop in the town that sold all kinds of goods, from French carpets to prayer books, and wine to stationery. He sold music and was an agent for Vienna's leading music publisher, Artaria. Much of the output of that firm in the 1780s became available in Bonn, including symphonies, quartets and piano music by Joseph Haydn, Michael Haydn, Leopold Kozeluch, Mozart and Rosetti.

Within the court itself Mozart's name was a familiar one. The elector and composer were exact contemporaries who had been acquainted since childhood, when Mozart had visited the Imperial and Royal court in Vienna. In 1775 the nineteen-year-old composer had written the opera, *Il rè pastore*, to commemorate the visit of the then archduke to Salzburg. When, in 1781, Mozart moved to Vienna, Maximilian Franz was a frequent advocate of his abilities in the gossipy world of imperial musical politics. Soon the composer was marking Maximilian Franz as a possible patron:

> I can say that he thinks the world of me. He shoves me forward on every occasion, and I might almost say with certainty that if at this moment he were Elector of Cologne, I should be his Kapellmeister. It is, indeed, a pity that these great gentlemen refuse to make arrangements beforehand. I could easily manage to extract a simple promise from him, but of what use would that be to me now.[7]

It is obvious from Mozart's letter, couched in a typical mixture of wishful thinking and obfuscation, that, at best, the possibility of employment at Bonn had been mentioned; there was no commitment. Certainly there is no evidence that, when the co-adjutor became elector two years later, Mozart was offered the position. History has been denied celebrating the artistic fellowship of Mozart and Beethoven in one court, but the elder composer soon became a talismanic figure for the teenage Beethoven, somebody whom Maximilian, Neefe and others regarded as a model for the development of the Bonn composer.

It should be remembered, however, that this view of Mozart was the product of the political link between Vienna and Bonn and did not reflect any kind of European perspective. If the court had wished Beethoven to become a court Kapellmeister who enjoyed international esteem then the clear role model would have been Joseph Haydn, still the hard-working Kapellmeister in the mid 1780s but a composer whose music was known and admired throughout Europe.

But within the political circles of the Bonn court several factors would have weighed against this choice: Haydn was not a familiar figure in Habsburg court circles (indeed, there is some evidence that Joseph II disliked his music); Haydn was not a performer and could not have nurtured that side of Beethoven's musicianship; finally, he was from an older generation than Mozart and the elector. Mozart, on the other hand, was young (only fourteen years older than Beethoven); he was known in Habsburg circles; and in the mid 1780s he was enjoying marked success as a pianist-composer in Vienna.

The Bonn–Vienna, Beethoven–Mozart axis resulted in 1787 in the composer being sent to Vienna to study with Mozart, a journey almost certainly encouraged and underwritten by the elector himself. Unfortunately, next to nothing is known about the visit. Beethoven probably arrived on 7 April and stayed a little longer than two weeks, leaving about 20 April because of the serious illness of his mother. It is not known where he stayed; it could have been with a member of the Waldstein family or, if formal lessons had begun, with the Mozart family, then living in the Landstrasse. A nineteenth-century anecdote relates that Beethoven played some piano music that left Mozart rather unimpressed, but when the sixteen-year-old improvised he remarked enthusiastically: 'Mark that man; he will make himself a name in the world.' Extant exercises by two regular pupils of Mozart, Thomas Attwood and Babette Ployer, indicate that Beethoven would have started with species counterpoint, moved on to the writing of canons and, then, over a period of a few months, to minuets and slow movements. If Beethoven was privy to what Mozart was composing and planning, then he might have caught him putting the final touches to the C major quintet (K515), contemplating a journey to London and enthusing about his latest opera commission, *Don*

Giovanni. As regards public concerts, Mozart himself had not given any that season and none was held during Beethoven's short time in the city. Had he gone to the opera it would have been to performances of *L' inganno amoroso* by Guglielmi or *Le gare generose* by Paisiello.

Beethoven's anxious return journey took him via Augsburg and he arrived in Bonn in late April. His mother died on 17 July. A few months later Beethoven wrote a letter to Joseph Wilhelm von Schaden, an acquaintance he had met in Augsburg. This is his first extant letter, written with some of the power and eloquence that were to characterize his correspondence in later years:

> I must confess that as soon as I left Augsburg my good spirits and my health too began to decline. For the nearer I came to my native town, the more frequently did I receive from my father letters urging me to travel more quickly than usual, because my mother was not in very good health. So I made as much haste as I could, the more so as I myself began to feel ill. My yearning to see my ailing mother once more swept all obstacles aside so far as I was concerned, and enabled me to overcome the greatest difficulties. I found my mother still alive, but in the most wretched condition ... She was such a good, kind mother to me and indeed my best friend. Oh! who was happier than I, when I could still utter the sweet name of my mother and it was heard and answered; and to whom can I say it now? To the dumb likenesses of her which my imagination fashions for me? Since my return to Bonn I have as yet enjoyed very few happy hours. For the whole time I have been plagued with asthma; and I am inclined to fear this malady may even turn to consumption. Furthermore, I have been suffering from melancholia, which in my case is almost as great a torture as my illness.[8]

This expression of filial affection is virtually the only first-hand evidence of Maria Magdalena Beethoven's part in her son's upbringing. These feelings of reverence remained with Beethoven for the rest of his life, causing him special pain when a bizarre rumour circulated in Germany and England that he was the illegitimate son of the King of Prussia. While the melancholy that Beethoven mentions was the understandable reaction of an adolescent to the death of his mother it was part, too, of a more general languor; as a teenager he seems to have lacked that sure determination that characterized him as an adult. While he was perfectly willing to be the protégé of Neefe, Maximilian Franz and others, and to undertake a journey to Vienna, there is little of the independence and ambition apparent in the teenage careers of Haydn and Mozart, for instance. Following his mother's death he immersed himself, quite contentedly, in the musical life of Bonn: playing the organ, piano and viola, and teaching keyboard instruments. His youthful attempts at composition decline after his return to Bonn, as if he had temporarily lost interest. If Neefe and Maximilian Franz still regarded Beethoven as Bonn's equivalent to Mozart then there was little striking evidence in 1787, either in achievement or aspiration, to justify the comparison.

Rather than a series of compelling events that presaged greatness, the remaining five years in Bonn constitute a period of quiet, though steady development. For several years Beethoven had taught the piano to two members of the Breuning family, aristocrats who had served the electoral court for several decades. Eleonore von Breuning was only a year younger than Beethoven and soon the formal piano lessons developed into love. Beethoven was never to marry, and the relationship with Lorchen, as she was affectionately called, was the first of many love affairs with ladies from a higher social class than himself. Lorchen later married a doctor from Bonn, Franz Wegeler, who was to record his reminiscences of Beethoven:

> Ludwig made his first acquaintance with German literature, especially poetry, in the von Breuning family in Bonn where he also received his first introductions to social life and behaviour...
>
> An unforced atmosphere of culture reigned in the house in spite of youthful high spirits...
>
> Beethoven was soon treated as one of the children in the family and not only did he spend the greatest part of the day there but even many nights. He felt free there, he could move around with ease, and everything combined to make him cheerful and to develop his mind.[9]

A prominent member of the Breuning social circle was Count Ferdinand Ernst Waldstein. Born in Bohemia in 1762, he arrived in Bonn early in 1788 and over the next few years established himself as the elector's most trusted adviser, with a roving ambassadorial role that involved him in practically all decisions that affected the relationship of the court with the outside world. As might be expected of someone who had gained the trust of the Habsburg family, he was a capable musician who even composed a little. He took an interest in Beethoven's career, recognizing a talent that could become an appropriate symbol of the ambition of the Habsburg dynasty. Near the end of the carnival season in 1791, Waldstein organized a ridotto in the court theatre. Members of the nobility turned up in old German dress and witnessed a ballet depicting some of the clichés of German nationhood: a march, a drinking song, a hunting song, a troubadour song, a war song and a peasant dance. Beethoven was entrusted with the composition of the music, the so-called *Ritterballett*, a notable step forward in his court career.

Waldstein was also a member of the *Lesegesellschaft* in Bonn, a reading circle open to all members of the town regardless of status; it satisfied the intellectual curiosity of its members in all manner of subjects including agriculture, geography, history and politics. In the last area the society remained wholly unaffected by the anti-monarchist views in France; indeed it rejoiced in the active patronage of the elector himself. When Maximilian Franz's brother, Emperor Joseph II, died in 1790 it was natural that this staunchly pro-Habsburg organization should want to mark the occasion. Severin Anton Averdonk, brother of Johann Helena the court singer, had already written a text. Waldstein – perhaps prompted by Neefe, who was also a member of the society – suggested that the task of setting it to music should be entrusted to the young Beethoven. The result, the 'Cantata on the death of Joseph II', was his most impressive composition to date, a five-movement work of great power and expressive range, framed by a chorus in C minor, 'Tot stöhnt es durch die öde Nacht' ('Death echoes through the empty night'). For reasons that remain unclear the cantata was not performed. It cannot have been because Beethoven had provided something that was fundamentally unsuitable, since he was asked to write a second cantata, to celebrate the succession of Leopold II to the Habsburg throne; this, too, remained unperformed in Beethoven's lifetime.

This notable year, 1790, ended with a brief visit to the Bonn court by Joseph Haydn. He arrived around Christmas, accompanied by the impresario Johann Peter Salomon; both were *en route* to London, where Haydn was to be the resident composer at the Hanover Square Concerts organized by Salomon. At the age of fifty-eight, Haydn was making his first visit outside Austria, and the journey had already become a highly gratifying one, as the composer was greeted with enthusiasm by local musicians in the towns where he stayed overnight. Bonn must have been particularly welcoming since it represented a homecoming for Salomon: he had been born there in 1745 and had played in the court orchestra for a few years before embarking on an international career. Salomon and Haydn attended mass at the court chapel, the setting of the Ordinary being by Haydn himself. Beethoven probably played the organ in the service, or perhaps the viola. The leading musicians at the court, a group that must have included Beethoven, dined with Salomon and Haydn, all paid for by the elector. Beethoven showed Haydn his most recent compositions, probably one or both of the cantatas, and the older composer was deeply impressed.

Only one work from Beethoven's years in Bonn is regularly played today, the B♭ piano concerto (itself heavily revised in the 1790s when a new finale was provided), which gives only the merest glimpse of the diversity of Beethoven's output by 1790, the time of Haydn's visit. A complete picture cannot be established. Alongside known completed works such as the two cantatas, three piano quartets, another concerto for piano (in E♭) and a collection of small pieces for piano, there are extant fragments of works, such as an oboe concerto and a violin concerto, that may once have been complete. There is a third, large category: works that were begun but never completed, including a symphony in C minor. Taking all the evidence – completed works, fragments, aborted works and sketches – it is clear that by the end of the decade Beethoven had at least attempted to compose in most genres: piano music, ensemble music, concerto, symphony, dance, liturgical music and operatic aria.

In November 1791 the journal *Musikalische Korrespondenz*, issued in Speyer, included a lengthy report by the musician and writer Carl Ludwig Junker on the abilities of court employees at Bonn following a two-day visit the previous month. It is an enthusiastic report, especially valuable for providing a contemporary assessment of Beethoven rather than one projected back from his later fame. On the first day of the visit Junker ate his meal to the sound of a wind octet in the background, including a performance of the overture to Mozart's *Don Giovanni*. He then went on to a performance of Paisiello's *Il rè Teodoro* which he thought well sung and even better played by the court orchestra under the direction of its leader, Franz Ries. The following morning there was a rehearsal at ten o' clock in Ries's rooms for the evening concert. Junker noticed the young average age of the players; one of them, Nicolaus Simrock, the horn player and shop owner, told him 'We don't have the usual cliques and double dealing here, the fullest unanimity prevails, we love each other as brothers, as members of a society.' It was the elector's nameday and shortly before the beginning of the rehearsal Ries was summoned to receive a gift of 1,000 thalers for the orchestra. The concert itself was at six in the evening and the assembled musicians were strikingly dressed in red and gold livery. Following a Mozart symphony (not identified), a vocal number, and a cello concerto, there was a symphony by Pleyel, an aria by Righini, a double concerto for violin and cello and, finally, a symphony by Wineberger. The performances could not have been more precise: 'Such an exact observance of *piano, forte, rinforzando*, such a swelling and gradual growth of sound, followed by a subsidence of the same, from the maximum intensity to the gentlest sound – this could otherwise be heard only in Mannheim.'

Beethoven probably played the viola in the orchestra but Junker took the opportunity too of hearing the composer improvise on the piano, providing the earliest eyewitness account – apart from Mozart's brief comment – of his extraordinary abilities in this area:

> The greatness of this amiable, light-hearted man, as a virtuoso, may in my opinion be safely estimated from his almost inexhaustible wealth of ideas, the altogether characteristic style of expression in his playing, and the great execution which he displays.

A comparison with the travelling virtuoso Abbé Vogler is offered, Junker maintaining that Beethoven is a much more expressive player, 'more for the heart'. All this remarkable musical talent and activity is supported by an elector, 'an enthusiastic lover of music' and 'the best and most humane of princes'. Maximilian Franz, Neefe, Waldstein, Mastiaux, the Breuning family and perhaps even the young Beethoven himself could have taken pride from Junker's penultimate observation:

> Until now it was customary to think of Cologne as a land of darkness, in which the Enlightenment had not taken hold. When one goes to the court of the elector, one forms an entirely different view. In particular amongst the members of the Kapelle I found entirely enlightened, healthily reflective and thinking men.[10]

There is no reason to suppose that Beethoven was other than wholly content with life as a courtier, a young conscientious member of a sophisticated and progressive musical environment. His broadly based employment as a viola player, organist, teacher, pianist and composer was beginning to show particular promise in the last two areas, ones that were likely to take him one day beyond Bonn. But in 1791 the glimpses of his personality that are offered – a rather shy individual, happy with close friends of all social classes, though otherwise awkward – do not suggest that he would ever have taken the initiative to broaden his horizons.

Eight months after Junker's article, Joseph Haydn called again in Bonn, on his way home to Vienna from his first, overwhelmingly successful journey to London. Six symphonies (Nos. 93–8) had been given their first performance in the two seasons of the Hanover Square Concerts organized by Salomon, and Haydn was expected to return for the following 1793 season. The idea was mooted that Beethoven should accompany Haydn to Vienna and then to London. Haydn himself had already been impressed by Beethoven's talents as a composer and perhaps he and Salomon were intrigued by the idea of promoting the unknown talent of someone from Salomon's birthplace. For Beethoven or, at least, for those who had an interest in his development, the advantages were twofold: lessons from a figure who was unequivocally recognized as the foremost composer in Europe and the opportunity to travel to London, a city whose richness and diversity of musical life made it the musical capital of Europe. With Haydn's guidance Beethoven's increasingly evident abilities as a composer and as a pianist would have been ideally suited to concert life in the British capital. Discussions with Haydn offered something more concrete than the putative connection with Mozart had ever yielded. After Mozart's untimely death the previous December the elector and his advisor, Waldstein, might well have come to reflect that Beethoven was not, after all, going to project the image they desired: a Habsburg protégé who was to move in court circles and strengthen the links between Bonn and Vienna. Instead, Beethoven was about to be taken on by a quite different figure, an outsider, much older, but paradoxically socially more free, and someone who had demonstrated that he could profit from the commercial opportunities that musical life in London offered. If Beethoven was excited by the prospect of a journey with Haydn to Vienna and to London, political events in the late summer and autumn of 1792 were seriously to weaken the comfortable certainties of life in Bonn.

From the earliest days of the French Revolution Bonn had been a favoured destination for fleeing émigrés. Drunk with savage idealism revolutionary leaders in France presided over, rather than controlled, a ghastly increase in the use of the guillotine in August 1792, while simultaneously expounding plans to extend the Revolution beyond France to the natural geographical boundaries of the Pyrenees and

Alps to the south and east, and to the Rhine to the north and east. Elector Maximilian Franz and the Habsburg regime in Bonn were in the middle of a potential battlefield. By deed and temperament he was one of the most enlightened of enlightened despots and the potential destruction of his humane idealism by the barbarism of France was deeply unnerving. Family loyalty meant that he had to support the Austro-Prussian alliance against France but, simultaneously, he hoped to appease the enemy by, for instance, indicating that Bonn was no longer willing to be a haven for French refugees. But 1792 was no time for old-fashioned Habsburg wheeling and dealing of the kind that had secured the electorate in the first place. By mid October the order had been given to leave Bonn, and the elector and his court spent most of the subsequent winter in Münster.

It was in this deeply unsettled atmosphere that Beethoven, himself a dutiful member of the *ancien régime* who had honoured Joseph II and Leopold II in two cantatas, prepared to leave Bonn for Vienna. In his last week in Bonn his friends compiled a *Stammbuch*, an autograph album of good wishes, reminiscences and injunctions to do well, written in the usual mixture of rhetoric and sentiment, and illustrated with the occasional drawing.[11] Eleonore Breuning (Lorchen) quotes three lines from Herder:

Freundschaft, mit dem Guten,
Wächset wie der Abendschatten
Bis des Lebens Sonne sinkt

(Friendship with the good grows like the evening shadows until the sunset of life)

Eleonore's brother, Christoph von Breuning, concentrates on the promised visit to London; 'bard' is probably a reference to Salomon:

See! Albion long beckons to you, O friend.
See the shady grove that it offers the singer.
Hurry then straight away
Over the surging sea,
Where a more beautiful grove offers its shade to you,

And the bard so kindly extends to you his hand,
[He] who fled
From our dominions to Albion's protection.
There may your song echo full of victory,
Loudly, wildly through the grove and over the sea's tumult
To the domain
From which you joyfully fled.

While it is possible to regard the urgency of Breuning's remarks as the product of the general unease in Bonn, none of the fifteen entries refers directly to contemporary events. Two, however, evoke the familiar Bonn metaphor, that Beethoven was to be the new Mozart. The physician Johann Heinrich Crevelt creates a picture of Beethoven's future success under the protective aura of Mozart's genius that 'hovers over you / And, smiling at you, lends its approbation'. Crevelt was writing on 1 November, the eve of Beethoven's departure, and almost certainly he took this image from a previous entry written by Count Waldstein:

Dear Beethoven!

You are going to Vienna in fulfilment of your long-frustrated wishes. The genius of Mozart is mourning and weeping over the death of its pupil. With the inexhaustible Haydn it has found refuge but not occupation; through him it wishes to be united once more with another. Through uninterrupted industry you will receive: *Mozart's spirit from Haydn's hands.*

The final *bon mot*, 'Mozart's spirit from Haydn's hands', has been quoted endlessly, signifying a moment in history when the young Beethoven assumed his role in the divine succession. But viewed in a less exalted manner, Waldstein's words are rather clumsy and uncharitable, if not meaningless. The idea of Beethoven becoming the second Mozart had been a long-held one, dashed by Mozart's premature death the previous December. However, the notion that his genius was now embodied in the unsuitable Haydn is awkward: Haydn as a mere conduit, or the keeper of the flame, does that composer's contemporary reputation scant justice, as Waldstein's contradictory 'inexhaustible' suggests. He never intended that these thoughts be quoted and they were not written as a testimonial or a letter of introduction; conceived quickly, they were merely meant to encourage the young Beethoven on his travels.

The *Stammbuch* reveals the affection in which Beethoven was held and the hopes that were entertained for his future. In musical terms this was highly promising. As a pupil of Haydn he was to go to Vienna and from there to London; meanwhile his position at court was to be kept open for his eventual return. Political events, however, were already threatening the very existence of the electoral court. The idyll of Beethoven's youth had come to an end. He was never to return to Bonn.

2 A new career in Vienna

During the journey from Bonn to Vienna Beethoven began entering incidental expenses in a pocket notebook.[1] The original intention may have been to keep a record of expenses to justify the continued support of Maximilian Franz. Although the volume was used until Beethoven's stipend stopped in 1794, its content soon became neither systematic nor comprehensive. After finding rooms in a house on the Alsergasse, some twenty minutes walk from the centre of the city, Beethoven spent the first few weeks in Vienna equipping himself for his stay: the notebook records the cost of buying wood for heating, various books, shoes, socks, underwear and an overcoat, everything, Beethoven ruefully remarked, that he had possessed in Bonn. Many of the items suggest that he was a young man concerned about his appearance and social manner in a way that he would later disdain. Only the older generation still wore wigs but Beethoven contemplated, at least, purchasing one; to emphasize the allure of his black hair he bought pomade; in readiness for the forthcoming carnival season, he noted the address of a dancing master, Andreas Lindner; he purchased a seal for his correspondence and about a year later sketched a design for a new one. For his studies he bought a desk and hired a piano. He also employed a maid who received half a gulden a day. An embarrassing legacy of Beethoven's poor schooling in Bonn was his inability to work out even the simplest arithmetical calculation. To determine how much the maid should be paid for eleven days

Beethoven wrote the figure '½' eleven times, added them up and noted the total as 10½ gulden! He subsequently bought a book on elementary arithmetic and over a year later seems to have taken lessons three times a week from a Herr Schuppanzigh; his son, Ignaz, was to become one of Vienna's leading violinists and a close friend of Beethoven.

A few weeks after his arrival Beethoven heard that his father, Johann, had died. Relations between father and son had been difficult for many years, the father's chronic disaffection with life at Bonn being aggravated by alcoholism. In response to a petition from Ludwig to Maximilian Franz some of Johann's salary from 1789 onwards had been paid to Ludwig to enable him to provide for his brothers. They were well cared for and, for the moment, it was not necessary either for Ludwig to return to Bonn or for the brothers to join him in Vienna.

Beethoven's lessons with Haydn began almost immediately, in the middle of December 1792, and were to last for a year until Haydn began preparing for his second visit to London. During the winter months the master lived in a house on the Wasserkunstbastei and the lessons were terminated by coffee in one of the many coffee houses in the city. Since coffee was rather expensive, the penny- or rather kreuzer-conscious Beethoven entered the expenditure in his note-book: 'coffee, 6x [kreuzer] for haidn and me'. Hot chocolate was even more expensive: '22x for haidn and me chocolate'. In May 1793 Beethoven went with Haydn to the principal palace of the Esterházy family in Eisenstadt, where he presumably stayed in a room in the palace. The glory days of the Esterházy court were over. The reigning prince, Anton, had reduced the musical retinue to the fashionable *Harmonie*, a wind group that played transcriptions of numbers from operas as well as original music. As a mark of their long and faithful service – nearly sixty years between them – Haydn and his leader, Luigi Tomasini, had been retained, but there was very little for them to do. When Beethoven was present at the court in the summer of 1793 he must have formed a mixed impression: an aura of magnificence, but with a level of musical activity much lower than back home in Bonn. Haydn's duties consisted of little more than sanctioning the retirement of a bassoon player, hardly the work of a Kapellmeister, let alone Europe's leading composer.

Haydn was an experienced teacher whose pupils had included Ignaz Pleyel, Fritz and Edmund von Weber (half-brothers of Carl Maria) and Anton Wranitzky. He set Beethoven working in methodical manner, using Fux's *Gradus ad Parnassum*. First printed in 1725, this had become the standard textbook for aspiring composers in the Austrian monarchy; Gregor Werner (Haydn's predecessor at the Esterházy court), Johann Georg Albrechtsberger and Antonio Salieri were only three composers who were weaned on its precepts. Mozart as well as Haydn used Fux's approach, even if they did not adhere slavishly to the old master's exercises or agree with every last detail of his comments. After some preliminary theory, musical craftsmanship was developed through species counterpoint, a graded and highly systematic approach to the writing of counterpoint. First, one note is set against one note, then two against one, four against one and so on. From two participating parts it moves to three and four parts until a complete vocabulary of contrapuntal practice is established, a natural basis for the writing of fugues and for good part writing in general. Such a methodical approach might give the impression of being wholly unmusical, and certainly a tone-deaf automaton can provide plausible results in the early stages, but it required a real musician to tap the usefulness of the exercises and it gave all students confidence in moving the notes around the page. Beethoven, of course, was already very adept at composition, often to eloquent effect. The real value to him of these exercises was their endemic emphasis on strongly shaped individual lines, which removed his dependency on harmonically based textures premised on figured bass and the fluency that derived from keyboard ability. It encouraged the mentality, latent in Beethoven's thinking but subsequently to become fundamental, that every note counts. There is no reason, therefore, to doubt that he recognized the value of the exercises; he may also have been fortified by knowing that Haydn had not subjected himself to this rigorous training until his middle thirties, some time after he had composed his first symphonies and quartets.

Fifty-three pages of Beethoven's exercises for Haydn exist, neatly copied by the pupil and with corrections, alternatives and improvements by Haydn. In keeping with the view of posterity that these exercises were beneath Beethoven, commentators have tended to exaggerate Haydn's casualness in marking the work. There are certainly plenty of uncorrected errors of a kind that would have been scrupulously marked by a dull pedant, but the many constructive remarks that appear could have come only from a practised composer. For Haydn, 1793 must have been one of the most relaxed years in his life. There were no duties at the Esterházy court, and life in Vienna and Eisenstadt was quite different from the hurly-burly of London. From being a celebrity fêted by the public he had slipped back to being an inactive Kapellmeister. He took the opportunity of preparing for his second visit to London, composing six quartets (later published in two groups of three, op. 71 and op. 74), one complete symphony (No. 99) and a portion of a second (No. 101). If Beethoven witnessed the composition of these works, and others written for Vienna, such as the remarkably focused variations in F minor for piano, it was to take him the best part of a decade to come to grips with their content. First-hand observation of the most acute musical mind in Europe at work was enhanced in December 1793 when three of the six symphonies (Nos. 93–8) Haydn had already written for London were given for the first time in Vienna, performances that Beethoven must surely have attended.

The regular exercises that Beethoven dutifully prepared for Haydn did not mean that he was inactive as a composer or as a promoter of his own compositions. On 18 May 1793, in the *Wiener Zeitung*, the music dealer Johann Traeg announced the availability of manuscript copies of Beethoven's variations for piano on a theme by Righini. It is possible that Traeg simply copied the music from the existing publication by Götz of Mannheim; more likely is that Beethoven instigated its availability. Whatever the truth, this set of variations was the first work by the composer to be sold in Vienna. As a completely unknown name Beethoven figures at the very end of a long list of advertised music that includes symphonies by Mozart, Eybler, Winter and Rosetti, concertos by Müller, Pleyel and Partzel, and German dances by Cibulka, Just, Ritter and Hagen.

At a time when most music in the Austrian monarchy was distributed in the form of manuscript copies, Traeg was Vienna's largest music dealer and copyist. The leading publisher of music was Artaria who, during the 1780s, had issued music by Vienna's principal composers including Haydn, Mozart, Dittersdorf and Vanhal. In addition the firm had established a network of agencies abroad that regularly sold its stock. It was almost certainly Haydn who introduced Beethoven to the firm that was to become the young composer's main publisher until the end of the decade, though, like Haydn before him, he was to complain frequently about their efficiency.

In Bonn, Beethoven had begun the composition of a set of variations for violin and piano on 'Se vuol ballare' from Mozart's *Le nozze di Figaro*, completing it under Haydn's supervision in Vienna. Variations represented little or no commercial risk for Artaria, and Beethoven's set joined dozens of others by the firm. Although the choice of theme had been made in Bonn, it fitted well with the sudden growth in Mozart's popularity that occurred in Vienna in the years immediately after his death, a growth evident in Artaria's catalogue. The title-page read 'XII Variations pour le Clavecin ou Piano-Forte avec un Violon ad lib. Composées et Dedies a Mademoiselle Eleonore de Breuning par Mr Beethoven. Oeuvre I. A Vienne chez Artaria Comp.'

The mention of 'Clavecin ou Piano-forte' (harpsichord or piano) was a typical publishers' ploy to maximize sales, attracting the older generation who could not afford to buy or rent the modern pianoforte. The dedicatee was Lorchen, his former pupil and friend Eleonore von Breuning. The designation 'Oeuvre 1' is interesting. Normally Artaria did not assign opus numbers to sets of variations, reserving them for larger works such as sonatas, trios, quartets, concertos and symphonies. It is likely, therefore, that Beethoven himself made the decision, regarding this work as the beginning to his official career. It turned out to be a false start.

Other works completed under Haydn's supervision in 1793 included an oboe concerto, a wind quintet for the unusual combination of oboe, three horns and bassoon, and a wind octet. Like the piano variations these works had been begun (even completed in certain cases) in Bonn but were revised under Haydn's tutelage. The emphasis on wind music may reflect the ready availability of the Esterházy *Harmonie* while Beethoven was staying in Eisenstadt in the summer of 1793.

A year on from arriving in Vienna it was necessary to prepare a progress report for Maximilian Franz. A couple of contemporary entries in Beethoven's notebook suggest that he was paying a copyist to provide neat versions of his latest compositions: one bill for 58 kreuzer, and a second for 25, at the typical going rate of 10 kreuzer per double sheet (four sides), is equivalent to about thirty-two pages of music. Two letters were sent simultaneously, one from Haydn, the other from Beethoven. Haydn's letter is a lengthy one in which he lists the compositions completed by his pupil, provides fulsome praise of his potential and hopes that the relationship can be continued. He also points out that Beethoven's expenses, including suitable attire for entry into society, had pushed the young composer into debt and that he had felt obliged to give him a loan. With emollient phrases of the kind that Haydn had directed at successive Esterházy princes he then tries to persuade the elector to pay these debts and to continue his patronage:

> As for the extravagance which one fears will tempt any young man who goes into the great world, I think I can answer for that to Your Serene Electoral Highness: for a hundred circumstances have confirmed me in my opinion that he is capable of sacrificing everything quite unconstrainedly for his art. In view of so many tempting occasions, this is most remarkable, and gives every security to Your Serene Electoral Highness – in view of the gracious kindness

that we expect – that Your Highness will not be wasting any of your grace on usurers as far as Beethoven is concerned. In the hope that Your Serene Electoral Highness will continue his further patronage of my dear pupil by graciously acceding to this my request, I am, with profound respect,

Your serene Electoral Highness's
most humble and obedient
Joseph Haydn.[2]

Beethoven's letter was much shorter and reveals an unease about the number and newness of the compositions mentioned by Haydn:

My sole endeavour is to render myself absolutely worthy of Your Electoral Excellency's highest favour. With this in view I have employed this year all the powers of my soul for the benefit of music in order to be able during the coming year to send to Your Electoral Excellency something that will resemble your magnanimous treatment of me and your sublime character in general more closely than what is being sent to Your Electoral Excellency by Herr Haydn.[3]

Beethoven's unease was well founded. The elector's reply to Haydn was tart. He noted that with the exception of a fugue he had 'composed and performed this music here in Bonn long before he undertook his second journey to Vienna'. He failed, too, to see why Beethoven was so short of money. He concluded:

I am wondering if he would not do better to begin his return journey here, in order that he may once again take up his post in my service; for I very much doubt whether he will have made any important progress in composition and taste during his present sojourn, and I fear that he will only bring back debts from his journey, just as he did from his first trip to Vienna.[4]

This was an enlightened despot in a despotic mood. Nevertheless, the elector must have relented, since Beethoven was allowed to remain in Vienna to continue his studies, though his stipend from the Bonn court was not increased to cover his expenses. None of the letters from teacher, pupil and patron mentions the journey to

London that had been part of the original understanding. As Haydn prepared for the return visit, which he had been obliged to postpone from 1793 to 1794, there is no hint that Beethoven was to accompany him. Whether a deliberate decision that he should not go had been made or whether the idea had been quietly forgotten is not known. Perhaps the cancellation of the promised journey to Europe's leading musical centre was another factor that fuelled Maximilian Franz's displeasure.

Haydn, however, ensured that his pupil was passed on to the leading teacher in Vienna, Johann Georg Albrechtsberger (1736–1809). Although he was four years younger than Haydn, he was one of many composers who had been at the cutting edge of musical style in the mid century but who had since lost this momentum. In his youth he had written symphonies, quartets and concertos (including several for mandolin) but from the 1780s onwards his output was increasingly dominated by church music. From a position as organist at Melk Abbey, he became, in turn, music director at the church of the Carmelites in Vienna, court organist, and, finally in 1792, Kapellmeister at St Stephen's. He was especially regarded as a teacher of composition and his many pupils included several names that were to figure prominently in Viennese musical life in the coming decades: Joseph Eybler, Joseph Nepomuk Hummel, Ignaz Seyfried and Joseph Weigl. His approach was firmly in the tradition of Fux. Indeed his own book, *Gründliche Anweisung zur Composition*, first published in 1790, was an up-dated *Gradus ad Parnassum*; to attain mastery of modern composition Albrechtsberger believed that all students had to be thoroughly prepared in theory, species counterpoint, counterpoint and fugue.

The progress of Beethoven's studies with Albrechtsberger matches the content of this volume. He began by revising some of the exercises prepared under Haydn's tutelage, moved on to fugue, invertible counterpoint at the tenth and at the twelfth, and then to vocal fugues. Again there is no reason to doubt that Beethoven found this instruction congenial; indeed Albrechtsberger, the church composer and organist, may well have reminded Beethoven of his own musical background in Bonn. Together with compositional discipline and a fascination with the intricacies of counterpoint, Albrechtsberger instilled in Beethoven an interest in religious music from previous eras; his treatise contains music examples taken from the works of renaissance and baroque composers such as Allegri, Bach, Caldara, Carissimi, Fux, Handel, Kirnberger, Lassus, Palestrina and Peri. Lessons were held as frequently as three times a week and lasted just over a year, probably until March 1795. Beethoven held Albrechtsberger in high regard, shown by his decision, over twenty years later, to give his grandson, Carl Friedrich Albrechtsberger, free lessons.

Formal tuition with Albrechtsberger constituted only part of Beethoven's musical life. During 1794 he worked on several ambitious compositions – string trios, piano sonatas and some songs – that reflected the new level of craftsmanship instilled by Albrechtsberger, though they were probably composed independently. Haydn's letter to the elector alludes to another element in Beethoven's life, gaining entry into high society, where he presumably played the piano. When Beethoven forwarded a copy of his 'Oeuvre 1', the variations on 'Se vuol ballare', to Eleonore von Breuning, he explained why he had decided to have the music published:

> I should never have written down this kind of piece, had I not already noticed fairly often how some people in Vienna after hearing me extemporize of an evening would note down on the following day several peculiarities of my style and pass them off with pride as their own. Well, as I foresaw that their pieces would soon be published, I resolved to forestall those people. But there was yet another reason, namely, my desire to embarrass these Viennese pianists, some of whom are my sworn enemies.[5]

It was probably Haydn who introduced his young pupil to Gottfried van Swieten; Beethoven's notebook records that he had an evening meal with him in the autumn of 1793. Swieten was a faithful servant of the Habsburg court, first as a diplomat in Brussels, Paris, London, Warsaw and Berlin and, from 1782, as chairman of the Court

Commission on Censorship and Prefect of the Imperial Library. In the short reign of Leopold II (1790–2) he temporarily lost his influence, only to regain it under Franz II. During his time in England and north Germany Swieten had amassed a substantial library of music from the early eighteenth century, especially the works of Bach and Handel. On his return to Vienna he established regular Sunday gatherings to explore this music and later organized semi-public performances of choral works by Handel, newly orchestrated by Mozart. By the time Beethoven met Swieten he had formed a group from among the nobility, the Gesellschaft der Associierten, to sponsor performances of Handel's choral works. During his first two years in Vienna Beethoven could well have attended performances of *Alexander's Feast*, the *Ode for St Cecilia's Day*, *The Choice of Hercules* and *Judas Maccabaeus*. It is not impossible that Beethoven took part in some of these performances; a rather cryptic comment 'concert auf der Orgel' ('concert on the organ') that he wrote in his notebook in December 1793 might refer to his participation in performances of the Ode and *The Choice of Hercules* that took place that month.

One member of Swieten's Gesellschaft was Prince Carl Lichnowsky, who was to play a determining role in Beethoven's career until the middle of the next decade. An old friend of Count Waldstein, Lichnowsky had been a notable patron of Mozart, accompanying him on a journey to Dresden, Leipzig and Berlin and lending him money. His main palaces were in Potsdam and Grätz (Hradec); unusually for someone who spent a considerable time in Vienna, he did not own a palace there. For four years between 1790 and 1794 he lived in a three-storey house in the centre of the city (now the Schauflergasse), where social and musical evenings of the kind mentioned in Beethoven's letter to Breuning were held.

Widening social and musical contacts, together with increasing confidence and ambition as a composer and a pianist, made 1794 a year of steady advancement. But it was also a deeply unsettling year, one that was to determine the entire course of Beethoven's life. Throughout this year his progress figured in a harsh and ultimately incompatible counterpoint with contemporary political events. The outcome was Beethoven's decision to stay in Vienna, rather than returning to Bonn. There was no single turning point, just a gradual realization that the security of Bonn was fast becoming a remembrance, replaced by the reality of an insecure yet challenging life in Vienna.

The whole process had begun in December 1793, the beginning of Beethoven's second year in Vienna, also marked by a change of teacher from Haydn to Albrechtsberger and by the composer's birthday. He wrote in his notebook: 'Courage, even in connection with weakness of the body, shall yet govern my spirit. 25 [sic] years you are here, this must determine the complete man – nothing must remain undone.' Whether this rather opaque annotation was prompted by an illness is not known, but the determination to succeed is clear enough, as is the sense that the next few years (until he was twenty-five?) were going to be crucial.

Elector Maximilian Franz was in Vienna from January to April, hoping to influence Habsburg policy towards the French following the guillotining of Louis XVI and Marie Antoinette. He was keen to act as mediator between France and Austria in the hope of saving Bonn from the French. Emperor Franz II, or rather the advisers of the twenty-five-year-old monarch, favoured confrontation, even though the prospect of war was not a popular one in Austria. It is not known whether Maximilian Franz and Beethoven met during this period, but Beethoven's allowance stopped in March, probably because of the general shortage of money at the Bonn court, which was on a war footing, rather than particular displeasure at the progress of one court musician.

Although the composer's brother, Carl, had recently moved from Bonn to Vienna, Ludwig was still hopeful of returning to Bonn. At the same time the resolve noted in December 1793 encouraged a new sense of strategy for the release of recent compositions, especially three ambitious piano trios. On 18 June he wrote to Simrock: 'The fact is that I had no desire to publish at the present moment any variations, because I wanted to wait until some more important works of mine, which are due to appear very soon, had first been given to the world.'[6] When Beethoven was writing this letter, political Vienna was in a state of crisis. Military defeats in the Austrian Netherlands had made the war deeply unpopular and a small but determined coterie of Jacobin sympathizers began to harness this unrest in order to unseat the Habsburg dynasty. Count Pergen, the minister of police, and his deputy, Count Saurau, held their nerve, arresting and subsequently prosecuting the ringleaders; dissidents from the military were hanged, while civilians were given jail sentences of up to sixty years. The crisis is referred to in a second letter from Beethoven to Simrock, one of the most fascinating letters of the composer's youth. There are some fashionable Jacobin sentiments and comments on the tense situation in Vienna; but, most strikingly, Beethoven is still hoping to return to Bonn:

> In my previous letter I promised to send you some of my
> compositions; and you treated my statement as if it were merely
> the fine phrases of a courtier. How on earth can I have merited such
> a description? – Faugh, who in these democratic times of ours
> would indulge in that kind of talk? Well, in order to clear myself of
> the epithet you have attached to me, you are to receive, as soon as I
> have made the grand review of my compositions, which is now
> about to take place, something which you will certainly engrave . . .
> We are having very hot weather here; and the Viennese are afraid
> that soon they will not be able to get any more ice cream. For, as the
> winter was so mild, ice is scarce. Here various important people have
> been locked up; it is said that a revolution was about to break out –
> But I believe that so long as an Austrian can get his brown ale and his
> little sausages, he is not likely to revolt. People say that the gates
> leading to the suburbs are to be closed at 10 p.m. The soldiers have
> loaded their muskets with ball. You dare not raise your voice here
> or the police will take you into custody.
> If your daughters are now grown up, do fashion one to be my
> bride. For if I have to live at Bonn as a bachelor, I will certainly
> not stay there for long.[7]

French success in the war in the Austrian Netherlands encouraged them to march south-east to Aachen and then towards Cologne and Bonn. The decision was taken to evacuate the electoral court. Ships were chartered to carry the silver plate, the expensive furniture, the library (including music) and the wine store to safety; much of the nobility fled eastwards; and Maximilian Franz himself left on 3 October.

For Beethoven this was the final event that convinced him that he should remain in Vienna. Seven months earlier he had lost his stipend as court organist; now the court itself had disappeared. In the autumn of 1794 the resolve of the young Beethoven must have stiffened as he contemplated his immediate future. How was his musical career going to unfold?

Had he turned to his teacher, Albrechtsberger, for advice he would have been told to specialize in one of the three traditional areas, church music, dramatic music or instrumental music:

> In modern times, unfortunately, an unjustifiable medley of these divisions has become prevalent, most injurious to their ultimate grand aims. We can hardly warn young musicians too strongly against this dangerous path: let every one who sincerely respects himself and real art, choose that branch for which he feels decided inclination, talent and vocation – then let him follow faithfully the banner under which he has enlisted, and never vacillate, like the mercenary soldier, who knows not what he will, nor to whom he belongs.[8]

Although this was a rather old-fashioned view in the 1790s, as the careers of Haydn and Mozart had shown, it was still a prevalent one. Beethoven's day-to-day experience in Bonn had made him well suited to a career in church music and his contact with Albrechstberger could have earned him a position as a church organist, but, while such a career would have guaranteed employment, church positions in Vienna were occupied either by musicians of local significance only, or by composers, such as Salieri and Albrechtsberger himself, who were in the later stages of their careers. It was not a career for a young ambitious musician who was expected to become as famous as Mozart and Haydn.

If a career in church music did not appeal, then one in opera was impossible; Beethoven had not had any contact with the operatic world since leaving the court in Bonn. Under the influence of his two teachers in Vienna Beethoven had already channelled his energies towards instrumental music, and it was almost inevitable that he should pursue a career in this area. Only a few years earlier a young composer of instrumental music in Vienna could have hoped to progress to the position of a Kapellmeister in an aristocratic court, but such opportunities were quickly disappearing in the 1790s as one aristocratic family after another disbanded its musical retinue. It was such a pronounced trend that a contemporary music yearbook, the *Jahrbuch der Tonkunst von Wien und Prag*, made special mention of it:

> It was formerly the strong custom that our large princely houses possessed their own house *Kapellen* whose splendid genius was built by one person (an example of this is our great Haydn). It can only be a coldness for the love of art, a change of taste, or economy, plus other reasons, in short to the shame of art, that this laudable practice has disappeared, and one *Kapelle* after an other has been extinguished, so that apart from that of Prince Schwarzenberg hardly any more exist.[9]

Although the author mentions 'coldness for the love of art' this was not a tenable reason, for music had lost none of its appeal for the aristocracy; it was simply no longer the fashion to employ large retinues of performing musicians. Instead, patronage had moved towards supporting musicians on a casual basis; in modern parlance there was a move to targeted support.

This gradual demise of the old order had not yet been replaced by a full flowering of modern trends in musical life. In comparison with London and pre-Revolutionary Paris, public concert life in Vienna was a haphazard, irregular business, with no regular subscription concerts featuring a constant core of performers and nurturing a faithful audience. Instead, spare evenings at the two court theatres, especially during Lent and Advent, could be hired by an individual or by a charitable organization for a concert. During Beethoven's first two years in Vienna, the violinist Franz Clement and the singer Josepha Dussek were only two performers who went through the arduous process of booking the hall, printing posters and tickets, selling the tickets, and paying fellow performers, all in the hope that there would be sufficient money left over to make the whole enterprise worthwhile. Twice a year the Tonkünstler-Societät (Society of Musicians) held two concerts to raise money for its members and beneficiaries, self-regarding social events that were the only regular feature of public concert life in the city.

It was in these unpromising circumstances of a private concert life that was changing and a public one that was underdeveloped that Beethoven embarked on a career in Vienna. That career was to be marked by ever-increasing ambition, but its course was inevitably conditioned by the vicissitudes of musical life in the city.

Beethoven had already told Simrock that he was not going to allow further sets of piano variations to be published until he had undertaken a 'grand review of my compositions'. The result of this review was the publication in the summer of a new opus 1, three piano trios. Replacing the previous 'Oeuvre 1', this was planned as the official launch to Beethoven's career in Vienna. The sense of a new beginning is shown by the unorthodox manner of publication. Instead of being printed and published by Artaria, Beethoven negotiated an agreement with the firm that allowed the composer to sell up to 450 copies himself, before the firm took over the sales at a lower price. While Artaria had occasionally printed a work on commission (such as Mozart's masonic cantata, *Die Maurerfreude*), there is no known precedent for this arrangement. The contract was signed by Beethoven but it is likely that Prince Lichnowsky played an important part in the whole plan, persuading friends and acquaintances to subscribe to the publication: 244 copies of the 450 were sold in advance to individuals whose names were printed in the piano part. Lichnowsky himself bought

3 First page of piano part of op. 1 no. 1 (1795)

twenty copies and members of his family a further nine copies.
Swieten purchased three copies as did the new Prince Esterházy,
Nicolaus. Most of the names are drawn from the cream of Viennese
aristocratic society, Count Apponyi, Count Browne, Countess
Brunswick, Count Erdödy, Prince Grassalkovicz, Count Harrach,
Prince Liechtenstein, Prince Lobkowitz, Count Razumovsky, Princess
Schwarzenberg and Count Thun; others, such as the second Earl of
Longford, who was on his Grand Tour, were temporary visitors to
Vienna. Many of these names were to figure in Beethoven's future
career in Vienna, but at this stage he was probably acquainted with
very few. For Prince Lichnowsky, persuading his friends to subscribe
was a novel way of promoting patronage and power while simultaneously sharing the financial burden. That it was designed as a matter of
prestige within Viennese society is suggested by the absence of any-
body from Bonn, including the elector; likewise there was nothing to
be gained from including the names of Beethoven's two teachers,

Haydn and Albrechtsberger. Thanks to Lichnowsky's efforts Beethoven made an immediate profit of over 880 gulden, a considerable sum of money and one that was not to be surpassed until the publication fee for the Missa Solemnis thirty years later.

The speculative venture of op. 1 could not easily be repeated and Beethoven's principal publications in the following years were issued in the normal way with the publisher bearing the full costs. A remarkable procession of published works appeared, advancing through to op. 21, his first symphony, in 1801. The vast majority of these published works with opus numbers involved the piano (solo sonatas, violin sonatas, cello sonatas, a horn sonata, a piano duet, piano trios and a piano and wind quintet), and were designed to further Beethoven's reputation as a pianist and a composer in the social milieu reflected in the subscription list attached to op. 1.

Artaria and other publishers in Vienna hardly ever allotted opus numbers to piano variations, dances and songs, genres that were regarded as less durable and primarily directed at the amateur market. Between 1794 and 1801 Beethoven secured the publication without opus numbers of a substantial number of works in these genres. Especially numerous are sets of variations on themes from operas and ballets that were popular in Vienna that decade: Grétry's *Richard Löwenherz* (*Richard Cœur-de-Lion*), Haibel's *Le nozze disturbate*, Paisiello's *La molinara*, Salieri's *Falstaff*, Süssmayr's *Solomon II*, Peter Winter's *Das unterbrochene Opferfest* and Wranitzky's *Das Waldmädchen*.

Many of these publications were dedicated to members of the Viennese aristocracy, including Count and Countess Browne, Countess Thun and Countess Odescalchi as well as Prince Lichnowsky. As Beethoven began to move freely in polite society he was often asked to give piano lessons, another source of income though not a reliable one because of the fickleness of some pupils and their frequent absence from Vienna, especially during the summer.

To these four elements – playing in salons, composition, publication and some teaching – Beethoven added a fifth in 1795, public performance. There is no record of him appearing as a soloist in public during his first two years in Vienna; the deliberate attempt to promote Beethoven as a virtuoso began in 1794–5 as soon as he realized that returning to the court at Bonn was not going to be possible. From this time on Beethoven worked as hard on his piano technique as he did on composition.

His public debut was intended to be as significant as the publication of op. 1: as a concerto soloist in one of the biennial concerts of the Tonkünstler-Societät held in the Burgtheater on 29 March 1795. The principal item was a performance of the first part of Anton Cartellieri's oratorio *Gioas, re di Giuda*. Beethoven played a piano concerto, and a symphony by Cartellieri was given too. Modern scholarship is divided about which piano concerto was played, with the balance of opinion favouring the B♭ concerto rather than the C major. On the following evening the second part of the oratorio was performed together with a symphony and a bassoon concerto by Cartellieri. There is no way of judging the impact of these concerts since Viennese newspapers of the time, especially the principal one, the *Wiener Zeitung*, hardly ever contained reviews of concerts and operas, another conservative feature of musical life in Vienna. On a third consecutive evening, 31 March, the Burgtheater was the venue for a benefit concert organized by Constanze Mozart to raise money for herself and her children, and to promote the music of her late husband. Mozart's *La clemenza di Tito* was performed and Beethoven played a concerto by Mozart.

With these two performances Beethoven embarked on a successful career as a pianist-composer in the mould of Clementi, Steibelt and, of particular interest to Constanze Mozart and Prince Lichnowsky, Mozart. At the end of the year Beethoven appeared for a third time in public as a soloist, another auspicious occasion, a concert in the small Redoutensaal organized by Haydn to present three of the symphonies composed during his second visit to London. Beethoven performed a piano concerto, possibly the premiere of the C major concerto. The following month he again played a concerto in the small Redoutensaal, at a benefit concert for a soprano named Maria Bolla.

The next natural step in Beethoven's career as a virtuoso pianist was to travel outside Vienna. Perhaps at Prince Lichnowsky's suggestion and certainly with his support, he travelled first to Prague, from where he wrote a cheerful letter to his brother, Johann, who had just moved to Vienna to continue his training as an apothecary:

> So that you may know at any rate where I am and what I am doing, I really must write to you. First of all, I am well, very well. My art is winning me friends and renown, and what more do I want? And this time I shall make a good deal of money. I shall remain here for a few weeks longer and then travel to Dresden, Leipzig and Berlin. So it will certainly be six weeks at least before I return –
> I hope that you will enjoy living in Vienna more and more. But do be on your guard against the whole tribe of bad women.[10]

Beethoven did, indeed, continue his journey northwards to Dresden, Leipzig and Berlin, the success of which may be judged from the fact that the planned 'six weeks at least' turned into five months. In Berlin Beethoven, like Mozart before him, visited the court of Friedrich Wilhelm II, an amateur cellist and notable patron of music who received or solicited new works from Haydn and Boccherini, as well as Mozart. The first cellist of the court orchestra was Jean-Louis Duport, who was later to publish an important treatise on cello playing, *Essai sur le doigté du Violoncello et sur la conduite de l'archet*. For this skilful player, and to the delight of his patron, Beethoven wrote two cello sonatas. The king subsequently offered him a position at court which he declined: 'Who can live among such spoiled children?', he later said to Czerny.

The cello sonatas were not the only works written during the journey: a concert aria was composed for Josepha Dussek ('Ah perfido'), a quintet for piano and wind instruments was written in Prague, and a quantity of music for the mandolin was composed for an eighteen-year-old countess from that city, Josephine de Clary. Although only one concerto performance is known, there must have been others; like all travelling virtuosos Beethoven would have carried sets of manuscript parts with him so that the typical one rehearsal and performance could be arranged quickly on the spot.

The artistic and financial success of this major tour must have encouraged Beethoven to contemplate a life of an itinerant virtuoso. At the end of 1796 he visited Pressburg (Bratislava) and Budapest, and the following year there was a return journey to Prague. However, any plans that Beethoven may have formulated to travel westwards to central Germany and beyond would have been checked by the realization that a concert tour through Europe's battleground was likely to be unrewarding, possibly dangerous.

In the same year as the five-month journey to Bohemia and northern Germany, a balanced assessment of Beethoven's standing was given in the *Jahrbuch der Tonkunst von Wien und Prag*. In a volume that has entries for over 200 performers and composers, Beethoven's entry is one of the fullest, exceeded only by those devoted to Clement (violinist), Eybler (in charge of music at the Schottenkirche), Häring (violinist), Haydn, Leopold Kozeluch (composer and publisher), Kreibig (violinist and director of the Hofkapelle), Wenzel Müller (composer of German opera), Therese Paradies (pianist and teacher) and Salieri. The initial statement is an interesting one, pointing out the significance of 1794 in Beethoven's career:

> Bethofen, a musical genius, who two years ago elected to stay in Vienna. He is universally admired for his particular virtuosity, the extraordinary difficulties which he executes with so much ease. In this short time he seems to have forced himself more or less into the inner sanctum of art, in which he excels through precision, expression and taste; in this way he has significantly elevated his fame. A telling proof of his genuine love of music is that he submitted himself to our immortal Haiden to be initiated in the hallowed secrets of composition. During his absence this great master has transferred him to our great Albrechtsberger. Much can be expected when such high genius as this submits itself to the guidance of such splendid masters. Already there are many beautiful sonatas by him, among which the last particularly excel.[11]

Contemporary comments on Beethoven's powers as a pianist invariably draw attention to the depth of expression he drew from the instrument, sometimes at the expense of technical accuracy. He was on friendly terms with Johann Andreas Streicher, a piano maker in Vienna. In a couple of letters to him Beethoven casually draws attention to the qualities needed by a good player and from a good instrument:

> There is no doubt that so far as the manner of playing is concerned, the *pianoforte* is still the least studied and developed of all instruments; often one thinks that one is merely listening to a harp. And I am delighted, my dear fellow, that you are one of the few who realize and perceive that, provided one can feel the music, one can also make the pianoforte sing. I hope that the time will come when the harp and the pianoforte will be treated as two entirely different instruments.[12]

In a second letter, dated 19 November 1796, Beethoven thanks Streicher for presenting him with a piano:

> I should be deceiving you if I didn't tell you that in my opinion it is far too good for me, and why? Well, because it robs me of the freedom to produce my own tone.[13]

'Freedom', 'feeling' and 'singing' occur over and over again in contemporary descriptions of Beethoven's piano playing, suggesting a new kind of pianism.

One of the most interesting observers of Viennese musical life at the turn of the century was Georg August Griesinger. Born in Stuttgart, he had studied in Tübingen and Leipzig before arriving in Vienna in early 1799 to be the tutor to the eldest son of Count Johann von Schönfeld, the Saxon ambassador in the city; Griesinger himself later joined the diplomatic representation in the city. A lover of music, he acted as the local representative for the Leipzig firm of Breitkopf & Härtel and provided regular accounts of Viennese musical life for its new journal, the *Allgemeine musikalische Zeitung*. Shortly after arriving in Vienna he wrote a report on the most popular pianists in Vienna, stressing that his views were not influenced by hearsay.[14] After commenting favourably on two of Vienna's leading female pianists, Josepha Auernhammer and Magdalene von Kurzbeck, Griesinger turns to the leading male pianists:

> Of these Beethoven and Wölffl cause the greatest stir. Opinion is divided here regarding the merits of the two; yet it would seem as if the majority were on the side of the latter. I shall try to set forth the peculiarities of each without taking part in this controversy. Beethoven's playing is extremely brilliant but has less delicacy and occasionally he is guilty of indistinctness. He shows himself to the greatest advantage in improvisation, and here, indeed, it is most extraordinary with what lightness and yet firmness in the succession of ideas Beethoven not only varies a theme given him on the spur of the moment by figuration (with which many a virtuoso makes his fortune and – wind) but really develops it. Since the death of Mozart, who in this respect is for me still the *non plus ultra*, I have never enjoyed this kind of pleasure in the degree in which it is provided by Beethoven.

Comparatively little is known about Beethoven's personal life during this period when he was the musical idol of aristocratic society and slowly accumulating a wider reputation through public concerts. His principal patron, Prince Lichnowsky, was a constant companion and their relationship was probably less formal than Beethoven would have experienced had he ever become Kapellmeister to Maximilian Franz, but there was still a social divide, a clear separation between patron and protégé that prevented real friendship.

The sense of a turning away from Bonn that is noticeable in the externals of Beethoven's life in 1794 is evident too in his private life. Any residual sense that he was responsible for his two brothers disappeared when both moved to Vienna where they developed their own careers, Carl as a musician, later banker, Johann as an apothecary. Although the correspondence with Eleonore von Breuning stops in 1794 her future husband, Franz Wegeler, was in Vienna from that year until the summer of 1796 when he returned to Bonn. An unknown incident momentarily clouded this friendship, prompting an anguished apology and a plea for forgiveness from Beethoven:

> Oh, try once more to throw yourself unrestrainedly into the arms of your B., and rely on the good qualities which you have always found in him. If you will do this, I guarantee that the new temple of sacred friendship which you will ever erect upon these qualities, will stand firmly and for ever, and that no misfortune, no tempest will be able to shake its foundations – firm – eternal – our friendship – forgiveness – oblivion – revival of our dying, declining friendship – Oh Wegeler, do not reject this hand which I am offering you in reconciliation, but place your hand in mine – Oh, God – But I will say nothing more – I am coming to see you, to throw myself into your arms, and to plead for the prodigal friend; and you will return to me, to your penitent Beethoven who loves you and will never forget you.[15]

Friendship with Beethoven could also generate a very different kind of behaviour, whimsical, superficial, even silly, as is apparent from his correspondence with Nikolaus Zmeskall von Domanovecz. Eleven years older than Beethoven, he was an official in the Hungarian Chancellery in Vienna. A rich man who owned wine estates in Hungary, he was a competent cellist who regularly held quartet parties; he also composed fourteen quartets himself. When Haydn prepared a new edition of his op. 20 quartets in 1800 it was dedicated to Zmeskall. Despite having a reputation for being rather stern, he seems to have responded readily to Beethoven's teasing. They met regularly at the tavern 'Zum weissen Schwann', in the Kärntnerstrasse; Beethoven cajoled him into giving him free bottles of Tokay wine, referred to him as the 'Conte di Musica' and, when Zmeskall objected to a short passage in a German dance, the composer summoned him to appear before a mock tribunal without delay: 'Handed out from our laboratorium artificiosum on October 20'.

Beethoven's letters during the 1790s often reveal a principled attitude to composition, a clear legacy of Neefe's outlook. He habitually refers to 'my art' rather than 'my music', is satisfied if only a few people rather than the multitude understand a particular work and is acutely conscious of the stylistic progress that he is making, to the extent that he is apologetic about earlier compositions. In August 1800 he wrote a letter to Friedrich von Matthisson, a poet whose 'Adelaide' he had set five years before:

I am sending you my Adelaide with a certain amount of apprehension. You yourself are aware what changes a few years may produce in an artist who is constantly progressing. The greater strides he makes in his art, the less is he satisfied with his earlier works.[16]

More than one commentator has remarked that Beethoven delayed writing his first quartet and his first symphony until he had assimilated fully the influence of Haydn and Mozart.

Beethoven began serious work on the six quartets of op. 18 in the summer of 1798 and completed the first version of the F major quartet by the following summer. Like Mozart before him, Beethoven found composing for four string instruments difficult, partly because both composers had to put to one side their facility as keyboard players. In the first version of the F major quartet Beethoven over-compensates, writing ensemble music that has so little padding that it sounds severe. In the revision, Beethoven lets the pendulum swing back a little so that there is greater variety and more air, as it were, in the texture. In this difficult task of writing naturally for the medium Beethoven sought the help of Emanuel Aloys Förster, a respected though not especially prolific composer of quartets.

There was a false start in the case of a symphony too. Beethoven worked assiduously on a symphony in C major in 1795–6; a few more months would have seen its completion. Instead it was abandoned, though some of its ideas found their way into the eventual first symphony. He may have become dissatisfied with the work as a composition but, more fundamentally, there was no real incentive for him to complete it in the mid 1790s. With no regular concert series in Vienna and no aristocratic orchestras, opportunities for the composition and performance of symphonies were limited. Haydn held a few concerts

4 Draft of aborted symphony in C major (1795–6); from 'Kafka' sketchbook

in the 1790s to present the symphonies he had written for London but even he did not contemplate adding to his tally of 104. The only other composer to make any kind of impact as a symphonist in Vienna in the 1790s was Paul Wranitzky. Most of his fifty or so symphonies were written in that decade when he was the leader of the orchestra at the court theatres and well placed to persuade the Tonkünstler-Societät and any passing singer or instrumentalist who was organizing a benefit concert to include a symphony by him. Beethoven had neither the esteem of Haydn nor the influence of Wranitzky.

Viewed against this uncongenial background, Beethoven's first benefit concert at the Burgtheater in April 1800, nearly six full years after he had decided to settle in Vienna, was daringly ambitious. He was aiming to present himself as a pianist and a major composer, something that had not happened in Viennese concert life since the heady days of Mozart's popularity in the mid 1780s. At first, Beethoven intended that the concert should include three new works: the first symphony, the septet and the C minor piano concerto. But the piano concerto was not

5   Engraving of Beethoven (c. 1801) (Johann Joseph Neidl)

finished in time and an earlier one, probably the C major, was played instead. Beethoven also gave the public a demonstration of his powers of improvisation. To complete the programme there were two numbers from Haydn's *Creation* and an unspecified symphony by Mozart.

Beethoven's friends and patrons no doubt congratulated him on a concert that was as much a landmark as the publication of the op. 1 trios five years earlier. For written testimony, however, Beethoven had to wait six months until October, when the *Allgemeine musikalische Zeitung* gave an account. Griesinger had offered to present a survey of musical life in Vienna, divided into the customary three areas of opera, instrumental and church music.[17] After indicating that regular public concerts were not a feature of Vienna's musical life, he notes the popularity of Haydn's *Creation*, mentions the morning concerts in the Augarten during the summer, comments favourably on a symphony by Méhul ('a man not only of genius but of considerable understanding'), disparages a concert given by the piano virtuoso, Steibelt and, finally, turns to Beethoven's concert:

> Herr Beethoven took over the theatre and this was truly the most interesting concert in a long time. He played a new concerto of his own composition, much of which was written with a great deal of taste and feeling. After this he improvised in a masterly fashion, and at the end one of his symphonies was performed in which there is considerable art, novelty and a wealth of ideas. The only flaw was that the wind instruments were used too much, so that it was more *Harmoniemusik* than orchestral music.

As a pianist and composer Beethoven had established himself as the leading figure in Vienna and he could look forward to the support of the wider public as well as the aristocracy. His first patron, Maximilian Franz, was now living in the city, a rather forlorn man who still styled himself Elector of Cologne and who clung to the hope that he might one day return there. In a touching mark of gratitude Beethoven instructed the publisher of the first symphony, Hoffmeister of Leipzig, to dedicate the work to the elector. Alas, Maximilian Franz died in July 1801, five months before it was published; in these sad circumstances the dedication was changed to Gottfried van Swieten.

3 Cursing his creator and his existence

Encouraged by the success of his first benefit concert Beethoven began work on his second symphony in the winter of 1800–1, with the intention that it should form a major item in his next concert. He worked on the content of the first movement in particular and, to a lesser extent, the scherzo and the finale, before placing the symphony aside in favour of a wholly unexpected commission, music for a ballet to be performed at the Burgtheater.

Ballet had experienced a chequered history in Vienna. In the 1760s and 1770s it had formed a regular part of theatrical entertainment, lavishly funded and enjoying a status equal to that of Italian opera; Asplmayr, Gluck and Starzer were the principal composers. Joseph II, however, disliked ballet and it did not figure in the court theatres, depriving posterity of Viennese ballet music by Mozart. His successor, Leopold II, reinstated the ballet company and from 1791 through to the nineteenth century it formed a regular and distinctive part of theatrical life in Vienna. By 1796 there was a company of nearly fifty dancers led by the ballet master Salvatore Viganò. Although he was replaced as ballet master two years later he remained active in the company until 1818. In one or two acts only, ballets never formed a complete evening of entertainment but typically followed a play or an opera; some had plots, others were a collection of dances with no binding narrative. The subject matter varied from the historical, such as Die wiedergefundene Tochter Otto des II. Kaisers der Deutschen (forty

55

performances), to the comical, such as *Das Waldmädchen* (130 performances). The leading composers in the 1790s were Joseph Weigl, first Kapellmeister at the court theatres, Paul Wranitzky, orchestral director at the theatres, and Leopold Kozeluch. How Beethoven came to compose ballet music is unclear. The court theatres were managed by Baron Peter von Braun, an acquaintance of Beethoven's for some years, with whom he must have negotiated the hiring of the Burgtheater for his benefit concert. Beethoven also knew the countess, dedicating two piano sonatas (op. 14) and the horn sonata to her. It was very likely this connection that led to the commission. The story was that of Prometheus, the bringer of fire, who gives life to two statues and enlightens them with knowledge and experience. With great enthusiasm Beethoven composed an overture and seventeen further numbers. After several years of studied composition of sonatas, trios, concertos and symphonies this score reflects the lighter, engaging side of Beethoven's creativity, up to now glimpsed only in piano variations and dances. He revels in the opportunity to explore new orchestral colours in a storm number, and in extended solo writing for cello, harp and basset horn (played by Anton Stadler, Mozart's clarinettist). Although it was performed on twenty-eight occasions, a respectable total, it was not judged a success and Beethoven was not asked to write further ballet music. The irony of this modest success is that it was to represent the largest number of performances in public of any work by Beethoven in Vienna during his lifetime.

The evident energy and enthusiasm with which Beethoven composed the ballet music was in sharp contrast to his mental and physical well-being during the winter of 1800–1. More than one letter from the period indicates that he was unwell. The first to provide reasonably full details was written on 29 June 1801 to his old friend, Franz Gerhard Wegeler in Bonn. It is a lengthy letter of six sides, carefully structured and eloquently written.[1] First, he greets Wegeler with great affection, becomes nostalgic about Bonn and indicates that he is now quite a different person from the one Wegeler had known in Vienna five years earlier. He then gives more details of his burgeoning success as a composer:

> My compositions bring me in a good deal; and I may say that I am offered more commissions than it is possible for me to carry out. Moreover for every composition I can count on six or seven publishers, and even more, if I want them; people no longer come to an arrangement with me, I state my price and they pay. So you see how pleasantly situated I am. For instance, I see a friend in need and if it so happens that the state of my purse does not allow me to help him immediately; well then, I have only to sit down and compose and in a short time I can come to his aid – Moreover, I live more economically than I used to; and if I remain in Vienna for good, no doubt I shall contrive to obtain one day every year for a concert.

From this rosy picture, Beethoven turns to the real purpose of the letter, the confession of a debilitating condition, one that was potentially far worse than the chronic stomach complaint that Wegeler knew about. As a trained physician who was eventually to become professor of medicine at Bonn university, Wegeler was a friend who would be able to respond appropriately to this devastating news:

> But that jealous demon, my wretched health, has put a nasty spoke in my wheel; and it amounts to this, that for the last three years my hearing has become weaker and weaker. The trouble is supposed to have been caused by the condition of my abdomen which, as you know, was wretched even before I left Bonn, but has become worse in Vienna where I have been constantly afflicted with diarrhoea and have been suffering in consequence from an extraordinary debility. Frank tried to *tone up* my constitution with strengthening medicines and my hearing with almond oil, but much good did it do me! His treatment had no effect, my deafness became even worse and my abdomen continued to be in the same state as before. Such was my condition until the autumn of last year; and sometimes I gave way to despair. Then a medical *asinus* advised me to take cold baths to improve my condition. A more sensible doctor, however, prescribed the usual tepid baths in the Danube. The result was miraculous; and my inside improved. But my deafness persisted or, I should say,

became even worse. During this last winter I was truly wretched, for I had really dreadful attacks of colic and again relapsed completely into my former condition. And thus I remained until about four weeks ago when I went to see Vering. For I began to think that my condition demanded the attention of a surgeon as well; and in any case I had confidence in him. Well, he succeeded in checking almost completely this violent diarrhoea. He prescribed tepid baths in the Danube, to which I had always to add a bottle of strengthening ingredients. He ordered no medicines until about four days ago when he prescribed pills for my stomach and an infusion for my ear. As a result I have been feeling, I may say, stronger and better; but my ears continue to hum and buzz day and night. I must confess that I lead a miserable life. For almost two years I have ceased to attend any social functions, just because I find it impossible to say to people: I am deaf. If I had any other profession I might be able to cope with my infirmity; but in my profession it is a terrible handicap. And if my enemies, of whom I have a fair number, were to hear about it, what would they say? – In order to give you some idea of the strange deafness, let me tell you that in the theatre I have to place myself quite close to the orchestra in order to understand what the actor is saying, and that at a distance I cannot hear the high notes of instruments or voices. As for the spoken voice it is surprising that some people have never noticed my deafness; but since I have always been liable to fits of absent-mindedness, they attribute my hardness of hearing to that. Sometimes too I can scarcely hear a person who speaks softly; I can hear sounds, it is true, but cannot make out the words. But if anyone shouts, I can't bear it. Heaven alone knows what is to become of me. Vering tells me that my hearing will certainly improve, although my deafness may not be completely cured – Already I have often cursed my Creator and my existence. Plutarch has shown me the path of resignation. If it is at all possible, I will bid defiance to my fate, though I feel that as long as I live there will be moments when I shall be God's most unhappy creature . . .

Beethoven also confided his condition to his friend Karl Amenda, in a letter written a couple of days later. This and a second letter to Wegeler have the same mixture of secrecy, anguish and a desperate desire to overcome the affliction. The deafness, which had started in the left ear, was treated by three doctors in Vienna, Frank, Schmidt and Vering, who variously prescribed all kinds of medicines, cold and tepid baths and compresses of bark tied tightly to the arms; Beethoven even contemplated the new wonder cure of galvanism, named after its inventor Luigi Galvani. At best these treatments alleviated a condition that tended to fluctuate anyway. Some relief from this private anguish was provided by 'a charming girl who loves me and whom I love'.[2]

This charming girl was almost certainly a seventeen-year-old pupil, Countess Giulietta Guicciardi. When, later in life, she was asked about her friendship with Beethoven she remarked only that he was a strict teacher and that he was 'very ugly, but noble, sensitive and cultured'. Maybe in this case the common infatuation of a teenage pupil for a teacher was reversed. Certainly, Beethoven seems to have idealized the relationship, once refusing a gift (probably an item of clothing) on the grounds that it made him feel indebted. To explain his position he resorted to coining an aphorism, an increasingly favoured and pompous way of challenging unwelcome behaviour: 'Friendship has no other reward than that which lies within it.'[3]

Even before Beethoven had confided in Wegeler and Amenda there were signs that the nature of his career was changing in a way that would enable him to adjust to worsening deafness. Unlike the situation in 1794–5 there was never a decisive moment when a new career plan was formulated, the severe bouts of depression revealed in individual letters exposing inner tension rather than signalling a drastic change of outlook. The most immediate effect was that a career as a performing musician who regularly travelled around Europe was not going to be possible. Increasing deafness would eventually make performance impractical but the more immediate problem that vexed Beethoven was a social one, embarrassment at not being able to hear conversation clearly and to respond appropriately, whether in formal or informal surroundings. A salon musician and travelling virtuoso was admired as much for his personality as for his playing. Always socially rather withdrawn, Beethoven had become increasingly unwilling to act the role of a celebrity and had already allowed the image of the difficult, unpredictable individual to evolve. Although he continued to perform in public for many more years the number of performances decreases markedly. Between the first benefit concert of April 1800 and the second in April 1803 he is known to have played in public on three occasions only, all of them performances of the horn sonata with Wenzel Punto, two in Vienna and one in Budapest. In addition there was no major journey abroad, not even a suggestion of one. Prince Lichnowsky had supported his first very successful virtuoso tour. From some time in 1800 Beethoven received an annual stipend of 600 gulden from the prince, which may have been intended to compensate for the fewer public performances given by him.

Beethoven continued to compose substantial quantities of piano music, especially sonatas and sets of variations, but in the latter in particular there is a widening gap between works intended for the seasoned musician and those for the amateur, the old *Kenner* and *Liebhaber*. For the *Liebhaber* he wrote entertaining variations on 'God save the King' and 'Rule, Britannia', whereas the *Kenner* were offered variations on original themes rather than popular tunes, and with structures that amended and expanded the pat repetitions traditionally associated with a set of variations. Beethoven himself referred to a 'method that is quite new' and altogether, whatever the genre, composition was already more intellectually rewarding than performing.

While further concert tours would have aided Beethoven's reputation beyond Vienna, there were plenty of signs that this was no longer necessary as far as his compositions were concerned. When Beethoven told Wegeler that he could 'count on six or seven publishers' he was not exaggerating. In Vienna his music was sought by five publishers, Artaria, Bureau des Arts et d'Industrie, Eder, Mollo and Traeg. These were now joined by three foreign publishers. The first to approach Beethoven was Franz Anton Hoffmeister of Leipzig. From the early 1780s he had been a prolific composer of instrumental music in Vienna, though the *Jahrbuch der Tonkunst von Wien und Prag* noted that he seemed to be more popular abroad than in Vienna itself. He was a new kind of composer who supported composition with a career as a publisher, becoming the principal rival to Artaria. The music of Haydn and, especially, Mozart had been published by the firm and Beethoven's *Sonate pathétique* and the variations on a theme by Süssmayr (WoO 76) were entrusted to Hoffmeister in 1799. Shortly afterwards Hoffmeister moved to Leipzig, where he founded a new publishing firm in partnership with Kühnel; although based in that city it retained a manager in Vienna too. From Leipzig Hoffmeister wrote to Beethoven asking whether he could publish some recent compositions. The proposal was doubly attractive to Beethoven: first, it enabled him to distribute his music in Germany's foremost musical city and, secondly, Hoffmeister, unlike his Viennese rival, Artaria, was willing to publish large-scale works such as concertos and symphonies. In the next eighteen months Hoffmeister was to issue the B♭ concerto (No. 2), the first symphony as well as the septet (a lengthy work of seven movements) and the B♭ piano sonata (op. 22).

Leipzig was also the home of Europe's leading music publisher, Breitkopf & Härtel. As an ordinary printer the family firm of Breitkopf had been active from the sixteenth century, and as a music publisher its activities can be traced back to the early eighteenth century; Johann Sebastian Bach was only one of many composers who figured in the output of the firm. It acquired a new lease of life in 1795 when Gottfried Christoph Härtel joined the firm. Together they sought a new authority in musical circles by marketing 'complete' editions of the music of Mozart and Haydn, the former with the co-operation of the composer's widow, Constanze, the latter with the co-operation of the composer and the local go-between Griesinger. In 1798 a new journal was founded by the firm that was to run for fifty years, the *Allgemeine musikalische Zeitung*. In double column format, it appeared every week and contained articles on composers, surveys of musical life, anecdotes, reviews of publications and of concerts in German-speaking Europe, plus the occasional music supplement. Beethoven was an enthusiastic reader, making notes on matters that interested him and reacting peevishly to any adverse comment on his music.

Probably at the instigation of Griesinger, Breitkopf & Härtel first made contact with Beethoven early in 1801, a few months after Hoffmeister. The composer was in the unfortunate position that major works such as symphonies, quartets and sonatas were already promised to other publishers, and so the first works issued by the firm were a string quintet (op. 29) and two sets of piano variations (op. 34 and op. 35). Nevertheless, the knowledge that Breitkopf & Härtel might, in principle, be interested in the composer's most ambitious works must have been of major encouragement at a time when Beethoven was obliged to emphasize composition rather than performance.

The publication of the string quintet by Breitkopf & Härtel in December 1802 occasioned a rift between Beethoven and Artaria, the Viennese publisher who had set his career in motion in 1795. Count Fries had purchased a manuscript copy of the quintet from Beethoven, which he handed over to Artaria to form the text of a printed edition. Beethoven was asked to correct the proofs, which he did, but in a deliberately careless manner. In order not to jeopardize his relationship with the illustrious firm of Breitkopf & Härtel, to whom he had promised the work, Beethoven seems to have decided to sabotage Artaria's edition. He went further. He inserted a notice in the *Wiener Zeitung* declaring Artaria's edition to be 'extremely faulty, inaccurate and quite useless for the performer; whereas Herren Breitkopf & Härtel, the lawful owners of this quintet, have done their utmost to produce the work as handsomely as possible'.[4] Artaria was understandably furious and instigated legal proceedings against the composer, who disingenuously commented that Haydn had always acted in this way. The court ruled against Beethoven and he was required to issue a public apology. He never did.

Other foreign publishers who contacted Beethoven at this time were Nägeli of Zurich, who subsequently issued the three sonatas of op. 31 as part of a continuing series entitled *Répertoire des Clavecinistes*, and André from Offenbach, with whom Beethoven was not able to make a deal.

Royalty payments were almost unknown at the time; instead publishers paid a single lump sum for a work or a group of works. Financial negotiations between composers and publishers were often tortuous; if successful, the composer usually supplied a manuscript copy (not the original autograph) at his own expense; and, finally, proofs had to be read, though they were not always supplied. For a while Beethoven's brother Carl, now a proud member of the Imperial and Royal bureaucracy, acted as the composer's secretary. Even in the eighteenth century major publishers like Artaria and Breitkopf had tried to take note of the most recent opus number applied by a fellow publisher in order to maintain some semblance of chronology. Beethoven, with Carl's assistance, was the first major composer to control the allocating of numbers himself, a small but significant indication of his ambition and self-esteem.

Music publishers in London were not to approach Beethoven until a few years later. However, the first public performance in London of a work by the composer took place in 1801. Salomon, the violinist and impresario who had twice brought Haydn to London in the 1790s, organized a subscription concert series in 1801.[5] Six concerts were announced, but in the event only five took place, the last of which was Salomon's own benefit. The Times announced that the 'most admired symphonies composed for Mr. Salomon by Dr. Haydn', that is, Nos. 93–104, were to be a regular feature, and that there were 'also several new Compositions lately received'. Salomon had written to Beethoven, asking him for new works, and the composer responded by forwarding manuscript parts of the septet in advance of its publication by Hoffmeister. It was performed in London on 23 April at the Great Concert Rooms of the King's Theatre, Haymarket, announced as the work of 'Luigi Van Beethoven'. Salomon's subscription series was a half-hearted attempt to revive the glory days of the Haydn concerts of the previous decade and was not a success. The septet, however, made a decided impact and was performed again, in Salomon's benefit, on 27 May.

Another small, but notable development in Beethoven's career at this time was the teaching of gifted young pianists intent on a professional career. From Bonn came the son of Franz Ries, a former violinist at the court; the seventeen-year-old Ferdinand was warmly welcomed by Beethoven, who taught him for four years. Even younger, aged only ten, was Carl Czerny, who, guided by his overprotective father, also had lessons with Beethoven. Both Ries and Czerny were to grow up to be stalwart advocates of his music.

At the age of thirty-two, Beethoven had developed a career, therefore, that was flourishing and promising. He maintained the general support of Viennese society and the particular support of Prince Lichnowsky; his music was increasingly distributed at home and abroad; he had completed a third piano concerto and begun a second symphony; and he had moved from being the interesting newcomer to a permanent figure of esteem. Overshadowing everything, however, was the continuing worry of deafness.

One of Beethoven's doctors, Schmidt, had encouraged him to seek a period of quiet rest, and in late April or May 1802 he moved to Heiligenstadt for six months. Three miles to the north-west of Vienna Heiligenstadt, even today, is a tranquil place. Beethoven's rooms, on the first floor of a house in the Probusgasse, are now a museum. The house stands on the brow of a gentle hill, except that the brow, too, is very gentle; turning to the right Beethoven could walk to the village square and the church in a couple of minutes, to the left was the way to the sulphur baths. Surrounded by fruitful fields and further hills, many covered with rows of vines for the local wine industry, the location was ideally suited to long country walks. Beethoven seems to have taken Dr Schmidt's advice seriously and to have reduced his working hours considerably.

While tranquillity, solitude and little work made for an idyllic existence, they must also have nurtured Beethoven's self-doubt and fears. As summer turned to autumn he became increasingly despondent as he realized that his stay in Heiligenstadt had not improved his hearing. On 6 October he wrote a document of four pages, with an addendum four days later. Alternately poignant and powerful, it would have been striking had it been written by a poet or a dramatist; it is doubly so coming from a musician.[6]

FOR MY BROTHERS CARL AND [JOHANN] BEETHOVEN

O you men who think or say I am hostile, peevish, or misanthropic, how greatly you wrong me. You do not know the secret cause which makes me seem so to you. From childhood on, my heart and soul were full of the tender feeling of goodwill, and I was always inclined to accomplish great deeds. But just think, for six years now I have had an incurable condition, made worse by incompetent doctors, from year to year deceived with hopes of getting better, finally forced to face the prospect of a lasting infirmity (whose cure will perhaps take years or even be impossible). Though born with a fiery, lively temperament, susceptible to the diversions of society, I soon had to withdraw myself, to spend my life alone. And if I wished at times to ignore all this, oh how harshly was I pushed back by the double sad experience of my bad hearing; and it was impossible for me to say to people, 'Speak louder, shout, for I am deaf.' Ah, how could I possibly admit weakness of the *one sense* which should be more perfect in me than in others, a sense which I once possessed in the greatest perfection, a perfection such as few in my profession have or ever have had.

Oh I cannot do it; so forgive me if you see me draw back when I would gladly have mingled with you. My misfortune is doubly painful to me as I am bound to be misunderstood; for me there can be no relaxation in human company, no refined conversations, no mutual outpourings. I must live quite alone, like an outcast; I can enter society practically only as much as real necessity demands. If I approach people a burning anxiety comes over me, in that I fear being placed in danger of my condition being noticed.

It has also been like this during the last six months, which I have spent in the country. My understanding doctor, by ordering me to spare my hearing as much as possible, almost came to my own present natural disposition, although I sometimes let myself be drawn by my love of companionship. But what humiliation for me when someone standing near me heard a flute in the distance and I *heard nothing*, or someone heard the shepherd singing and again I

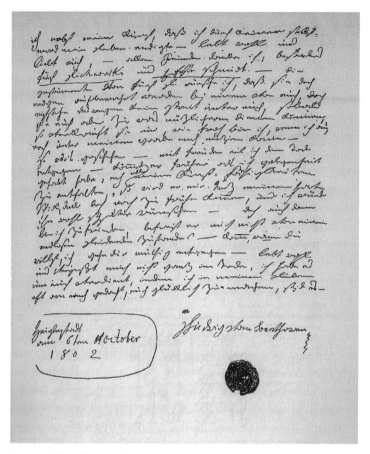

6 Part of the Heiligenstadt Testament (1802)

heard nothing. Such incidents brought me almost to despair; a little more and I would have ended my life.

Only *my art* held me back. Ah, it seemed to me impossible to leave the world until I had produced all that I felt was within me; and so I spared this wretched life – truly wretched for so susceptible a body, which by a sudden change can reduce me from the best condition to the very worst.

Patience, they say, is what I must now choose for my guide, and I have done so – I hope my determination will firmly endure until it pleases the inexorable Parcae to break the thread. Perhaps I shall get better, perhaps not; I am ready. Forced to become a philosopher already in my 28th year, it is not easy, and for the artist harder than for anyone else.

Divine One, thou lookest down on my inmost soul and knowest it; thou knowest that therein dwells the love of man and inclination to do good. O men, when at some point you read this, then consider that you have done me an injustice; and the unfortunate may console themselves to find a similar case to theirs, who despite all the limitations of nature yet did everything he could to be admitted to the ranks of worthy artists and men.

You, my brothers Carl and [Johann], as soon as I am dead, if Dr Schmidt is still alive, ask him in my name to describe my disease, and attach this written document to his account of my illness, so that at least as much as possible the world may be reconciled to me after my death.

At the same time, I here declare you two to be the heirs to my small fortune (if one can call it such); divide it fairly, and bear with and help each other. What you have done against me you know was long ago forgiven. You, brother Carl, I thank in particular for your recent proven attachment to me. My wish is that you have a better, more trouble-free life than I have had. Recommend *virtue* to your children; it alone, not money, can provide happiness. I speak from experience; virtue was what raised me in my distress. Thanks to it and to my art, I did not end my life by suicide.

Farewell and love each other.

I thank all my friends, particularly *Prince Lichnowsky* and *Professor Schmidt* – I want the instruments from Prince L. to be preserved by one of you, but not to cause strife between you; as soon as it is more useful to you, just sell them. How happy I am if I can still be of use to you in my grave – so let it be. With joy I hasten towards death. If it comes before I have had the chance to develop all my artistic abilities, then despite my harsh fate it will still be coming too soon and I should probably wish it later – yet even so I should be content, for would it not free me from a state of endless suffering? Come when thou wilt, I shall approach thee bravely.

Farewell, and do not completely forget me when I am dead. I have deserved this from you, since I often thought of you during my life, and of ways to make you happy; do be so.

Ludwig van Beethoven

Heiglnstadt [sic]
6 October 1802

For my brothers Carl and [Johann]
to be read and executed after my death
Heiglnstadt [sic], 10 October 1802, thus I take leave of thee – and indeed sadly. Yes, the fond hope, which I brought here with me, to be cured at least to some degree – this I must now wholly abandon. As the leaves of autumn fall and wither, so too has my hope dried up; I go away almost as I came. Even the high courage which often inspired me in the fine summer days has disappeared.

O Providence – grant me some time a pure day of joy. For so long now the heartfelt echo of true joy has been strange to me. Oh when – oh when, oh Divine One – can I feel it again in the temple of nature and of mankind – Never? No – oh that would be too hard.

Part letter, part will, even for some people part suicide note, this document refuses to be categorized. Its initial paragraphs suggest a letter to his brothers, rather like the ones he had sent to Wegeler and Amenda, admitting the extent of his disability; the second part, with its specific instructions on how to act following his death, have the character of a will. If it was intended as a letter it was one that was never sent; on the other hand if it was a will, then it is very incomplete. Beethoven carefully kept the document for the rest of his life, through several dozen changes of abode. It was discovered after his death and published in the *Allgemeine musikalische Zeitung* where it was described as 'a testament';[7] it soon became known as the Heiligenstadt Testament. It is a testament not in the narrow legal sense of a will but as a statement of character, a mixture of the rational, the impulsive, the meandering and, in the postscript, the angry. For the modern psychologist it is the next best thing to Beethoven on the couch. Perhaps this was its value to the composer, a tormented souvenir from a difficult period in his life, and why he kept it long after it had ceased to have any validity as a will.

Some aspects of Beethoven's personality revealed in the document are familiar ones: the sense of duty to his art, the moralizing ('Virtue alone can make a man happy') and the fear of being misjudged. Also, the document reveals a warm, humane side to his character ('the love of man and inclination to do good'), especially if it involved his art. He had floated the idea to Breitkopf & Härtel of issuing a new work on subscription, the proceeds going to the impoverished daughter of J. S. Bach, 'the immortal god of harmony'; and, taking one of the more impracticable ideas thrown up by French enlightenment thinkers, he had proposed that there should be a music store ('Magazin de Musique') where his compositions could be exchanged for everyday goods. In the latter stages of the main document and in the disjointed rhetoric of the addendum there is a heartfelt plea for happiness and joy ('Oh Providence – grant me some time a pure day of joy').

Beethoven's musical inheritance was one where optimism and a positive outlook constituted the final impression in most compositions, whether a rondo in a Haydn symphony or a *lieto fine* in a Mozart opera. But the sense of a struggle to achieve an artificially joyous state that is apparent in the Heiligenstadt Testament is a clear harbinger of the content of many of Beethoven's future works, *Fidelio*, *Egmont* and, most directly, the ninth symphony. Perhaps Beethoven retained the document because it was, in some measure, an artistic testament too.

One of the disappointments of the earlier part of the year was Beethoven's failure to secure the Burgtheater for a presentation of his recent music, including the third piano concerto and (he hoped) the second symphony. Of all Beethoven's endeavours, the organizing of public concerts was the most wearingly difficult; he might well have mused that it was easier to ensure the publication of a major work than it was to ensure a performance. A new opportunity became apparent in the winter of 1802–3. There was a new theatre in Vienna, the Theater an der Wien, replacing the old Freihaus (or Theater auf der Wieden). Located across the Glacis in the Laimgrube it was a splendid building, founded on the financial and artistic success of Emanuel Schikaneder, the librettist of *The Magic Flute*. Outside the direct control of the court, it was soon regarded as the premier theatre in Vienna, with a programme of serious and comic opera (usually in German), ballets and pantomimes, as well as plays. It was also the largest theatre in Vienna, holding about 2,200 people of which about 1,500 were standing places. Shortly after its opening in June 1801 an enthusiastic commentator wrote as follows:

> For carriages there is a designated gate and entrance. From there we stepped into the most elegant building, in which stairs lead on either side to the upper floors. A few steps towards the centre brings one to the box office, and from there one is directed to appointed places along very fine corridors and comfortable, wide stone stairways; the two court theatres cannot match the many advantages and conveniences of this theatre . . .
>
> The entire theatre is decorated in the most beautiful blue and with silver. It has four floors, of which the first two are divided half in boxes and half in galleries that reach right over the stalls, giving the viewers more room and bringing them closer to the stage. All the seats are as comfortable and as roomy as those in the equivalent categories in the court theatres, the boxes are charming and advantageous . . . Walls, pillars, the railings of the boxes and both upper floors are covered with blue and rich silver decorations, antique borders, medallions, paintings etc. The boxes have curtains made of blue silk and the two principal boxes, intended for the use of the imperial aristocracy, are magnificent.[8]

Given that Beethoven's relationships with the manager of the court theatres, Peter von Braun, was a difficult one, he must have been delighted to be asked by Schikaneder to become a house composer at this new independent theatre. Ignaz Seyfried was the permanent Kapellmeister at the theatre and Beethoven's post was not a fixed one with wide responsibilities, but was linked with the composition of one work, to be decided; Abbé Vogler was engaged at the same time on a similar basis. No doubt the association could be continued if the work was successful. Both Beethoven and Vogler were given accommodation at the theatre, rather cramped rooms with little daylight. As

7 The Theater an der Wien

in the two court theatres run by Braun, the Burgtheater and the Kärntnertortheater, three or four concerts per year were given, in Advent and Lent–typically an oratorio for charity, sometimes benefits for individuals. Occasionally, concertos and other single items of music were played between the acts of the main stage work. Beethoven, however, was not likely to be satisfied with single performances; neither was Abbé Vogler, who was a prolific composer of all kinds of music and an irrepressible showman.

Three major concerts were given at the Theater an der Wien in Lent 1803. On 25 March Süssmayr's oratorio *Moses* was performed; the following evening a concert of works by one of the house composers, Abbé Vogler, was presented; and on 5 April a concert by the other house composer, Beethoven, was arranged. The last included the long-awaited first performance of the second symphony and of the third piano concerto, only the second known performance in Vienna of the first symphony, and the premiere of a recently completed oratorio, *Christus am Oelberge*.

Oratorio was an entirely new departure for Beethoven but, as with the ballet *The Creatures of Prometheus*, it shows a typical eagerness to explore unfamiliar musical territory. In November 1802, just as Beethoven was taking up his position in the Theater an der Wien, Carl Beethoven had claimed in a letter to Johann André that his brother no longer wished to compose piano sonatas (described as 'trifles'), 'only oratorios, operas etc.'[9] In 1795 Beethoven had made his public debut as a pianist in the middle of an oratorio performance and there was a healthy local tradition of oratorio composition, dominated by the two late oratorios of Haydn, *The Creation* and *The Seasons*. The former, in particular, was regularly performed; indeed, there was a performance at the Burgtheater on the same evening as Beethoven's concert. Süssmayr's *Moses* was also a familiar part of the repertoire. It was only natural, therefore, that a composer of Beethoven's ambition should want to tackle the genre, though the duration of the work, fifty-five minutes, suggests that he was anxious to avoid direct comparison with Haydn. The subject matter, too, Christ's sufferings on Calvary, is very different from that of Haydn's masterpieces. A determining element in the choice of the text was its explicit sense of universal suffering, something that resonated deeply with the author of the Heiligenstadt Testament. Barry Cooper has drawn attention to some striking parallels between the text of the oratorio, on the one hand, and the content of the Testament and the letters to Wegeler and Amenda on the other; he further proposes that the composer helped in the drafting of the text, even to the extent of supplying some of the phraseology.[10]

The concert received the customary one rehearsal. Among the interested onlookers were the faithful Prince Lichnowsky and the eager Ferdinand Ries. The latter recorded his impressions:

> Prince Carl Lichnowsky, who attended the rehearsal from the beginning, sent out for great hampers of bread and butter, cold meats and wine. In a friendly way he invited everybody to help themselves, which they did even with both hands, so that everyone was once again in a good humour. Then the Prince requested that the oratorio be tried out once more, so that it might come off well in the

evening and Beethoven's first work of this kind be presented to the public in a worthy manner. So the rehearsal began again.[11]

The concert was a modest success. One commentator remarked that the first symphony was a better work than the second, which was judged too forced, and that Beethoven's piano playing did not satisfy everyone. Another thought the oratorio 'too drawn out, too contrived in construction and lacking in expressive relevance'.[12] Despite this lukewarm reception Beethoven made 1,800 gulden, three times his annual stipend from Prince Lichnowsky and enough to keep the composer supplied with hampers of food and wine for a year. The despair of the previous autumn had been overcome.

4   Drama and symphony

Three days after the concert at the Theater an der Wien Beethoven wrote a buoyant letter to Breitkopf & Härtel.[1] The proper labelling of the constituent sections of the 'Eroica' variations for piano was posing a problem for composer and publisher; Beethoven wanted to change the dedication from Abbé Stadler to Count Moritz Lichnowsky ('He is the brother of Prince Lichnowsky and only recently did me an unexpected kindness . . .'); he confirms, too, that another set of variations is to be dedicated to Princess Odescalchi; thanks the publisher for a volume of Bach's music and enquires about a sequel; and, finally, signs off with the request 'If you have a fine text for a cantata or any other vocal work, do let me see it.'

The same positive outlook is found in other letters over the next few months, confirmation that the concert had banished the self-doubt and despondency of the previous autumn. A violinist from London, George Polgreen Bridgetower, was visiting Vienna. He had already played for Prince Lobkowitz and the banker, Fries, and Beethoven introduced him to other members of Viennese society: Baron Wetzlar, Therese Schönfeld, Countess Guicciardi and Count Deym. The composer accompanied his performances, and in a matter of a few weeks wrote a new and challenging sonata for him (op. 47 in A major); it was given its first performance on 24 May at one of the morning concerts in the Augarten. Work on an even more challenging composition began in the summer, a new symphony in E♭, the Eroica Symphony.

Apart from the scale of the work, which builds on the experience of the second symphony as well as the A major violin sonata, this symphony reflects two other recent preoccupations. First, the finale was to use the same compositional approach found in the piano variations being prepared for publication by Breitkopf & Härtel: essentially a set of variations on a theme taken from the *Prometheus* ballet, preceded by sections that prefigure the theme itself, variations in search of a theme as well as on a theme. (This was the section that caused the labelling confusion between composer and publisher.) The symphony expands further on the standard approach to the writing of variations, allowing them to overspill the structural boundaries of the original theme, with the result that the movement has an unprecedented sense of expansive discovery. Whether the entire symphony was conceived in order to accommodate the possibilities that Beethoven glimpsed when writing the piano variations, or whether the idea of using the same material arose after he had conceived the earlier movements cannot be answered.

Secondly, Beethoven's ultimate title for the work, 'Sinfonia Eroica' ('Heroic Symphony'), reflects an equally forward-looking feature: the composer's intense contemporary interest in music with a programmatic content, the belief that music could – indeed should – deal with issues beyond the notes on the page. He had just composed an oratorio, was awaiting a libretto from Schikaneder and had asked Breitkopf & Härtel to pass on any suitable texts for a cantata. Patriotism, closely related to heroism, was a popular subject matter, recently given voice in such diverse works as Haydn's specially composed national anthem, 'Gott erhalte Franz den Kaiser', Beethoven's own song with refrain, 'Kriegslied der Oesterreicher' ('Warsong of the Austrians'), Salieri's cantata *Der Tyroler Landsturm* (*The Tyrolean Home Guard*) and Paul Wranitzky's 'Grande sinfonie caractéristique pour la paix avec la République française', written to celebrate the signing of the Peace of Campo Formio in 1797.

The summer of 1803 was a relatively relaxed period for Austria in the continuing European conflict. It had declared itself neutral at the most recent outbreak of fighting between France and Britain, a situation that encouraged Beethoven to contemplate a journey to Paris and to attach the title 'Bonaparte' to his newest symphony. In a way that many of his aristocratic patrons in Vienna would have thought indulgent or irresponsible Beethoven admired some of the republican ideals that Napoleon as First Consul practised. It was an innocent illusion that was to be broken a year later when Napoleon declared himself emperor, and Beethoven, having already decided against a journey to the French capital, famously tore up the title-page of the autograph manuscript (now lost). It was then that the symphony acquired the more general title 'Sinfonia Eroica'. While the severe Austrian censorship laws would never have allowed the specific title, artistically the general one was much more suited to Beethoven's achievement: an evocation of a heroic ideal rather than of one heroic figure.

Most of the composition of the symphony was undertaken at Oberdöbling, a village between Vienna and Heiligenstadt, where Beethoven spent the summer of 1803. He was still waiting for a libretto from Schikaneder whose managerial duties at the Theater an der Wien prevented him from completing it as quickly as both he and the composer would have liked. During these months Viennese operatic taste changed almost overnight in a way that had not happened since the accession of Leopold II over a decade earlier. At the Theater an der Wien old favourite operas by Mozart (Die Entführung aus dem Serail), Martín y Soler (Das Liebesfest in Catalonien and Die Insel der Liebe) and Peter Winter (Das Labyrinth, billed as a sequel to Die Zauberflöte) continued to be performed, but the imagination of the public had been caught by a new style, operas from France translated into German. The trend had started the previous year with performances of three works by Cherubini, Lodoiska, Les deux journées and Eliza. Their success prompted a wave of similar works, especially by Méhul; his Le trésor supposé, Une folie, L'irato and Héléna were all given between May and December 1803, joined by a fourth opera by Cherubini, La prisonnière. Most of this repertoire was intensely serious rather than frivolously comic; the action tended to be governed by the heroic intent of individuals rather than the chance intervention of the magical or the supernatural; and the settings were recognizably real, even contemporary, rather than escapist or mythological. This turn-of-the-century *verismo* captured Beethoven's imagination as it did everybody else's, and it could not have been more timely. Beethoven had always sought to be high-minded and resolute in his musical outlook, qualities that made him appear priggish in his daily life. After the energy and drama that inform the second symphony, *Christus am Oelberge* and the Eroica Symphony, all completed in a matter of twenty-one months, suddenly to have these characteristics displayed on the operatic stage in situations that were grippingly theatrical, even histrionic, was a revelation. All of a sudden the Schikaneder tradition in opera seemed old-fashioned and irrelevant. Schikaneder finally produced a text for Beethoven: *Vestas Feuer* (*Vestal Flame*), set, like many an old Metastasio opera, in ancient Rome with roles for a magistrate, a tribune, a couple of soothsayers and a slave. With severe misgivings Beethoven began setting the libretto, virtually completing the opening number, 'Blick, O Herr'. At about the same time he received the first act of another libretto, from Johann Friedrich Rochlitz, the editor of the *Allgemeine musikalische Zeitung*. On 4 January Beethoven wrote a polite reply to Rochlitz:[2]

> However fortunate I should have counted myself to be allowed to compose the music for this text, yet it would have been quite impossible to do this now. *If the subject had not been connected with magic*, your libretto might have extricated me this very moment from a most embarrassing situation, for I have finally broken with Schikaneder, whose empire has really been entirely eclipsed by the light of the brilliant and attractive French operas. Meanwhile he has kept me back for fully six months, and I have let myself be deceived simply because, since he is undeniably successful at creating stage effects, I hoped that he would produce something more brilliant than usual. But how greatly have I been misled. I hoped at least that he would have the verses and the contents of the libretto corrected and

considerably improved by someone else, but in vain. For it was impossible to persuade this fellow, who is so infatuated with his own opinion, to do this. Well, I withdrew from my arrangement with him, although I for my part had composed several numbers. Just picture to yourself a Roman subject (of which I had been told neither the scheme nor anything else whatever) and language and verses such as could proceed only out of the mouths of our Viennese *apple-women* – Well, I have quickly had an old French libretto adapted and am now beginning to work on it. If your opera had not been an opera with magic I would have snatched it with both hands. But the public here is now as prejudiced against a subject of that kind as it formerly looked for and desired it.

With a mixture of genuine idealism and ruthless opportunism Beethoven had decided that he wanted to compose a modern opera. His choice of librettist was a fortunate one, an old and trusted supporter named Joseph Sonnleithner. Four years older than the composer, he was to become one of the most influential figures in Viennese musical life in the first decades of the century. His father, Christoph Sonnleithner, had been a prolific composer; his quartets were regularly played at the court of Joseph II, and he wrote symphonies for the Esterházy family. Joseph trained as a diplomat and, like Swieten before him, developed a strong interest in the history of music. He organized a historical anthology of music jointly edited by Albrechtsberger, Haydn and Salieri; unfortunately publication was thwarted in 1805 when the invading French army melted the engraved plates for munitions. He helped found a new music publishing business, the grandly named Bureau des Arts et d'Industrie; devoted almost entirely to small-scale piano pieces, it made an exception in the case of Beethoven, publishing such works as the second, third and fourth symphonies, the third and fourth piano concertos and the violin concerto. As a loyal servant of the Habsburg dynasty he also nurtured the increasing sense of Austrian, rather than old-fashioned German, identity in musical life. He was a leading figure in the setting up of Vienna's Gesellschaft der Musikfreunde in 1812, becoming its first secretary; he initiated plans for a collection of 'data on the life and works of composers and performers of the Fatherland' that would form the basis of a new encyclopedia; like the earlier anthology this project was never realized, though the preliminary material is extant, as is Sonnleithner's treasured collection of oil paintings of Austrian composers from the baroque period onwards. In February 1804 Sonnleithner was appointed as the new secretary of the court theatres plus the Theater an der Wien. Over the next ten years he translated or arranged over twenty plays and operas; his first project is the one referred to in Beethoven's letter, the translation and adaptation of Bouilly's *Leonore ou l'amour conjugal*. At first, Beethoven thought he could complete the opera by the summer of 1804. But it was a much larger project than he anticipated and the re-organization of the administration of the three leading theatres in Vienna also delayed the project.

Opera was not the only genre that concerned Beethoven during these winter months. Griesinger had been trying to coax a new oratorio from Haydn, *Polyhymnia oder die Macht der Töne*, but the increasing frailty of the composer meant that he had to turn it down. Griesinger then offered the text to Beethoven who rejected it also; he observed that there was insufficient action and variety, and, conscious that odious comparisons with Haydn's *Creation* and *Seasons* were bound to be made, noted that there was an excess of word-painting.[3]

Having completed the Eroica Symphony in 1803, Beethoven might well have hoped for a benefit concert at the Theater an der Wien in March or April 1804 to follow on the success of the previous concert. Nothing is known of any such request. Abbé Vogler, however, was given an evening on 26 March, when the audience was offered a gaudy ragbag of items including 'The evocation of the midnight sun in Lapland', which was an unaccompanied vocal trio, and 'The Praise of Harmony', a work in the form of variations for chorus and orchestra (in shape and content rather like Beethoven's later Choral Fantasy). The following evening was devoted to a benefit concert for Sebastian Meyer, a stage manager, actor and occasional singer at the Theater an der Wien, at which a revised version of *Christus am Oelberge* was given together with the composer's first symphony, a violin concerto by Viotti and extracts from operas by Cherubini. Beethoven, no doubt, was content with this opportunity, though he would have been even more content had it been a concert for his own benefit.

Soon, however, the composer had a private opportunity of hearing the new symphony, courtesy of Prince Lobkowitz. As one of the most fanatical supporters of music in Vienna, Lobkowitz had always taken a keen interest in Beethoven. His name had appeared on the op. 1 subscription list; Beethoven is known to have played at the prince's palace on at least one occasion; Lobkowitz purchased twelve copies of the op. 9 string trios; and in 1799 he rewarded the composer with a gift of 200 gulden for the dedication of the op. 18 quartets. Up to 1804 Beethoven was only one of several composers who figured in Lobkowitz's musical life. For the next ten years Lobkowitz was Beethoven's principal patron, eclipsing the long-standing support of Prince Lichnowsky whose annual stipend of 600 gulden probably lapsed soon after the beginning of this relationship.

The Lobkowitz family, together with a small permanent retinue of musicians, moved regularly from its principal palaces in Vienna and Prague to country estates in Raudnitz (Roudnice) and Eisenberg (Jezeří) in Bohemia. In each of these places local musicians were engaged to supplement the court musicians for performances of anything from dance music to symphonies, operas to oratorios. The main palace in Vienna, between the Kärntnertortheater and the imperial residence, had several music rooms, the principal one of which was rebuilt and refurbished to make it suitable for performances of operas and oratorios. It was about 50 feet long and 26 feet wide with a high ceiling that reached up to the next storey. Temporary staging was available, and the invited audience sat on benches covered with red linen. It was in this music room in May or June 1804 that the Eroica Symphony and the recently completed Triple Concerto were played for the first time.

8   Prince Lobkowitz

The timely support of Lobkowitz that enabled the composer to hear these two works is typical of the unpredictable nature of Beethoven's life at this time. However many plans the composer formulated to further his career, its actual course was characterized by dashed hopes and the grateful seizing of passing opportunities. It reveals itself too in the number and variety of works that Beethoven contemplated writing at this time. The sketchbook that is largely devoted to the Eroica Symphony also contains random ideas for over fifty potential works, from songs to symphonies. Some of these works such as the 'Waldstein' sonata and the Pastoral Symphony were to be completed, others such as a mass in A major and a symphony in D minor were never realized. Ambitions as a composer co-existed with insecurity as to how he was to earn a living. Although Lobkowitz had taken over as Beethoven's principal aristocratic patron, the composer was keen to point out that he did not enjoy the salaried security of a Kapellmeister. The increasing instability of the Austrian currency was an aggravating factor. To finance the war effort the Austrian government had printed paper money (*Bankozettel*), intending that it should have parity with the metal currency. For a few years it did, but by 1803–4 the paper currency had two-thirds the value of the metal currency. The foreign fees that Beethoven received from Simrock in Bonn, Nägeli in Zurich and Hoffmeister and Breitkopf & Härtel in Leipzig were paid in paper currency and, though the situation was going to deteriorate considerably over the next few years, he was already very conscious of his declining income. While more and more of his music was being published, its monetary value was falling; financially he was obliged to publish more in order to stand still. The first few years of the century had also seen a steep rise in the cost of food and rented accommodation in Vienna. Again, this was only a worrying beginning of a trend that was to become much worse. To a certain extent, the casual patronage that gave Beethoven free accommodation in the Theater an der Wien and meals at the palaces of the aristocracy meant that he was not as badly affected as some people not on the fringes of social patronage, though the summer months, when he lived a more isolated and financially independent existence, were bound to be more difficult.

While Beethoven clearly gained artistic fulfilment in ambitious works such as symphonies, concertos, the new opera and large sonatas such as the 'Waldstein', he could not devote himself entirely to such music. Indeed, he probably welcomed the opportunity to relax and compose music such as the three marches for piano duet (op. 45) and the eight songs of op. 52, music that he knew would be published more or less immediately.

The increasingly tetchy tone of Beethoven's correspondence with

Breitkopf & Härtel reflects these circumstances. It was partly a clash of view between what the composer thought ought to be published and the pragmatic, commercial outlook of Breitkopf & Härtel, partly an understandable concern to maximize income; it was almost always aggravated by irascibility. Negotiations concerning the Eroica Symphony, the 'Waldstein' sonata, the 'Appassionata' sonata, the F major sonata (op. 54) and the Triple Concerto were especially difficult. After a long delay, which itself annoyed the composer, Breitkopf & Härtel evidently made an offer that was derisory:

> The *fee* is much lower than what I usually accept – Beethoven is no braggart and he despises whatever he *can not obtain solely* by his art and his own merits – Send me back, therefore, all the manuscripts you have had from me, *including the song* – I cannot and will not accept a lower fee.[4]

The manuscript copies of the works were duly returned to Beethoven, who turned to Sonnleithner and his Bureau des Arts et d'Industrie, which proceeded to publish all five works.

A striking feature of Haydn's relationship with publishers in the last twenty years of his life was his ability to negotiate separate publication rights in more than one country, so that there are often several equally authentic 'first' editions. Beethoven's letters from this period on reveal a consistent attempt to follow Haydn's example, but with limited success. The publishing scene was becoming more international, with individual firms acting as agents for music publishers from other countries. In this way publishers rather than composers began to control negotiations, deciding whether it was more advantageous to have direct contact with a composer or to act as an agent for another company.

Beethoven's music was not systematically available, for instance, in London, and performances of his music were comparatively rare, even after the notable success of the septet in 1801. The former virtuoso pianist and composer Muzio Clementi had redirected his energies towards piano manufacturing and music publishing. He travelled to Vienna in 1804, hoping to arrange a meeting with Beethoven. Ferdinand Ries, Beethoven's piano pupil, reported how they did, indeed, see each other, but never spoke:

> When Clementi came to Vienna, Beethoven wanted to call on him at once; his brother, however, put it into his head that Clementi had to visit him first. Clementi, despite the fact that he was much older, would probably have done this anyway, if some gossip about it had not arisen. So it came about that Clementi was in Vienna for a long time without knowing Beethoven other than by sight. We frequently ate lunch at the same table at the Swan, Clementi with his pupil Klengel and Beethoven with me. Everyone knew who everyone was, but no one spoke with each other or even nodded a greeting. The two pupils had to imitate their masters, because presumably each one risked losing his lesson otherwise. I certainly would have done that, since with Beethoven compromises were never possible.[5]

Apparently cold-shouldered, Clementi tried a different way of bringing Beethoven's music to London. Over the next few months he purchased the rights from Nägeli of Zurich for the piano sonata in E♭ (op. 31 no. 3) and began discussing with Breitkopf & Härtel the possibility of the two firms sharing the cost of printing and publishing Beethoven's music. When the composer came to know of this plan, which would have greatly reduced his room for manoeuvre, he attempted to sink it by offering the British rights for the Eroica Symphony, the Triple Concerto and several other works to another publisher, George Thomson of Edinburgh:

> Some time ago I had the pleasure of quoting to you the lowest prices for those works of mine of which you desired to be the sole owner; and now I take the liberty of informing you of another plan, that is to say, provided that my works can appear simultaneously in Paris, London, Vienna or in some other towns in Germany, I can then quote more moderate prices, such as you will see from the attached note; and I promise to send you everything I create unless it is something or other which you cannot make use of; and of that you must inform me.[6]

Nothing came of the Thomson plan nor of Clementi's discussions with Breitkopf & Härtel.

Publishers, patrons, public concerts, fees and inflation were continuing concerns in Beethoven's life. In the winter of 1804–5 they were supplemented by a love affair. Beethoven had known the Deym family for over five years. Count Joseph Deym owned one of Vienna's most popular attractions, an art gallery in the square adjacent to St Stephen's cathedral, where he displayed wax figures, sculptures, paintings and carvings. Mozart had written some pieces for a mechanical organ that provided musical background to an exhibition dedicated to the memory of Field Marshal Loudon. Beethoven, too, wrote piped music for Deym's gallery. In 1799, at the age of forty-nine, after four weeks of courtship the count married Josephine Brunsvick, aged only twenty, a marriage encouraged by her mother. Josephine, her sister Therese, and their brother Franz were all accomplished musicians, and the Deym household soon became a favourite venue for musical parties at which Schuppanzigh and Zmeskall as well as Beethoven appeared regularly. In January 1804 the death of the count temporarily halted the musical soirées, but by the following winter the household was once again at the heart of polite society. It was at this time that Beethoven seems to have undertaken some of the practical arrangements for the musical evenings, making sure, for instance, that Schuppanzigh was able to turn up. He also wrote a simple, but eloquent song for Josephine, 'An die Hoffnung' (op. 32). Friendship turned to deep affection, as the following exchange of letters reveals.[7] Josephine wrote:

> You have long had my heart, dear Beethoven; if this assurance can give you joy, then receive it – from the purest heart. Take care that it is also entrusted into the purest bosom. You receive the *greatest* proof of my love [and] of my esteem though this confession, through this confidence! It is that which most ennobles you, that you know to appreciate it – of which you acknowledge the value, of whose possession I herewith [give] you – of the possession of the noblest of my *Self*, of which I herewith assure you.

Beethoven replied:

> Oh, beloved J., it is not desire for the other sex that draws me to you, no, *it is just you, your whole self* with all your peculiar qualities – this has compelled my regard – this has bound all my feelings – all my emotional power to you. When I came to you – it was with the firm resolve not to let a single spark of love be kindled in me. But you have conquered me – The question is whether *you wanted to do so?* or whether *you did not want to do so?* – No doubt J. could answer that question for me sometime – Dear God, there are so many things I should love to tell you – how much I think of you – what I feel for you – but how weak and poor are those words – at any rate my words.

Over the summer months passion receded and the previous *politesse* was resumed. Maybe Josephine's mother interfered once more. For, while it was perfectly in order for a daughter of the aristocracy to be forced into a marriage with someone twenty-nine years older, it was not socially acceptable for her to marry a musician who was nine years older. Even in this intensely personal correspondence Josephine and Beethoven preserved the social convention of addressing each with the polite 'Sie' and not the familiar 'Du'. Beethoven and Josephine remained acquaintances until 1809 when she married Baron Christoph Stackelberg, from whom she separated three years later.

This love affair occurred while Beethoven was composing the opera *Leonore*, whose subtitle was *Conjugal Love* (*Die eheliche Liebe*). A single incident, the timely arrival of Don Fernando, saves Florestan from death, but the abiding power of the work derives from Leonore's superhuman devotion and physical courage. Plenty of commentators have analysed in detail the double parallel present in the work: between Florestan's false imprisonment and Beethoven's social isolation because of deafness; and between Leonore's ardour and Beethoven's idolized view of marriage. Josephine was certainly not the model for Leonore – there is nothing in Leonore's personality that reflects a music-loving countess from Vienna – but it would be a mistake, too, to hide behind the convenient platitude that Beethoven's art was not informed by his life or not to acknowledge the reverse, that his actions were sometimes prompted by the idealism that he had discovered in his music. Beethoven had always placed his art on a pedestal; he was increasingly placing himself on a pedestal also. The most striking juxtaposition of art and life in his entire career was about to occur with the premiere of *Leonore*.

Beethoven had completed his opera by the end of the summer of 1805, except for the overture (*Leonore No. 2*), which he was going to write during the rehearsals. The first night was set for 15 October, at the Theater an der Wien. As well as supervising the preparation of the orchestral and vocal parts and attending the rehearsals, Beethoven had to wait for the approval of the official censor. From the early 1790s, the court had exerted the most rigorous control over published material of all kinds: books, pamphlets, posters, timetables, tickets, games, pictures and, naturally, musical texts, from single songs to opera and oratorio. Working from the offices of the state police, the censor judged stage works on three counts: the subject matter of the piece, any explicit or implied moral, and the dialogue. Religious and political themes were not allowed; the military were to be treated sympathetically with no mention of cowards or deserters; certain emotive words such as 'freedom', 'equality' and 'enlightenment' were rarely permitted; a loving couple was not allowed to leave the scene together, unless accompanied by a third person; and so on. With so many rules, the censor held absolute authority and the fact that judgments were often arbitrary and inconsistent mattered little as long as the fabric of the Austrian state remained unthreatened by revolution. To ensure that the dictates of the censor were followed an official attended the final rehearsal and all performances; minor indiscretions were followed by reprimand, major ones by police arrest.

As it happens the text of *Leonore* contained the inflammatory word 'Freiheit' ('freedom', in the prisoners' chorus at the end of Act II) but the censor was more worried about the general subject matter: an individual wrongly imprisoned by a tyrannical state. Approval was denied. Sonnleithner, as the author of the text, secretary of the court theatres and someone who moved in the innermost circles of the imperial court was ideally placed to seek a review of the decision. On

2 October he wrote a letter to the censor's office, making full use of his connections:[8]

> On the 30th of last month, I received the opera *Fidelio* back with the decision that it is not acceptable for performance.
> Since:
>> First, I have thoroughly adapted this opera from the French original of Bouilly (entitled *Leonore ou l' amour conjugal*), primarily because Her Majesty the Empress and Queen finds the original very beautiful and assured me that no opera text had ever given her so much pleasure, and since
>> Second, this opera, with music by Kapellmeister Paer, to an Italian text, has already been given in Prague and Dresden, and since
>> Third, Herr Beethoven has spent over a year and a half with the composition of my libretto and (since there was no fear in the least of a ban) has already held rehearsals, and all other preparations have been made, since this opera is supposed to be given on the Name Day of Her Majesty the Empress, and since
>> Fourth, the action itself, which I had forgotten to mention on the title-page, is set in the 16th Century (thus there can be no association [with current events]), and, finally, since
>> Fifth, there is such a great lack of good opera librettos, and [since] the present one features the most touching portrait of wifely virtue, and the malicious Governor exercises only a private revenge, like Pedraria in *Balboa*,
> I therefore request that the Roy. and Imp. Roy. Police Direction deign to allow the performance of this opera and to indicate the changes that may perhaps be found necessary as soon as possible.

Three days later Sonnleithner received permission for the performance, subject to some changes in the dungeon scene. The first night was now set for 20 November.

Austria's war against the French in Bavaria was going badly. In a two-week campaign the French under Bernadotte occupied Bavaria and took 49,000 Austrian prisoners. They continued eastwards along the Danube with alarming speed. The Habsburg family fled the imperial city. Johann Carl Rosenbaum, a former senior clerk in the service of the Estérhazy family, noted in his diary that 'On the Josephplatz there are more than a hundred draught-horses ready to be harnessed to baggage coaches standing in the Winter Riding School. They are laden with gold in casks, the crown jewels, the coin and natural science collections, silver, linen etc.' The Viennese negotiated a peaceful surrender and the French entered the city on 12 November. Napoleon established his headquarters in the summer palace at Schönbrunn while his generals billeted themselves in the aristocratic palaces in the centre of the city. As Beethoven walked around Vienna, to and from rehearsals for *Leonore*, he would have experienced a tense stand-off between the Viennese and the occupying forces. On Friday 15 November Rosenbaum wrote in his diary:

> A beautiful day... There is nothing at the market; yesterday a pound
> of butter cost between 2 and 3 Gulden – No one risks bringing
> anything, since it will be confiscated, and the horse unharnessed and
> taken... At about 12 o' clock midday at the Laimgrube, a Frenchman,
> whose shoes were torn, seized a journeyman and attempted to take
> his boots off by force. When he resisted, the Frenchman slashed him
> across the mouth with his sabre. Some of our people came running
> immediately, disarmed the Frenchman... and led him off to the
> nearest guard-room... Except for whores, one sees very few women
> at the theatres.

As Rosenbaum indicates, the theatres were still open, and five days later he attended the first night of *Leonore*. He was an enthusiastic and regular opera-goer and his mixed impressions must have been coloured by the presence of invading forces in his beloved Vienna:

> In the evening I went to W. Th. to hear Louis Beth.'s opera... The
> opera has pretty, ingenious, difficult music and a tedious libretto of
> little interest. It had no success and the theatre was empty.[9]

Three performances only were given. The second was attended by a visiting English physician, whose reaction to the music was similar to that of Rosenbaum:[10]

The story and plan of the piece are a miserable mixture of low manners and romantic situations; the airs, duets, and choruses equal to any praise. The several overtures, for there is an overture to each act, appear to be too artificially composed to be generally pleasing, especially on being first heard. Intricacy is the character of Beethoven's music, and it requires a well-practised ear, or a frequent repetition of the same piece, to understand and distinguish its beauties. This is the first opera he ever composed, and it was very much applauded; a copy of complimentary verses was showered down from the upper gallery at the end of the piece. Beethoven presided at the pianoforte and directed the performance himself. He is a small dark young-looking man, wears spectacles, and is like Mr. Koenig. Few people present, though the house would have been crowded in every part but for the present state of public affairs.

The French occupation of Vienna lasted sixty-seven days. Following the brutal defeat of joint Austrian and Russian forces at Austerlitz Emperor Franz I of Austria was compelled to sign the humiliating Peace of Pressburg in which he ceded territory to Bavaria, to the new sovereign states of Baden and Württemberg, and to the new kingdom of Italy; and, especially humbling to the Habsburg dynasty, he was forced to renounce the title of Holy Roman Emperor.

Following the departure of French forces in January, the Habsburg court returned to Vienna, the aristocrats reclaimed their palaces, and theatrical life began to regain its former energy. Sonnleithner was engaged in the writing of a libretto for Cherubini, *Faniska*, first performed at the Kärntnertortheater on 25 February; from that he moved on to *Zum goldenen Löwen*, one of Seyfried's most popular stage works. At the Theater an der Wien plans were made to re-present Beethoven's *Leonore*. The composer responded to the general criticism that the work was too long by reducing the three acts into two and making some strategic cuts. Because Sonnleithner was so busy, the libretto was adjusted by Stephan von Breuning, though Sonnleithner was still named as the author. Beethoven composed a new overture, *Leonore No. 3*, probably the most thrillingly dramatic movement in his entire orchestral output and confirmation of the fervour with which he approached the revision. Following a rehearsal of the opera he complained bitterly that the orchestra did not pay proper attention to the many volatile changes in dynamics:

> I shall not say anything about the wind-instruments but – that all *p*, *pp*, *cres*, all *decres*. and all *f*. and *ff*. should have been deleted from my opera! In any case they are not all observed. All desire to compose anything more ceases completely if I have to hear my work performed like that![11]

Despite his worries, the revised version of the opera was warmly received and might well have established itself in the repertory of the Theater an der Wien. According to one source, Beethoven was to receive a percentage of the box office receipts rather than a fee, but he suspected that the money was not being properly calculated and, consequently, the opera was withdrawn after two (possibly three) performances. He had already vacated his rooms in the theatre; with the withdrawal of *Leonore* Beethoven's operatic career came to a sudden halt.

The difficulties with the management of the theatre did not stop Beethoven from maintaining friendly relations with the leader of the orchestra, Franz Clement. He had led the orchestra in the first public performance of the Eroica Symphony as well as the performances of *Leonore*. Clement occasionally played concertos in benefit concerts at the theatre and solo items after the main operatic fare. Violin concertos had never been a prominent feature of Viennese concert life but 1806 saw a sudden increase in their number. In March, Clement played a concerto of his own at a benefit concert for an orchestral colleague; in June two performances of a concerto by Rode were given, one by a gifted thirteen-year-old boy, Joseph Strauss; and in August a concerto by Blumenthal was performed. It was against this background and with real admiration that Beethoven composed a violin concerto for Clement; it was first performed at his benefit in December 1806. It was part of a lengthy programme that also included overtures by Méhul and Cherubini, an aria by Mozart, a vocal quartet by Cherubini, extracts from Handel's *Ode for St Cecilia's Day* (in Mozart's instrumentation) and, in the freak-show tradition of many of Vienna's public concerts, a composition for a violin that had one string and was held upside-down.

In addition to the concerto for Clement, Beethoven had been commissioned to write three quartets for Count Razumovsky, and by June 1806 had completed a fourth piano concerto. To accord with the practice he had established in his two benefit concerts Beethoven now needed a new symphony to go with the concerto before he could book a vacant evening at one of the theatres. During the later summer of 1806, therefore, he began work on a fourth symphony.

For the first time in seven or more years Beethoven did not rent accommodation in a village outside Vienna for the summer months. He had been invited by Prince Lichnowsky to his estate in Grätz, the longest journey that Beethoven had undertaken since his tour as a piano virtuoso ten years earlier. From here Beethoven and Lichnowsky travelled north-east to Ober-Glogau in Upper Silesia (now Glogówek in Poland) to the estate of Count Oppersdorff. He was one of the few aristocrats that still maintained a full orchestra (not even Prince Lobkowitz did that) and Beethoven was presented with a performance of the second symphony. The count was anxious to be associated with new works by the composer and so Beethoven sold him the fourth symphony for 500 gulden, giving him exclusive performance rights for six months.

It was during this stay with Lichnowsky that patron and composer fell out, apparently because Beethoven would not play the piano for some visiting guests. At the end of his stay Beethoven wrote a curt note, or perhaps openly exclaimed:

Prince, what you are, you are by circumstance and birth, what I am, I am through myself; there are, and there always will be, thousands of princes; but there is only one Beethoven. [12]

1 January 1807 witnessed an exciting new venture in the history of the theatre in Vienna. A group of nine aristocrats, including

Lobkowitz and three members of the Esterházy family, assembled a stock fund of 1,200,000 gulden to lease the two court theatres and the Theater an der Wien, the former for twelve years, the latter for ten. Increasing inflation soon affected the commitment of each individual as well as the commercial and artistic plans of the consortium and, when the second and more disruptive occupation of Vienna by French forces took place in 1809, the plans became even more insecure. By 1811 the consortium had been dissolved. It was an interesting experiment, however. Setting aside the semi-public activities of Swieten's Gesellschaft der Associierten, this was the first time aristocrats had supported public events, a notable broadening of social patronage.

For Beethoven it augured particularly well. Lobkowitz, as well as being the largest stock holder (a full quarter of the total) assumed special responsibility for operas and concerts. Not surprisingly, Beethoven's ambitions as an opera composer began to stir again, but, more immediately, there was the likelihood of a benefit concert; as well as the fourth symphony and the fourth piano concerto, the concert would no doubt have featured the recently completed *Coriolan* overture, padded out by vocal items from *Leonore*. Beethoven seems to have wanted his favourite venue, the Theater an der Wien, but the authorities were anxious to establish the small and large Redoutensaal as venues for concerts, even though the acoustics and sight lines were not as good as in the theatres. Negotiations dragged on through to mid March, and petered out when it became too late to organize a concert that season. Meanwhile, Lobkowitz had organized performances of the same works at his Viennese palace, partly designed, as in the earlier performance of the Eroica Symphony, as trial runs for the planned public performance.

Frustrated once more by the lack of a public concert, Beethoven turned his attention to the plan of having his music published in several European countries simultaneously. This was prompted by a return visit to Vienna by Clementi, who on this occasion managed to meet the 'haughty beauty', as he called him, and established a business arrangement that was to last four years. Clementi became

Beethoven's sole publisher in Britain, issuing the violin concerto and, later, the fifth piano concerto, the Choral Fantasy and the 'Les Adieux' sonata, the whole venture marking the real beginning of the composer's popularity in that country. Encouraged by this, Beethoven set about attempting to organize a similar deal with Pleyel in Paris and with his old friend Simrock in Bonn. In Vienna itself the Bureau des Arts et d'Industrie was to remain his main publisher. The plan was only partially realized: Simrock was not as ambitious as Clementi and published only small-scale works like piano variations and songs, while nothing came of the approaches to Pleyel; indeed, Beethoven was never to achieve this fourfold, country-by-country, simultaneous issue of his compositions.

The president of the consortium that ran the theatres in Vienna was Prince Nicolaus Esterházy, the last of Haydn's four patrons. While regular concerts and operatic performances were no longer a feature of life at the Esterházy court, music was by no means non-existent there. Haydn was still nominally the Kapellmeister but his duties were undertaken by a Vice-Kapellmeister, Johann Nepomuk Fuchs, and a Konzertmeister, Johann Nepomuk Hummel. Opera, performed by visiting troupes, was given at the palace in Eisenstadt and special occasions, like family weddings and the nameday of Prince Marie Hermenegild Esterházy, were celebrated with operas, plays and church services. Haydn's six late masses, composed between 1796 and 1802, were performed (and with one exception actually written) to celebrate the nameday in September of the princess. From 1803 masses by Hummel and Fuchs featured in this well-established local tradition. For the 1807 nameday Beethoven was asked by the prince to compose a new mass. He accepted readily. It was a new challenge, his first contact with liturgical music since his employment at the Bonn court, an opportunity to show that he could compose for the church, as well as the theatre and the concert room. He approached the task with 'considerable apprehension, since you, most excellent Prince, are accustomed to have the inimitable masterpieces of the great Haydn performed for you'.[13] He studied Haydn's masses in great detail, but progress was delayed by a severe and persistent headache in the early summer. Dr Schmidt was consulted once more and, after removing a troublesome tooth, offered the view that the headaches were due to gout, that Beethoven should avoid strong summer breezes, wear compresses of bark on his arms, 'take healthy walks, work little, and sleep; also eat well and drink spirits in moderation'.[14] Most of the composition of the Mass in C was done in August which, according to Rosenbaum, was an exceptionally hot month. Rosenbaum attended the nameday church service on the morning of 13 September and remarked in his diary that Beethoven's mass was 'unsuccessful'. For reasons that later generations have always found difficult to comprehend this seems to have been the general reaction. Prince Nicolaus was to write to Countess Henriette Zielinska: 'Beethoven's music is unbearably ridiculous and detestable; I am not convinced that it can ever be performed properly. I am angry and ashamed.'[15] Not for the first time in his life Beethoven queried the commitment of the performers; his own commitment to the work, however, was heartfelt, equal to that felt for any symphony, concerto, quartet or sonata. Following endless cajoling Breitkopf & Härtel agreed to publish it; it was dedicated not to Prince Nicolaus but to Prince Kinsky.

After this disappointing foray into sacred music Beethoven returned to instrumental and theatre music, both of which seemed to be offering new openings. His contacts with the administration of the theatres led him in early December to write a letter outlining his ambitions as a theatre composer. It is one of Beethoven's most dignified letters, sure in its self-esteem, yet pragmatic and, for the most part, diplomatic too.[16]

He begins by noting that his music has already achieved a certain respect in Vienna and elsewhere, and that he is anxious 'to develop his talents to an even higher degree of perfection which must be the aim of every true artist, and to secure for an independent future the advantages which hitherto have been merely incidental'. Without any malice or paranoia he alludes to the difficulties of pursuing a career as an independent artist in Vienna; nevertheless, 'the patriotism of a German make his present place of residence more to be valued and desired than any other'. He offers to compose one opera per year for a stipend of 2,400 gulden plus the proceeds of one performance; in addition he is willing to provide smaller works free of charge, such as an 'Operette' or a 'Divertissement' and choruses, as long as he is allotted an evening for a benefit concert at least once a year. Only in the subsequent paragraph does Beethoven's tone become rather insistent:

> If one considers what an expenditure of time and energy the making of an opera demands, inasmuch as it completely excludes every other mental exertion; furthermore, if one bears in mind that in other places where the composer and his family are entitled to share in the takings at each performance, one single successful work establishes once and for all the whole reputation of a composer; furthermore, if one remembers what little advantage, owing to the unfavourable money currency and the high prices of all commodities, accrues to an artist living in Vienna who, moreover, can easily betake himself to some other country; then the above conditions can certainly not be regarded as exaggerated or excessively grasping.

He ends the letter by stating that if his proposals are not acceptable he still expects the promise of an evening for a benefit concert to be honoured.

From a modern perspective it seems surprising that Beethoven, the composer of symphonies, concertos, quartets and sonatas, should be anxious to devote himself to opera, especially as Leonore had made only a limited impression. From Beethoven's perspective, however, it is less surprising. His completed symphonies and concertos (four of each) had not made a sustained impact in Vienna, mainly because public concert life was so undeveloped; operatic life, on the other hand, was much more active and offered financial security of a kind unimaginable to a composer of instrumental music. Also Beethoven may have been reflecting the still prevalent view that opera, not instrumental music, constituted the basis of international fame; Haydn's success as a composer of symphonies and quartets was still very much the exception in 1807 and, moreover, Beethoven's own instrumental music had not yet achieved the same status. Given these circumstances, it seemed reasonable to pursue operatic ambitions. Beethoven's own letter carefully makes no mention of *Leonore*, impulsively withdrawn at the point when it could have formed a sound beginning for the career he was now seeking. Ignaz Seyfried (1776–1841) and Joseph Weigl (1766–1846) were two composers in Vienna who had secure livelihoods from the composition of opera, writing over 100 stage works between them. Their careers reveal an eye and an ear for what was likely to be popular, also a willingness to battle or worm their way through opera-house politics, qualities that were alien to Beethoven. Such thoughts may well have occurred to the directors of the theatre, because the composer's letter made only limited impact. A clerk noted that the composer could not be engaged until a topic for an opera had been agreed. For a year Beethoven discussed various operatic plans with the local playwright Heinrich Collin (author of *Coriolan*) but nothing eventuated. Certainly Beethoven never received his stipend and the theatre authorities continued to be as dilatory as ever about a date for a benefit concert.

Ironically, just as Beethoven was formulating his operatic ambitions, a new development was taking place in the concert life of Vienna, one that was to shape his identity in the city as a challenging composer of orchestral music. A group of aristocrats, Trauttmansdorff, Spielmann, Dietrichstein and, inevitably, the musically insatiable Lobkowitz, had come together to organize a subscription concert series, twenty concerts between November 1807 and March 1808, that became known as the Liebhaber Concerte. Seventy subscribers were enlisted and they could purchase as many tickets as they liked. Through this network of patronage a regular audience of over 1,000 people was secured; the first concert was held in the Mehlgrube on the Neuer Markt, where Mozart had given concerts twenty years earlier, but pressure of space forced a move to a larger hall at the university. The orchestra was handpicked and the players had to attend two rehearsals per concert, rather than the normal one. The guidelines for the content of each concert could have been dictated by Beethoven himself: 'Every concert must be distinguished by the performance of significant and decidedly splendid music, because the institute has the intention to uphold the dignity of such art and to attain an ever higher perfection.'[17]

Mozart's music featured the most, with twenty performances of fourteen works. Beethoven had eleven performances: the first three symphonies and the *Coriolan* overture were performed twice in the series and there were single performances of the *Prometheus* overture, the fourth symphony and the first piano concerto. The series ended with a special performance of Haydn's *Creation*, to celebrate the composer's seventy-sixth birthday.

While this notable series of concerts was in progress Beethoven completed his fifth symphony. Although it had been commissioned by Oppersdorff, the success of the Liebhaber Concerte must have encouraged Beethoven to anticipate performances in a future series. Towards the end of the series and in this positive frame of mind Beethoven took up the ideas he had for another new symphony, the Pastoral Symphony. It was completed by June 1808. Preliminary plans were indeed made for a second series of Liebhaber Concerte in which Beethoven's two newest symphonies as well as other works not yet played in the series, such as the third and fourth piano concertos, the triple concerto, the violin concerto and the two *Leonore* overtures, might well have figured. But once more the ebb and flow of the Napoleonic wars adversely affected musical life in Vienna.

Following Napoleon's unsuccessful campaign in the Spanish peninsula, anti-French sentiments in Austria grew ever more strident, leading inexorably, in April 1809, to a declaration of war. In the increasingly bellicose atmosphere of the previous autumn, organizing a concert season seemed unimportant and the Liebhaber Concerte fell by the wayside. No doubt disappointed, Beethoven redoubled his efforts to secure an evening at the Theater an der Wien for a benefit concert. He was finally allotted the date of 22 December.

Six years had elapsed since his last benefit concert and he had a number of unplayed or comparatively unfamiliar works ready for performance; he must, too, have been conscious that a similar opportunity might not arise for some time again. This state of affairs largely explains the enormously ambitious nature of the concert, the most impractical in Beethoven's career. It began with the first public performance of the Pastoral Symphony; then came the concert aria 'Ah, perfido' (possibly the first performance in Vienna), the Gloria from the Mass in C (with German words to disguise the liturgical origins so as not to offend the censor) and the fourth piano concerto. The second half contained the first performance of the fifth symphony, the Sanctus from the Mass in C, an improvisation on the piano by Beethoven and, finally, the first performance of a work hurriedly written in the previous few weeks, the Choral Fantasy.

Naturally, the faithful Prince Lobkowitz attended. In his box in the Theater an der Wien he had a most interesting guest, Johann Friedrich Reichardt. Now aged fifty-six, Reichardt had earned a respectable reputation in north Germany as a composer of Italian opera first, then German opera and German song. He was also an eloquent writer on music who, after loyally serving at the court of Friedrich William II, espoused fashionable republican sentiments in the 1790s, airing them in a volume entitled *Vertraute Briefe über Frankreich* (*Confidential letters on France*). When, in 1807, Napoleon established the new kingdom of Westphalia he made his youngest brother Jerome Bonaparte king; Reichardt was appointed *Directeur général des théâtres et de son orchestre*. However, within a year, Reichardt was deeply unhappy and set out on a journey that took him to Vienna. He arrived there on 24 November 1808, only to learn the astonishing news that Beethoven had been offered his post in Westphalia. He spent nearly five months in the city, becoming familiar with its musical patrons, leading composers and performers, and recording his impressions in another volume of letters, *Vertraute Briefe geschrieben auf einer Reise nach Wien und den Österreichischen Staaten zu Ende des Jahres 1808 und zu Anfang 1809*. His enthusiasm for the city and its music was spoilt only by the early onset of wintry weather (the first heavy snowfall occurred at the beginning of December) and the imminence of war with France.

Reichardt reported that the evening of Beethoven's concert, 22 December, was extremely cold and that the concert lasted four and a half hours. This discomfort must have coloured his response to a concert that was already under-rehearsed:[18]

> [Pastoral Symphony.] Each number was a very long and fully realized movement replete with lively tonepainting and splendid thoughts and figures; this Pastoral Symphony already lasted as long as a complete concert at court with us.

> ['Ah, perfido',] sung by Mademoiselle Killitschky, the beautiful Bohemian with the beautiful voice. That this dear child today rather shivered than sang can only be blamed on the bitter cold; for we shivered in the comfortable boxes wrapped in our fur coats and cloaks.

> [Gloria from the Mass in C. The] performance was, unfortunately, completely unsuccessful.

> [Piano concerto in G] of frightful difficulty, the fastest tempos of which Beethoven performed to astonishment. The adagio, a masterly movement of beautiful and continuous lyricism, he sang with his instrument with a deep, melancholy feeling that really thrilled me.

> [Symphony No. 5,] a large, very protracted, overlong symphony. A nearby gentleman assured us that at the rehearsal he had seen the cello part, which is very active, and it alone consisted of thirty-four leaves. The copyists here, like the scriveners and lawyers' clerks at home, know how to maximize their income. [Both were paid by the page.]

> [Sanctus from the Mass in C.] Unfortunately, like the Gloria, the performance was completely unsuccessful.

> [Improvisation by Beethoven.] A long fantasy in which Beethoven showed his complete mastery, and, finally, to end, another fantasy,

> [Choral Fantasy.] The special nature [of this piece] had the misfortune in performance to be spoilt by mistakes in the orchestra.

Beethoven, who thought more of his holy artistic fervour than of the public and of the occasion, stopped and called out to start again. You can imagine how all his friends and I suffered thereby. At the time I certainly wished that I had had the courage to leave earlier.

On the morning of the concert Reichardt had attended a quartet concert given by Schuppanzigh and his colleagues that included works by Haydn, Mozart and Beethoven. His final comment was a weary one: 'I had, therefore, my fill of music for the day.'

5 Patrons and patriotism

The invitation extended to Beethoven from Jerome Bonaparte, to be director of music at Cassel, is one of the strangest incidents in the composer's life. Jerome was only twenty-three years old, rather reckless and self-indulgent, but happy to be a player in his brother's dynastic ambitions, which were as calculating as any executed by the Bourbons and Habsburgs in the previous two hundred years. A marriage was arranged with Catherine, daughter of the Duke of Württemberg, and in 1807 he was placed on the throne of an entirely new kingdom, Westphalia. While promoting many of the humanitarian aspects of the Napoleonic Code, this *nouveau riche* king also spent ostentatiously on himself and on his court in Cassel. He did not know a word of German (in later years he is said to have picked up 'lustig') but encouraged the arts. The new royal librarian was one of the Grimm brothers, Jacob Grimm, and Reichardt was one of Germany's most respected elder statesmen of music. Beethoven was a much younger man, clearly ambitious and, moreover, a French speaker, three qualities that no doubt attracted him to Jerome. For a salary of 600 ducats plus 150 ducats for travelling expenses Beethoven was to direct concerts by the court orchestra and compose such works as he wished.

That Beethoven, the composer who had deleted a dedication to Napoleon on learning that he had declared himself an emperor, should seriously consider an offer from somebody who was no more a king than Napoleon was an emperor is strange, if not incomprehensible. Early in 1809 Beethoven actually accepted the offer. Ultimately, however, advancing his musical career was more important to Beethoven than political ideology. Cassel offered ideal conditions for artistic creation: a lavish patron, a steady income, a good orchestra and a trouble-free environment. It is what he might have gained at Bonn in the early 1790s and what, as many asides in his correspondence indicate, he still regarded as the ideal: Kapellmeister to an enlightened ruler. In this sense Beethoven was happy to be a prisoner of the eighteenth century and, if part of that patronage meant a certain amount of artistic exclusiveness – the freedom, as Haydn had once put it, 'to be original' – then that suited Beethoven too.

Many of Beethoven's aristocratic patrons in Vienna became concerned that the composer would, indeed, desert them – a concern that he skilfully exploited over the next few months. Baron Ignaz von Gleichenstein had been acting as Beethoven's secretary since the marriage of Carl in 1806, stoically putting up with his unpredictable changes of mood and willingly running messages. Between them Gleichenstein and Beethoven persuaded three patrons, Prince Kinsky, Prince Lobkowitz and Archduke Rudolph, to provide an annual stipend of 4,000 gulden. Although this amount represented about half the value of the offer from Westphalia, it was considerably more (even allowing for inflation) than Beethoven had requested from the directors of the theatres just over a year before. It offered a comfortable living standard and could, of course, be supplemented as before by income from the occasional benefit concert and from publishing. Other clauses in the agreement were equally generous. The stipend was to be paid until Beethoven received a permanent appointment that yielded the same amount; further, it would be paid as a pension should he 'be prevented from practising his art by an unfortunate accident or old age'.[1] For his part the composer was obliged to live in Vienna or, alternatively, any of the other major cities in the Austrian lands, and to request permission for any significant journey. This generous arrangement remained in force until the composer's death in 1827, though delayed payments, renegotiated contributions and even lawsuits were to change *noblesse oblige* into something much more shabby.

Reichardt's account of his stay in Vienna does not mention Beethoven's acceptance of the king's invitation, nor his subsequent change of mind when he secured financial support. He does, however, give a full account of musical life in aristocratic and middle-class salons in Vienna; detailed documentation of this kind is very rare, for the obvious reason that these private events were not publicised in the way that operas, oratorios and public concerts were. Reichardt's snapshot of activity in the winter of 1808–9 is of a continuing tradition that featured prominently in Beethoven's musical life.

During his stay of five months in Vienna, Reichardt attended over 120 musical events, of which well over a half were private concerts at the homes of the aristocracy. Sometimes the musical entertainment was impromptu, a few songs performed casually in a gathering of half-a-dozen or so; at other times the guests numbered several hundred with a pre-planned concert of piano music, quartets and extracts from operas, the whole evening lasting several hours and culminating in a lavish *souper*. Private subscription concerts of quartets were organized by the violinist Schuppanzigh and the cellist Kraft, at which Beethoven's works were played. Reichardt attended four concerts at the home of Countess Erdödy, a gifted pianist and a patron of Beethoven, where he heard performances of two piano trios recently completed and subsequently dedicated to the countess (op. 70); with the composer at the piano, Reichardt was particularly taken with the 'heavenly singing' of the third movement of the E♭ trio. The sight and sound of Beethoven improvising at the piano was even more notable. 'He improvised for us, for a full hour, from the innermost depth of his artistic feeling, exploring the highest heights and the deepest depths of heavenly art, and with a masterly strength and fluency that repeatedly reduced me to tears; I could find no words to express to him my heartfelt rapture.'[2] The most active sponsor was Prince Lobkowitz. Reichardt describes his palace as a 'veritable academy of music'. Reichardt's own opera *Bradamante* was performed there, as well as Paer's *Camilla*; quartet parties were held every Thursday; and a series of concerts was presented featuring Archduke Rudolph as a pianist, including a performance of a piano concerto by Beethoven. Music could be heard at almost any time of day in the palace and, very often, two or three performances or rehearsals were going on simultaneously.

Reichardt's account also refers eloquently to the new nationalist fervour sweeping Austria, leading ineluctably to a declaration of war in April 1809. The poet Collin wrote a series of patriotic texts for songs, one of which, 'Östreich über alles', was given to Beethoven to set. For whatever reason, he abandoned the task after a few sketches (a plausible completion was made in 1996) and Joseph Weigl took over the job. It and several other xenophobic works were performed at two concerts in the Burgtheater. Although Austria had never experienced such rampant jingoism, laced with a fair share of bravado, the state was, in reality, poorly equipped to fight a war against one of the most efficient land armies in history. Barely a month after Austria had declared war Napoleon's troops were within sight of Vienna, and the imperial court had left to take refuge in Hungary. In one last defiant act of vainglory instructions were given that Vienna was to repel the invaders rather than surrender as it had done in November 1805. Rosenbaum wrote in his diary:

THURSDAY 11TH: Ascension . . . It was only just quarter past 9 [in the evening] when the French began . . . the bombardment; there was heavy firing until midnight, then it slackened until 3. As dawn began to break, they . . . stopped. Our batteries fired only very little, for they were without effect . . . The fires that broke out were dreadful to see . . . The poor city suffered great damage, for no one was prepared, no one conceived of such misfortune . . . One cannot walk about due to the broken glass . . . At our house . . . everyone fled to the cellar . . . I had nothing but my light dressing gown, and consequently froze . . . With a thousand consolatory arguments . . . I attempted to calm . . . the wailing group . . . From time to time I went out on the street, onto the Graben to see how far the ravaging flames had advanced and how our house was to be saved . . . I called everyone together, we carried water . . . and in this way managed to save our house.[3]

In the southern suburb of Gumpendorf, Haydn and his servants were caught in the crossfire between the defending Viennese and the attacking French; a cannon ball fell in the courtyard and Haydn's bedroom door was blown wide open. At the age of seventy-seven, and only three weeks before his death, he consoled his servants with the words 'Children, don't be afraid, for where Haydn is, nothing can happen.' Beethoven was in the inner city, sheltering in the cellar of his brother's house, covering his head with pillows. Early on Saturday morning the city surrendered. For the next five months, until October 1809, Vienna was an occupied city, ruled by Napoleon from the comfort of Schönbrunn palace.

For a while freedom of movement was severely curtailed, which meant that Beethoven was not able to spend the summer months outside the city as he liked to do, though he did manage to get to Baden and to Hungary for a few days in August. 'What a destructive, disorderly life I see and hear around me, nothing but drums, cannons, and human misery in every form', he reported to Breitkopf & Härtel.[4] Amidst all this oppression there were moments of comedy that would have appealed to Beethoven's gruff sense of humour and lack of deference. A Franco-Prussian officer reported that

On 15 August Napoleon's birthday was celebrated with great pomp in the Austrian capital; all ships on the Danube were colourfully bedecked with flags; the thunder of the cannons announced the high feast of the Dictator of the European 'Festland' in all the districts. In Schönbrunn there was a large parade, with shooting and with the pealing of bells that went on endlessly . . . The townspeople had to stand in line with the troops. As night fell all Vienna and its suburbs were lit up, and splendid fireworks crackled in the air. Amongst the many appropriate cut out and illuminated transparencies prepared by the Viennese townspeople, one could read 'Zur Weihe An Napoleons Geburtstag' ['Dedicated to Napoleon's Birthday']. Anyone who was not nearby read it as 'Z W A N G' [coercion] because the other letters were so small that they disappeared.[5]

During the French occupation only one work by Beethoven is known to have been played in public; at a charity concert in the Theater an der Wien on 8 September the Eroica Symphony – of all pieces – was given in a concert that included a violin concerto by Clement, the overture to *Anacreon* by Cherubini, two operatic numbers by Mozart and the 'Hallelujah' chorus from Handel's *Messiah*. Beethoven may well have been despondent, even lonely, in these months but he was not inactive. As well as some songs and small piano pieces he completed three major works, all in E♭, a quartet (op. 74), a new piano concerto and the 'Les adieux' piano sonata. The quartet was dedicated to Prince Lobkowitz, and the concerto and sonata to a patron who was soon to become central to Beethoven's creative life, Archduke Rudolph. He also became a close friend in a way that Lobkowitz never did.

Born in 1788, Archduke Rudolph Johann Joseph Rainer was the youngest brother of Emperor Franz. Like many members of the Habsburg family through the generations, Rudolph received an extensive musical education, but he was undoubtedly the most gifted Habsburg musician since Leopold I (1640–1705). His first teacher was the court composer Anton Teyber (1756–1822), but as early as the winter of 1802–3 he had been passed on to Beethoven for piano lessons. Because of a weak constitution and occasional epilepsy, a traditional military career was changed to a church career, a parallel progress to that of his uncle, Maximilian Franz. He was appointed coadjutor of the archbishopric of Olmütz (Olomouc) in 1805, finally becoming archbishop in 1820. As a pianist he performed frequently in private concerts in Vienna and together with Ferdinand Ries and Carl Czerny became one of Beethoven's most faithful disciples.

The year 1809 saw a blossoming of the relationship between Beethoven and the archduke. First, Archduke Rudolph was one of the three figures who had guaranteed the composer an annual income to remain in Austria. Rudolph seems to have been the leading player in this arrangement and over the next few years, as Kinsky and Lobkowitz defaulted on the agreement, he often shouldered the burden of additional payments. Secondly, Beethoven's teaching moved from piano playing to composition. During the next twelve years or so the archduke produced some twenty-seven completed works, including piano music, several compositions involving the clarinet and a fine violin sonata in F minor. Many of the autograph manuscripts of these and other works have alterations in Beethoven's hand. Although Beethoven was sometimes to complain that teaching interrupted his own work (not a particularly original complaint), he was genuinely interested in the progress of the archduke.

Quite why Beethoven began a new piano concerto in 1809 is not known. As with its predecessors, there may have been the intention that it should feature in the composer's next benefit concert, though in the event he never played the work. There may, too, have been the intention that the work should be played by the archduke, its ultimate dedicatee. Certainly, around this time Beethoven wrote cadenzas for the first, third and fourth piano concertos, probably for Rudolph. The piano sonata in E♭ (op. 81a) owes its programme to Rudolph. When the archduke fled from Vienna to avoid the French invasion Beethoven wrote the first movement of the sonata, inscribing it 'The Farewell [Das Lebewohl], Vienna 4 May 1809, on the departure of His Imperial Highness the Honourable Archduke Rudolph'. During his absence and in anticipation of his return Beethoven added the two remaining movements, 'Abwesenheit' and 'Das Wiedersehen'.

During this period Beethoven began compiling material for Rudolph's instruction as a composer. He copied extracts from a variety of textbooks, including Fux's *Gradus ad Parnassum*, Kirnberger's *Die Kunst des reinen Satzes* and Türk's *Kurze Anweisung zum Generalbassspielen*. The exercises that he gave Rudolph show the same pedagogical thoroughness he had experienced with Haydn and, especially, Albrechtsberger.

In one aspect of musical experience Rudolph was probably more knowledgeable than Beethoven, at least in a dilettante way. He had amassed one of the most wide-ranging private music libraries in Vienna, housed in his apartments in the Hofburg. He began collecting when he was thirteen years old, meticulously entering details of every acquisition in his own handwritten catalogues. The principal catalogue gives an almost annual statistical survey of the growth of the collection; in 1808 Rudolph noted that there were 2,000 works by 370 composers; by 1812 this had grown to 5,000 compositions by 700 composers; and in 1814 there were over 5,700 works by 825 composers. Contemporary composers featured prominently include Cherubini, Salieri, Seyfried and Vogler, as well as Beethoven; not surprisingly Rudolph had an almost complete collection of his teacher's music, both in manuscript and printed form. From the earlier generation of Austrian composers, Joseph Haydn, Michael Haydn and Mozart are well represented, but he also owned substantial quantities of music by Dittersdorf, Dussek, Gassmann, Kozeluch, Pleyel, Pichl, Steffan and Zimmermann. Although Rudolph was a pianist, the material is not dominated by keyboard music but includes everything from violin sonatas to symphonies, and operas to oratorios. It is especially interesting for the number of antiquarian items, music from the past that was not generally known but increasingly regarded as the sign of educated taste in the new century: Allegri, Albinoni, Johann Sebastian Bach, Wilhelm Friedemann Bach, Charpentier, Graun, Handel, Leo, Palestrina, Pachelbel, Rameau and Vivaldi. There was also a collection of some 250 books on music, ranging from Zarlino's *Le istitutioni harmoniche* (1558), through Daube's *Der musikalische Dilettant* (1773) to Niemetschek's life of Mozart (1798). For Beethoven this was a real treasure trove, one, moreover, that was being added to all the time. Since he never kept a systematic library of his own compositions, he often borrowed items from the archduke's library. More illuminating, access to the library encouraged Beethoven's latent interest in older music, one that becomes increasingly evident over the next decade and which was, eventually, to feed itself into his own compositions.

In Archduke Rudolph, Beethoven had found the perfect patron: generous, liberal, protective and musically educated. Pursuing a public career in Vienna as a composer was to remain difficult, but Rudolph's patronage fed the mind as well as the purse. There was an old-fashioned sense of indebtedness in the relationship, one that is apparent in the correspondence between the composer and the archduke. While Beethoven's letters are deferential without being sycophantic, they are also demanding without being peremptory. The following extract from a letter concerning arrangements for a private concert in the archduke's apartments is typical:

> I ask Your Imperial Highness to have the orchestra summoned for a quarter to three tomorrow afternoon, so that these worthy m[usicians] may come earlier and so that we may have enough time to rehearse the two overtures as well. Should Y.I.H. desire to have the latter rehearsed, then I should require four horns. But in the symphonies, of course, there are only two of them. For instruments in the symphonies I would like to have at least four violins (four seconds, four firsts), two double basses, two violoncellos – All I ask you is kindly to let me know today what you have decided. There is no greater pleasure for me than to let my eminent pupil hear my works. May God soon restore your health. For I am most anxious about it.[6]

The stability and generosity of the archduke's support was crucial in a period when the Austrian economy was veering out of control. From 1800 to 1809 Vienna had experienced gently rising inflation which produced hardship but which was socially containable. From 1809, as a result of the French occupation of the city, there was a sudden increase in inflation, with food and rent prices being particularly hit. By 1811 inflation had moved to hyperinflation and the currency was virtually worthless, forcing the government to declare the state bankrupt and to devalue the currency by 80 per cent. For a while inflation was halted before it began moving upwards again, to a point that a second state bankruptcy was contemplated in 1816. Like everybody else in Vienna, Beethoven had never experienced such savage economic instability – between 1809 and 1814 the cost of living increased by a staggering 542 per cent – and, though it affected food and rent most directly, it undermined the confidence of the whole of society, affecting its way of life including musical life, already in a state of suspended animation because of the continuing Napoleonic wars.

When Archduke Rudolph, Kinsky and Lobkowitz agreed to the annual payment of 4,000 gulden, they assumed, like imperial and princely patrons for a century or more, that it would be a fixed amount; as landowners all three were buttressed against the more severe effects of inflation. Nevertheless, two of the three benefactors, Kinsky and Lobkowitz, found it difficult to maintain the payments. Early in November 1811 Prince Kinsky went riding on his estates in Bohemia, fell awkwardly and suffered head injuries; he died the following day at the age of only thirty-one. His sons were too young to assume control of the estate, and its affairs were entrusted to the princess and to her uncle, Franz Anton von Kolowrat-Liebsteinsky. Before the end of the year Beethoven wrote a lengthy letter to the princess. After some dutiful condolences he cites the 'bitter duty of self-preservation' as justification for a plea that her late husband's support be maintained and the accumulated arrears be paid in full. Although the legal situation was unclear Beethoven pursued the matter, testing the elastic patience of his lawyers, until it was settled in his favour in 1815.

The history of Lobkowitz's payments was even more sensational. Beethoven was only one of many musicians who had benefited from this prince's unquenchable thirst for music. At the time of the signing of the agreement with Beethoven, Lobkowitz was spending over 8,000 gulden per annum on the copying of music alone; his promised contribution of 700 gulden was, therefore, a very small part of his total expenditure. Like most aristocrats Lobkowitz had no real understanding of income and expenditure and, certainly, not the faintest comprehension of the likely consequences of state bankruptcy. He continued to spend until he himself was declared a bankrupt and prevented from any further expenditure. In one of the saddest tales of musical Vienna, this former leading figure became something of a pariah in aristocratic circles, spending most of his time on his estates in Bohemia. An increasingly dejected man, he became seriously ill and died in December 1816 at the age of forty-four.

Lobkowitz's payments to Beethoven had been suspended in 1812 and for three years the composer received nothing from the prince. Again Beethoven's reaction was to enforce the 1809 agreement with the 'princely rascal', as he called him; as with the Kinsky family, legal agreement was reached in 1815 when the allowance was reactivated together with payment of the arrears.

Financial worries can only have aggravated Beethoven's health in the years after 1809. His deafness was becoming progressively worse, and he began to rely more and more on ear trumpets to carry on any kind of conversation. In appearance, the striking, well-dressed young man of ten years before became rather shabby and unkempt. Letters written in the winter months of 1811, 1812 and 1813 continually refer to various illnesses that prevented him from working; headache, gout and stomach pains were the main afflictions, and a modern doctor might well have diagnosed depression too. His personal relationships with women continued to be marked by true tenderness, on occasions consuming love, but they were also marred by gauche behaviour and impractical idealism. Through his friend Gleichenstein Beethoven met an eighteen-year-old girl, Therese Malfatti. As a token of his friendship he presented her with a rather wistful short piano piece in A minor inscribed 'Für Therese'; when the autograph was rediscovered later in the nineteenth century the inscription was misread as 'Für Elise', thereafter the title of the piece. Beethoven apparently proposed marriage using Gleichenstein as a go-between; not surprisingly Therese rejected him.

Two years later, in 1812, Beethoven fell in love with another woman, and penned her an intense love letter. Along with the Heiligenstadt Testament, this document is one that has fascinated generations of biographers. As well as a highly emotional content, it shares with the Heiligenstadt Testament two further characteristics: it was never, apparently, sent (at least in its surviving form) and for that reason may have been another act of catharsis; and it was carefully preserved by the composer as a poignant memory. There is an added mystery in the case of the love letter. Its recipient is not identified; indeed, Beethoven takes great care to avoid mentioning her name, variously addressing her as 'my angel, my all, my very self', 'my true, my only treasure' and 'my Immortal Beloved'. Maynard Solomon has proved beyond reasonable doubt that the 'Immortal Beloved' was Antonie Brentano, a

9 The Malfatti family. Therese is playing the piano; Joseph Malfatti, one of Beethoven's doctors, is seated right

married lady ten years younger than Beethoven. More speculatively, it has been suggested that the composer was the father of her youngest child.[7]

From the middle of 1812 Beethoven began keeping a notebook, now usually referred to as the *Tagebuch*, in which favourite passages of poetry and prose plus some proverbs mingle with thoughts of his own, both melancholy and hopeful, and mundane reminders to buy shoe brushes and move the stove into the attic.[8] The tenor of many of the confessional passages is a familiar one: his fateful existence, a determination to overcome circumstances, and fulfilment through art. As well as the virtuous idealism of the struggle there are some passages that allude to the solace of contemplation: 'Learn to keep silent, O friend. Speech is like silver, but to be silent at the right moment is pure gold' (Herder). Many of Beethoven's letters from this period reveal, sometimes in a very self-conscious way, his reading of Greek

mythology and ancient literature in general. From a German translation of *The Iliad* Beethoven copied into the *Tagebuch*, 'For Fate gave
Man the courage to endure to the end.'

During these years of increasing tensions and worries, the tranquillity that Beethoven's regular visits to the countryside in the
summer months provided became more and more crucial to his well-
being. Baden, fifteen miles to the south of Vienna, was a particularly
favoured resort. In 1813 Beethoven left Vienna for Baden at the end of
May, rather early in the season. Archduke Rudolph, nevertheless, was
already there, and Beethoven was anxious to remind him of his arrival.

I have the honour to inform you of my arrival at Baden, which indeed
is still very empty so far as people are concerned; but all the more
fully and lavishly is Nature decked out in her profusion and ravishing
beauty – If I am doing anything wrong or have done so, kindly make
allowances for me, for a number of unfortunate incidents occurring
one after the other have really driven me into a state bordering on
mental confusion. However, I am convinced that the glorious
beauties of Nature and the lovely surroundings of Baden will restore
my balance and that a twofold calm will take control of me, seeing
that by staying here for a while I am fulfilling also Y.I.H.'s desires –
Would that my longing to hear soon that you are enjoying perfect
health were fulfilled also. That is indeed my most ardent desire. And
how grieved I am that just now I am neither permitted nor able to
contribute in any way to your recovery and your welfare by means of
my art. That privilege is reserved for the goddess *Hygeia* alone. After
all I am only a poor mortal who sends his compliments to Y.I.H. and
ardently desires to be allowed soon to visit you at Baden.[9]

Two years earlier Beethoven had intended making an extended visit
to Italy to improve his health but his doctor, Joseph Baptist Malfatti
(Therese's uncle), suggested that he take the cure in Teplitz (Teplice),
some fifty miles north of Prague. Beethoven had often visited the
baths in Heiligenstadt and Baden, but there was a particular reason
for the costly journey to Teplitz. The oldest of the Bohemian spa
towns, it had been known for the healing properties of its warm

spring waters from Celtic and Roman times; in the early nineteenth century the waters were noted for their beneficial effects on lameness, gout and, improbably, deafness. Although Beethoven was at first rather reluctant to make the journey, he spent six weeks in Teplitz, from early August to mid September 1811 and reported an improvement in his general well-being. Not surprisingly, therefore, the following summer saw a return visit to Teplitz; from here Beethoven made shorter visits to further spas, Carlsbad (Karlovy Vary) and Franzensbad (Františkovy), staying a total of ten weeks from July to September. In terms of Beethoven's health, this second visit was a failure. Towards the end of the stay he had a debilitating bout of illness, a final impression that together with the high cost of the stay ensured that he never again visited the spa towns of Bohemia.

Many people visited Teplitz, Carlsbad and Franzensbad for social reasons as much as medical reasons. The first two towns, in particular, were noted as venues where princes, monarchs, aristocrats, poets, artists and musicians gathered, and where new political, cultural and personal liaisons were formed. Beethoven, for whom the prospect of socializing was often more painful than the actual experience, forged a number of new friendships in these spa towns, including the Brentano family, Giovanni Battista Polledro (a violinist with whom he gave a charity concert), Elisa von der Recke (author), Amalie Sebald (singer), Christoph August Tiedge (poet), Joseph Varena (musician) and Karl August Varnhagen (diplomat). Pre-eminent amongst these new acquaintances was Goethe. Beethoven had long admired him, regarding him as a hero, and a poet and playwright whose rhythm and rhetoric almost willed a musical response. The years 1809 and 1810 had produced a number of settings of Goethe: three of the six songs from op. 75 (including 'Kennst du das Land' and Gretchen's fable 'Es war einmal ein König' from *Faust*), the three songs of op. 83 and incidental music to the play *Egmont*. For his part Goethe was only dimly aware of Beethoven's reputation; in musical matters he tended to rely on the judgment of the Berlin composer Carl Friedrich Zelter. On this occasion, however, the person who made Goethe aware of Beethoven's artistic stature was the extraordinary Bettina Brentano.

Half-sister to Franz Brentano, the husband of Antonie (the supposed 'Immortal Beloved'), she craved the company of creative artists, pampered and flattered them, and wrote extravagant and indulgent appreciations of their work. Eventually, she was to marry the poet Achim von Arnim, but her real literary idol was Goethe. On a visit to Vienna in 1810 she met Beethoven and wrote an embarrassingly lavish – some might say psychologically disturbed – letter to Goethe:

> When I saw him of whom I shall now speak to you, I forgot the whole world – as the world still vanishes when memory recalls the scene – yes, it vanishes . . . It is Beethoven of whom I now wish to tell you, and who made me forget the world and you; I am still not of age [she was twenty-five], it is true, but I am not mistaken when I say – what no one, perhaps, now understands and believes – he stalks far ahead of the culture of mankind. Shall we ever overtake him? I doubt it, but grant that he may live until the mighty and exalted enigma lying in his soul is fully developed, may reach its loftiest goal, then surely he will place the key to the heavenly knowledge in our hands so that we may be advanced another step towards true happiness.[10]

Goethe was in Carlsbad in 1811 when Beethoven was in Teplitz, and so the long-anticipated meeting between poet and musician did not take place until 1812 when both were in Teplitz. Over a period of many weeks, they met on almost a daily basis but mutual admiration never developed into friendship and they never again met. Both recorded their impressions and both were right. Goethe, a generation older than Beethoven and a seasoned social diplomat, wrote to Zelter:

> His talent amazed me; unfortunately he is an utterly untamed personality, who is not altogether in the wrong in holding the world to be detestable but surely does not make it any the more enjoyable for himself or others by his attitude. He is easily excused, on the other hand, and much to be pitied, as his hearing is leaving him, which perhaps mars the musical part of his nature less than the social. He is of a laconic nature and becomes doubly so because of this lack.[11]

Beethoven's thoughts, which were certainly laconic, were given in a letter to Breitkopf & Härtel:

> Goethe delights far too much in the court atmosphere, far more than is becoming to a poet. How can one really say very much about the ridiculous behaviour of virtuosi in this respect, when poets, who should be regarded as the leading teachers of the nation, can forget everything else when confronted with that glitter.[12]

Beethoven's status within the private musical circles in Vienna in this period changed very little. His public reputation, however, underwent a sea change. From being a composer whose six symphonies (to date), five piano concertos, single opera and single oratorio represented the most challenging aspect of Viennese musical life, he moved, by accident rather than by design, to a position where he was a permanent and popular presence. In terms of public acclaim 1814 was to be the most successful year in his entire career; it was also the year that he was at his most Austrian.

Up until the mammoth concert in the Theater an der Wien in December 1808, symphonies and concertos had formed the cornerstone of his compositional plans. Between 1809 and 1812 he completed three more works of this kind, the fifth piano concerto, and the seventh and eighth symphonies, enough to form the main content of a benefit concert. But the actual premiere of the fifth concerto had taken place in Leipzig, and Beethoven allowed the first Viennese performance, given by Czerny in February 1811, to be given as part of a mixed entertainment whose principal feature was a series of *tableaux vivants* based on paintings by Poussin, Raphael and Troyes. In April 1813 Beethoven tried to secure the hall in the university for a benefit concert, and after that either the Kärntnertortheater or the Theater an der Wien.

Both the seventh and the eighth symphonies had been rehearsed in private at the apartments of Archduke Rudolph, but they still remained unperformed in public. An incorrigible showman named Johann Nepomuk Maelzel ensured their eventual performance in public. Maelzel had been born in Regensburg in 1772. He was an accomplished musician who soon developed an enthusiasm for inventing and building mechanical instruments of all kinds, including a robotic arm, an audio-visual realization of extracts from Haydn's *Seasons*, a mechanical chess player and a life-size mechanical trumpet player. His house in Vienna was a veritable amusement arcade, and he took his exhibits on European tours too. His most popular invention was the panharmonicon, a mechanical orchestra that reproduced the sounds of violins, cellos, trumpets, flutes, clarinets, drums, cymbals and triangle, all activated by a barrel organ mechanism. Early in 1813 Maelzel was contemplating a trip to London and prepared new barrels for the panharmonicon that reproduced the overture to Cherubini's *Lodoiska*, Haydn's 'Military' symphony and two numbers from Handel's *Timotheus*; in addition Cherubini and Moscheles agreed to write some especially composed music.

During the summer news reached Vienna of the Duke of Wellington's stunning victory over the French at the Battle of Vittoria. Maelzel, who had known Beethoven for over twenty years, supplying him with various ear trumpets and interesting him in the chronometer (a forerunner of the metronome), now asked him to write a new work for the panharmonicon: 'Wellington's Victory or the Battle of Vittoria'. Beethoven agreed and responded with the most grandiloquent of compositions, one that apparently challenged the physical capabilities of the instrument to the utmost. Maelzel soon felt that the work would make even more impact if it were rewritten for orchestra. Beethoven might well have been persuaded by the worldly-wise impresario that it might establish a new reputation for the composer and give him the opportunity to present other works in the wake of its success. Beethoven's attitude to public acclaim was always more ambivalent than he sometimes averred, and certainly more ambivalent than that which posterity has claimed on his behalf. A large quantity of piano music had always been aimed at the amateur market, including variations on 'God save the King' and 'Rule, Britannia' (both tunes feature in *Wellington's Victory*); he had written over eighty dances for the annual carnival season in Vienna; from 1809 he began setting folksongs for the Scottish publisher George Thomson; and he frequently sanctioned (in some cases prepared) arrangements for piano, piano duet, piano trio and quartet of works like the second symphony and the ballet music to *Prometheus*. Public recognition and money were as important to Beethoven as the self-imposed intellectual challenges of composition, and there was a side to his gruff, unsophisticated personality that would have found the composition and many performances of *Wellington's Victory* hugely entertaining. Beethoven's willingness to play to the gallery is shown by his (and Maelzel's) decision to present the work at a charity concert on 8 December 1813 in aid of Austrian and Bavarian soldiers wounded in the recent Battle of Hanau that had driven the French out of central Germany. The composer took this opportunity to present the seventh symphony for the first time, a work completed a year before but whose jubilance matched this patriotic occasion. The concert was so successful that it had to be repeated four days later. A glowing account of the concerts appeared in the *Allgemeine musikalische Zeitung*:

> Long honoured at home and abroad as one of the greatest instrumental composers, Herr von [sic] Beethoven celebrated his triumph at these performances. A large orchestra, comprising the first and choicest of local musicians, had united voluntarily to co-operate out of patriotic zeal and heartfelt gratitude for the blessed success of the universal exertions of Germany in the present war and afforded, under the direction of the composer and through his precise involvement, a general pleasure that rose to ecstasy.[13]

The actual subject matter of *Wellington's Victory* was the triumph of the British over the French, but the fervour that the work aroused was not so much pro-British, or even anti-French, but breast-beatingly Austrian.

The success of the concerts with Maelzel led to Beethoven appearing at three further concerts in as many months. On 2 January at the large Redoutensaal and for Beethoven's own benefit, Wellington's Victory was given once more, together with three numbers from The Ruins of Athens, ending with the patriotic, pro-Habsburg declamation 'Heil, unserm König, Heil'; a second benefit concert for Beethoven at the Redoutensaal followed on 27 February, when the programme consisted of the seventh and eighth symphonies (the latter being given in public for the first time), a vocal trio, 'Tremate, empi, tremate' and, once more, Wellington's Victory; and on 25 March, at the Kärntnertortheater, for the benefit of retired and destitute theatre personnel, Beethoven directed the Egmont overture (which has its own victory symphony in the coda) and, inevitably, Wellington's Victory, the fifth public performance in four months.

In France a defiant Napoleon was attempting to delay inevitable defeat at the hands of advancing Austrian, British, Prussian and Russian troops. For once the Allies managed to withstand his skilful attempts at dividing and ruling, and entered Paris on the last day of March. In Vienna the management of the court theatres decided to celebrate the good news with a hastily thrown together Singspiel with that very title, Die gute Nachricht. Hummel provided three of the eight musical numbers, four were adapted from existing music by Gyrowetz, Kanne, Mozart and Weigl, and Beethoven was asked to compose the final chorus, a mainly strophic number in which a bass soloist leads the choir in a brisk, heavily accented march, 'Germania, Germania, how splendid you now stand' and ending 'Kaiser Franz, Victory, Praise him, Hail to thee Germania'. Beethoven even headed the movement in German rather than the customary Italian, 'Feurig, jedoch nicht zu geschwind' ('Fiery, but not too fast'), a patriotic habit evident in many works from 1814.

Welcome though this sustained public acclaim must have been Beethoven was especially gratified by the unexpected proposal made by the administration of the court theatres that his opera, Leonore, not heard for eight years, should be revived. Beethoven agreed, on condition that he could revise the work. Although Joseph Sonnleithner, the original author, and Stephan von Breuning, its first reviser, were still

10 Engraving of Beethoven (1814) (Höfel)

living in Vienna, Beethoven was happy to entrust the task to another person, Georg Friedrich Treitschke, an experienced Viennese playwright. He was the author of *Die gute Nachricht* but, in much the same way as the composer could produce populist music when required, Treitschke was capable of the opposite, highly crafted individual work. His revision of the text of *Leonore* was masterly, giving it a dramatic focus that the two earlier versions lacked. Beethoven was enthused by the task, conscious of the effects that local changes would have on the whole but worried that he was being forced to compose against the clock. He wrote to Treitschke:

> Now, of course, everything has to be done at once; and I could
> compose something new far more quickly than patch up the old with
> something new, as I am now doing. For my habit when I am
> composing even instrumental music is always to keep the whole in
> view – But in this case the whole of my work is – to a certain extent –
> scattered in all directions; and I have to think out the entire work
> again – To produce the opera in a fortnight is certainly out of the
> question. I am convinced that it will take us four weeks . . . Had you
> not taken so much trouble with it and revised everything so
> satisfactorily, for which I shall ever be grateful to you, I would hardly
> bring myself to do my share – but by your work you have salvaged a
> few good bits of a ship that was wrecked and stranded.[14]

The new ship, renamed *Fidelio*, was launched on 23 May at the Kärntnertortheater and was an immediate success, for the complementary reasons that it mirrored the heady social and political mood of the time, and was the work of a composer who was now the undoubted favourite of the Viennese. Six further performances followed, the last a benefit performance for Beethoven.

Beethoven was not alone in providing music for this new era of liberation. Hummel, as well as his contribution to *Die gute Nachricht*, composed a one-act opera to celebrate the return from the peace negotiations in Paris of Emperor Franz, *Die Rückfahrt des Kaisers*. For their part, Joseph Weigl and his librettist Joseph Sonnleithner looked forward to a new world order in *Die Weihe der Zukunft* (*The Inauguration of the Future*). The many pianists in Vienna could amuse themselves and their guests with a 'characteristic tone painting for the piano' by Diabelli called 'The Glorious Return of the dearly-loved Franz to his Court on 16 June 1814', a work that ends with a mock spontaneous rendition of Haydn's anthem, 'Gott erhalte Franz den Kaiser'.

Emperor Franz had invited the heads of all the European states to a conference in Vienna, the Congress of Vienna, designed to map out the future of Europe after a quarter of a century of fighting. For five months from October 1814 Vienna was home to the crowned heads of Europe, together with their retinues of countless diplomats, civil servants and messengers. While the real business of the congress featured the rival diplomatic skills of Metternich for Austria, Castlereagh for Britain and Talleyrand for France, hundreds of people took part in the associated festivities. There were specially arranged dances, hunts, military tattoos, sleighrides, banquets, *tableaux vivants*, operas, concerts and church services. Beethoven's music played a prominent part in these festivities.

To greet the assembled heads of states Beethoven was asked to compose a chorus, 'Ye prudent sagacious founders of happy states' (WoO 95), another unremittingly energetic movement, rather reminiscent of the finale of the seventh symphony. The opera *Fidelio* was given in the presence of foreign heads of state on 26 September, followed by several more performances in the following months. Beethoven's prominence in Viennese public life even caused him to figure in the reports of Austria's secret police, delivered every morning to Metternich: 'There are two camps, pro and contra Beethoven. Opposite to Razumovsky, Apponyi and Kraft who idolize Beethoven, stands a much larger majority of connoisseurs who do not want any music by Beethoven.'[15]

While still in the ascendant, Beethoven planned a further benefit concert, the fourth in a year and one more than he had achieved in his entire career to date. The original date was to be Sunday 20 November, but the secret police reported that Castlereagh and his colleagues would not attend on a Sunday because 'The English are so religious.'[16] The concert was finally given on Tuesday 29 November at the large Redoutensaal in the presence of several heads of state. The centrepiece was a new, six-movement cantata, *Der glorreiche Augenblick* (*The glorious moment*). Beethoven preceded this work with the seventh symphony and followed it with yet another performance of *Wellington's Victory*. The success of the concert prompted two repetitions, the first for Beethoven's benefit and the second for the benefit of St Marx hospital.

In one hectic year Beethoven had been catapulted to fame. He had also become very wealthy, earning more in 1814 than at any other time in his life, despite the fact that the Kinsky and Lobkowitz families were not paying their share of the annuity. Much as the composer welcomed this popularity, its nature was at odds with what he had hoped to accomplish and was based, with the notable exception of the seventh symphony and *Fidelio*, on works that posterity was to regard as irredeemably banal. Rather than Beethoven the animated and poetic pianist or Beethoven the questing symphonist, it promoted Beethoven the showman and Beethoven the patriot. After a lifetime of self-consciously standing apart from Viennese musical life he was now at its very centre.

6 Empires of the mind

The assembled crowned heads of Europe remained in Vienna until March 1815, when their deliberations were abruptly halted by the news that Napoleon had left Elba, landed at Antibes and was marching menacingly towards Paris. Diplomatic and social manoeuvring in the gossip-ridden congress was quickly put to one side as the parties were forced to tackle once more the common enemy. Early on the morning of 18 June, on the slopes of Mont Saint-Jean near Waterloo in Belgium, Napoleon was defeated for the final time.

Napoleon's actions had meant that the Congress of Vienna had dissolved quickly without reaching a grand, ceremonial conclusion. Perhaps this too denied Beethoven one last public occasion to impress Vienna and the assembled world with his music. Apart from an impromptu performance with the tenor Franz Wild of the song 'Adelaide' at a concert for the birthday of the Russian empress in January, Beethoven had taken no part in the festivities after December 1814.

Beethoven's unprecedented popularity in Vienna encouraged plans for new works of all kinds and, had these plans been realized, the period from 1815 to 1819 would have rivalled the five years up to 1809 in the number of major works composed; at various times an opera, an oratorio, a piano concerto, a piano trio and a symphony were contemplated. None was completed and, instead, the five years from 1815 to 1819 became one of the most fallow in the composer's career;

the 'Hammerklavier' piano sonata and the two cello sonatas of op. 102 are the only substantial works written in this period. Many of the reasons for this decrease in creativity were the usual ones – increasing deafness and general ill health, financial concerns, extreme self-criticism, and the unsupportive nature of public concert life in Vienna – but there were new factors too, an obsessiveness about his domestic situation, especially his relationship with his nephew Karl, and a general indecision about what he wanted to do. For twenty-three years the European conflict had affected Beethoven's life and music. Ironically, the end of the Napoleonic wars initiated a period of tortured rather than liberated creativity.

Given the success of *Fidelio*, it is not surprising that Beethoven and Georg Treitschke planned a new opera, *Romulus und Remus*. At first the composer was very enthusiastic about the project but this was soon undermined by a local composer named Johann Fuss, who claimed that he had prior rights to the story, and then completely derailed when he could not agree financial terms with the director of the court theatres, Ferdinand Pálffy; a few sketches were made before the project was abandoned.

Another project for which Beethoven showed considerable enthusiasm but which did not result in any real achievement was a projected second oratorio to follow *Christus am Oelberge*, a work that was frequently performed in Vienna. In 1812 a group of musical enthusiasts had established the Gesellschaft der Musikfreunde (Society of the Friends of Music) dedicated, as its statutes declared, 'to the promotion of music in all its branches'. A conservatoire was to be established, so-called 'classical works' performed, prize essays on the state of music organized, a music journal set up, a public music library established and outstanding talent supported. It was an ambitious manifesto at a time when war and inflation made all artistic life difficult, and it was to take the best part of a decade for the Gesellschaft der Musikfreunde to become a dominant force in the musical life of the city, a position it holds to this day. In the first few years its patronage of concerts was restricted to promoting annual oratorio concerts given by forces up to 1,000 strong and featuring Handel's *Timotheus*, *Samson* and *Messiah*, and Maximilian Stadler's *Die Befreyung von Jerusalem*; the last had been written by one of Vienna's most respected musical figures. As the Gesellschaft sought to expand its role in Viennese musical life it was natural that it should turn to the city's most popular composer for a new oratorio. Beethoven readily agreed, was later formally commissioned, but nothing ever came of the project.

More conducive to Beethoven's talents, it might be thought, was a new piano concerto in D major, begun in the winter of 1814–15. A draft score for almost the entire first movement was completed, its contents suggesting a work on a grand scale, a worthy successor to the fifth concerto. Almost certainly Beethoven intended to play the work in a future benefit concert. Gradually, he may have come to realize the impracticality of this and, since imagining a public performance had always been a vital stimulus for the composition of concertos, much more so than for a piano sonata, quartet or even symphony, he abandoned the work. This was the final, rather disconsolate episode in Beethoven's long transition of some fifteen years from pianist-composer to composer.

About a year later, in the winter of 1815–16, Beethoven worked on a substantial piano trio in F minor, to the extent of offering it for publication, but again it was never completed. There may have been a particular compositional problem that the composer was unable to solve, though the extensive sketches reveal a fierce determination to will the notes into a finished composition. Again the element of personal involvement as a performer may have been an issue; he could not envisage a performance and was unable to complete the work. Apart from settings of folksongs for George Thomson of Edinburgh, Beethoven was never again to attempt a chamber work for piano and strings.

As well as revealing the widening gap between Beethoven the pianist and Beethoven the composer, the abandoned F minor trio is part of a second, long-term trend in his output, the opening of a gap between composer and listener. His latest string quartet, also in F minor, had been composed in 1810–11 and was dedicated to his old friend, Nikolaus Zmeskall. As a connoisseur of quartet writing and one of Beethoven's most supportive friends, Zmeskall was presented with a work that was at the cutting edge of the composer's style, a work that is by turn brutal and elliptical. It was not published until 1816 and even then Beethoven warned Sir George Smart of London: 'The Quartett is written for a small circle of connoisseurs and is never to be performed in public. Should you wish for some Quartetts for public performance I would compose them for this purpose occasionally [i.e. specifically].'[1] The 'Archduke' trio, by far the largest of Beethoven's piano trios, has a similar history to the F minor quartet; written in 1810–11 for a sympathetic and loyal patron, Archduke Rudolph, it was not published until 1816.

The period 1817–19 saw another stage in this continuing and deepening exclusivity, the 'Hammerklavier' sonata, a four-movement work of extraordinary practical and intellectual difficulty that lasts fifty minutes. Once more the concerns of the listener are set aside; so too are those of the pianist, as Beethoven finally eradicates a lifetime of performing instincts in favour of rigorously cerebral and exalted composition.

Incongruously, it was while Beethoven was at the height of public success, during the Congress of Vienna, that he articulated this rarefied side of his artistic make-up most tellingly. From the bustle and intrigue of Vienna he wrote to his lawyer Dr Kanka in Prague, urging him to resolve the continuing dispute with the Kinsky family:

> I shall not say anything to you about our monarchs etc., or about our monarchies etc., for the papers report everything to you – I much prefer the empire of the mind, and I regard it as the highest of all spiritual and worldly monarchies.[2]

Empires of the mind are evident too in Beethoven's reading at the time, as shown in the extracts he copied into the *Tagebuch*.[3] His abiding belief in the liberating power of reason and the healing powers of nature are reflected in his reading of Kant's *Allgemeine Naturgeschichte und Theorie des Himmels* (*Universal History of Nature and Theory of the Heavens*):

> It is not the chance confluence of the [Lucretian] atoms that has formed the world; innate powers and laws that have their source in wisest Reason are the unchangeable basis of that order that flows from them not by chance but inevitably. When in the state of the world order and beauty shine forth, there is a God. But the other is not less well founded. When this order has been able to flow from universal laws of Nature, so the whole of Nature is inevitably a result of the highest wisdom.

The nature of the Divine fascinated Beethoven as he expanded his own conception based on his inherited Catholicism towards that of eastern religions. He read German translations of the writings of the English orientalist, Sir William Jones:

> *Free from all passion and desire, that is the Mighty One. He alone. No one is greater than He.* [Brahm,] His spirit, is enwrapped in Himself. He, the Mighty One, is present in every part of space. His omniscience is self-inspired and His conception [comprehends] every other. Of all comprehensive attributes omniscience is the greatest . . . For it there is no [threefold time, no threefold] type of existence . . . It is independent of everything.

Spiritual passivity for Beethoven was a counterpoise to industry, especially his consuming sense of duty to his art, which he exerted to the point of self-sacrifice. Some time in 1815 he considered setting the following lines from *The Iliad*:

> But now Fate catches me!
> Let me not sink in the dust unresisting and inglorious,
> But first accomplish great things, of which future generations too
> shall hear!

Beethoven's increasing sense of intellectual detachment was encouraged by his worsening deafness and by bouts of illness. A persistent cold or bronchial infection (Beethoven's term is the unhelpful 'inflammatory catarrh'), that today would be quickly dispelled by anti-biotics, troubled the composer from the autumn of 1816 through to the late summer of 1817 and caused him to think that he might not ever recover. His deafness, meanwhile, had reached a critical stage. Normal conversation was impossible and could be carried out at all only by speaking into cupped hands adjacent to Beethoven's ear or into one of the half-a-dozen or so ear trumpets of different sizes that he owned. Illness and deafness made him irascible and his actions were often unpredictable, sometimes frighteningly so. Servants were engaged and sacked at an alarming rate while, at the same time, he was becoming increasingly dependent on them, as this letter to Zmeskall illustrates:

> I shall soon see you again in town. In the interest of economy I have a question to ask you, namely, what does one pay *now to have a pair of boots soled and heeled*? For indeed I have to pay my servant, who often walks into town and back, *for this*. –
>
> Let me add that it drives me to despair to think that owing to my poor hearing I am condemned to spend the greater part of my life with this class of people, the most infamous of all, and partly to depend on them.[4]

For some time acquaintances had taken to writing their part of the conversation on scraps of paper or a slate; in 1818 Beethoven began habitually to provide homemade books of scrap paper for that purpose. Measuring approximately 18 cm × 10 cm, they could be carried around in the composer's coat pocket; indeed, he often had two such books, one for musical jottings, the other for conversations. Over 100 conversation books have survived from 1818 to Beethoven's death in 1827 and they provide a fascinating glimpse of the composer at his most human and mundane; they are frequently tantalizing too, since only one side of the conversation is usually given because Beethoven replied orally. They are an invaluable reminder that the increasingly private man could also be very sociable with old friends and with new acquaintances who engaged his interest and trust. Conversations in inns and taverns are common, presumably because Beethoven did not have an ear trumpet with him and found it particularly difficult to hear if there was a constant babble of background noise. He is once touchingly reassured that he is not speaking too loudly; he worries about the quality of the wine; he is prompted to reminisce about an incompetent timpani player in a rehearsal of *Egmont*; he discusses a rare performance of Mozart's *Idomeneo*; and is asked whether he wants to play a game of chess. Occasionally, the conversation books were used for other purposes: musical ideas were scribbled on quickly drawn staves, advertisements from the *Wiener Zeitung* were copied, especially for new books on nature or on hearing difficulties; items for sale, such as a new piano or organ, were noted, as was rented accommodation; and there are simple domestic accounts (Beethoven had still not learned to multiply) and reminders to buy blotting paper and candles. One subject of conversation occurs more regularly than any other in this period, Beethoven's guardianship of his nephew, Karl. In a troubled personal life, the dispute over who should assume responsibility for Karl's upbringing crystallizes in one sorry saga the many contradictions in Beethoven's personality: affectionate, caring, honourable and principled, he could also be ruthless, calculating, self-centred and obsessive.

Early in 1815 Carl Beethoven, the composer's brother, was taken ill with tuberculosis; he was refused leave of absence from his job as a civil servant and worked until shortly before his death at the age of thirty-eight on 16 November. Two days earlier he drew up a last will and testament. His principal concern was the welfare of his nine-year-old son, Karl. The original wording made Johanna, his wife, and Ludwig, his brother, joint guardians. The composer and his sister-in-law had never seen eye to eye and when Beethoven chanced to see the will he persuaded Carl to amend the clause with the effect that it made him the sole guardian. Other visitors must have persuaded Carl of the perils of the wording and encouraged him to add a codicil later the same day: 'in as much as the best of harmony does not exist between my brother and my wife, I have found it necessary to add to my will that I by no means desire that my son be taken away from his mother'. His clear intention was that the boy should live with his mother but that Ludwig should take an active interest in his education and general welfare. The codicil ends with a plea, which even Carl must have thought hopeless: 'I recommend compliance to my wife and more moderation to my brother. God permit them to be harmonious for the sake of my child's welfare. This is the last wish of the dying husband and brother.'[5]

Within a fortnight of his brother's death Beethoven began legal proceedings to ensure that he became sole guardian, on the grounds that the will had been altered following pressure by Johanna and, since she had been previously prosecuted for embezzlement and had not always been faithful to her husband, that she was not a fit person to bring up a child. This was the beginning of a protracted legal battle that lasted four years and which Beethoven eventually won. It had all the vindictiveness of a modern divorce couple fighting for the custody of a single child. Although uncle and mother does not seem a just equivalent to the modern father and mother, Beethoven had a perfectly reasonable case according to the laws of the time. A child who had lost its father was deemed an orphan who could be entrusted to the guardianship of a nominated man – that is, a substitute father – until adulthood; moreover that guardian had the prime responsibility if it could be proved that the mother was not a suitable person to bring up the child.[6]

Beethoven won the first round of the legal battle in February 1816 when the boy was taken from his mother and entered as a pupil, at Beethoven's expense, at a highly regarded private school run by the Giannattasio family. The school was near the Landstrasse, on the eastern side of the city, and Beethoven moved to the area in order to be close to his nephew. Conveniently, it was the opposite end of the city from the Alsergasse, where Johanna lived. To Beethoven's annoyance she, nevertheless, began visiting her son at the school. Even after he had persuaded the school that the mother should be allowed only one visit per month, he remained convinced that she was having a corrupting influence on the child, and referred to her as the Queen of the

Night (presumably he was the wise Sarastro) or, occasionally, the raven mother.

Beethoven was touchingly solicitous about the welfare of Karl, making sure that he had new clothes, arranging for Czerny to give him piano lessons, caring for him when he had treatment for a hernia and, above all, ensuring that he had the best possible education, whether at a boarding school or with private tutors. There was a severity too that was, in part, typical of the age and, in part, the product of Beethoven's own temperament. On the first anniversary of the death of Karl's father Beethoven asked permission to take the son from school for the day; it does not take much psychological insight to recognize in the following letter that Karl's avowed reason for his sadness was not the true one, rather the one he knew his uncle wanted to hear:

I should like to have Karl for tomorrow, for it is the anniversary of his father's death and we want to visit his grave. I shall come and fetch him perhaps at about twelve or one o'clock – I should like to know what has been the result of my treatment of Karl after your recent complaints – Meanwhile I have been very much touched at finding him so sensitive about his honour. While we were still at your house I dropped some hints about his tendency to be lazy. We walked along together more seriously than usual. Timidly he pressed my hand but found no response. At table he ate practically nothing and said that he felt very sad; but I failed to find out from him the cause of his sadness. Finally during our walk he explained that he was feeling very sad because he had not been able to work as hard as usual. I then did my share and was even more friendly than before. This certainly shows his feeling of delicacy; and it is precisely traits of this kind that lead me to entertain hopes of his developing a fine character.[7]

On two occasions the boy ran away to his mother and Beethoven encouraged the police to collect him. The slowly swinging pendulum of the legal process moved in Johanna's favour in January 1819, when the boy was allowed to return to his mother. By now Beethoven was at least as interested in defeating Johanna as in winning the affection of

11 Steiner's music shop in the Paternostergassel

Karl; he appealed and a year later the boy lived with his guardian once more.

Preoccupation with Karl's guardianship, ill-health and an increasing insecurity about the nature of large-scale works explain why the years immediately after the end of the Congress of Vienna were comparatively unproductive. It should not be assumed, however, that, following the acclaim that the composer had received during the Congress, his music suddenly fell out of favour, that he had been pigeon-holed as a congress composer whose music was no longer required. On the contrary his compositions were frequently played in Vienna, and elsewhere too.

In April 1815, a month after the end of the Congress of Vienna, Beethoven signed a major contract with a new force in Vienna's music publishing scene, S. A. Steiner & Comp. Sigmund Anton Steiner had been born in Weitersfeld, Lower Austria in 1784, trained as a choir boy, and then worked at the firm of the general publisher (including music) Chemische Druckerey. By the age of thirty he had worked himself up the business ladder and established himself as the principal publisher of music in Vienna, acquiring the back-catalogues of Chemische Druckerey, Hoffmeister, and Haslinger. His contract with Beethoven reflected this leading status. The firm agreed to publish most of the composer's recent successes as well as some older works that had remained unpublished: *Fidelio, Der glorreiche Augenblick*, the F minor quartet, 'Tremate, empi, tremate', *Wellington's Victory*, the seventh and eighth symphonies, the 'Archduke' trio, the G major violin sonata (op. 96), three overtures (*The Ruins of Athens, Namensfeier* and *King Stephen*) and some folksong settings. Steiner became, therefore, Beethoven's third major publisher in Vienna, following on from Artaria and the Bureau des Arts et d'Industrie.

Rather like Zmeskall, Steiner brought out the whimsical side of the composer's personality. He was the frequent butt of Beethoven's laboured punning over his name (Stein=stone) and, especially, on 'Noten' and 'Nöten' (notes and needs). The two maintained a continuing and feeble comparison between music publishing and fighting a war: Beethoven was Generalissimo, Steiner the Lieutenant General, the shop was the military headquarters, shoddy work was the subject of a court martial, and so on.

When *Wellington's Victory* and the two symphonies were published over the next two years Steiner issued full scores of the works (a comparatively recent development reflecting the increasingly common use of a conductor) as well as several arrangements for piano, piano duet, piano trio, string quintet and wind band, all of which suggests an eager market in Vienna for the music. Large-scale works such as these (together with their arrangements) were very much the exception in Steiner's catalogues, which were overwhelmingly devoted to solo piano music and to salon arrangements of operatic arias. In fact Beethoven's symphonies are the only examples in his catalogue, partly reflecting the traditional commercial caution of Viennese publishers and, more fundamentally, the fact that very few symphonies were then being written by local composers.

Steiner's contract with Beethoven authorized him to distribute the music throughout Europe 'with the sole exception of England'.

As had been the composer's practice since the early 1800s, he hoped to secure a separate publisher in London to maximize his income. It was a particularly propitious time, for Beethoven's popularity had reached new heights in England. Virtually all his published music was available in London, either as a result of the first editions Clementi prepared with Beethoven's hard-won co-operation or as pirated, secondary editions. Performances of his symphonies, concertos and overtures had taken place with increasing regularity during the previous ten years, the establishment of the Philharmonic Society in 1813 playing a major part. The oratorio *Christus am Oelberge* (rendered as *The Mount of Olives*) was given ten times in London in 1814, followed by a single performance in Liverpool. Beethoven's music was at least as familiar to British musicians as to the Viennese, though his artistic profile was differently constituted. Whereas in Vienna Beethoven's reputation was, in part, built on *Fidelio*, the Mass in C and the various pieces spawned by the Congress of Vienna, these were unknown in Britain. On the other hand Beethoven had regularly provided settings of folksongs of various nationalities for the Scottish publisher George Thomson; these settings made Beethoven a favourite in the genteel drawing rooms of early nineteenth-century Britain, but they were not widely known in Vienna.

Old friends of Beethoven such as Johann Peter Salomon ('my honoured fellow countryman') and Ferdinand Ries, who had settled in London, were encouraged to sound out publishers and to promote performances, but two native musicians played even more important roles, Charles Neate and Sir George Smart. Both were involved in persuading the firm of Robert Birchall to publish some of the music that was simultaneously being issued in Vienna by Steiner: the G major violin sonata (op. 96), the 'Archduke' trio and piano arrangements of *Wellington's Victory* and the seventh symphony. On a visit to Vienna in the early summer of 1815 Charles Neate met the composer, who gave him manuscript copies of the three overtures that were being published by Steiner. This gift marked the beginning of a continuing relationship between Beethoven and the leaders of musical life in London that was to last until his death. It always promised to deliver much more than it was finally able to, and must count as one of the most tantalizing of unfulfilled opportunities in the composer's life. A formal invitation to visit London arrived in 1817. Ferdinand Ries had been given the welcome task of writing to Beethoven on behalf of the Philharmonic Society:

> The Philharmonic Society, of which our friend Neate is now also a director, and at whose concerts your compositions are preferred to all others, wishes to give you evidence of its great esteem and its gratitude for the many beautiful moments that we have so often enjoyed in your extraordinarily ingenious works; and I feel it really a most flattering compliment to have been empowered with Neate to write to you first on the subject. In short, my dear Beethoven, we would very much like to have you among us here in London next winter.[8]

The sum of 300 guineas was offered, for which Beethoven had to write two new symphonies and promise not to appear with another organization in London before or during the visit. Ries also reminded Beethoven that Sir George Smart had previously offered 100 guineas for a new oratorio and held out the prospect that a new, Italian opera might be commissioned too. Beethoven was certainly attracted by the idea of a visit, and actually began work on a new symphony (the beginnings of the ninth) while, at the same time, haggling about the main fee. In the end his health and domestic circumstances plus what was now an endemic reluctance to leave the city whose characteristics, good and bad, had fashioned his career compelled him to decline. Had Beethoven travelled to London in 1818 he would have been fully eleven years younger than Haydn when he had first visited London in 1791; posterity might have gained a ninth symphony that was rather different from the one he completed in 1823 and a tenth symphony too, plus an opera and an oratorio, but it might also have lost the 'Hammerklavier' sonata and the 'Diabelli' variations. In his late forties Beethoven was quite different from his former teacher: cautious, self-interested and suspicious rather than curious, open-hearted and trusting.

January 1817 saw the launching of a notable new venture in musical Vienna: a weekly journal devoted exclusively to music. It was quite blatantly modelled on the *Allgemeine musikalische Zeitung* published in Leipzig. It followed the Leipzig journal very closely not only in its title – *Allgemeine musikalische Zeitung mit besonderer Rücksicht auf den österreichischen Kaiserstaat* (*Universal Musical Journal with particular consideration of the Austrian Imperial State*) – but also in the format and content: two columns in roman type, a leading article (sometimes spread over several issues), reviews of publications and concerts, anecdotes, music supplements and, occasionally, an information sheet (*Intelligenz Blatt*) listing new publications. Published by Steiner, it soon established a keen readership and from its third year was issued twice a week. The main article in the first three issues was a critical appraisal of Stadler's oratorio *Die Befreyung von Jerusalem*. The next work to be treated in this extended manner was Beethoven's seventh symphony, followed a year later by the eighth. Operatic life in Vienna was increasingly dominated by Rossini, especially his serious operas, and the journal reported, often at length, on performances of *Tancredi*, *Elisabetta*, *regina d'Inghliterra*, *Otello*, *L'italiana in Algeri* and *Il barbiere di Siviglia*. When the journal was established, public concert life was still largely represented by benefit concerts. Beethoven's music featured extensively, including performances of *Christus am Oelberge*, the overtures to *Prometheus* and to *Egmont*, the fifth piano concerto, the Triple Concerto and the fourth symphony. Subscription concerts of chamber music that were reported in the journal likewise included quartets by Beethoven, alongside works by Haydn, Mozart, Romberg and Forster. The most frequently performed work by Beethoven in the post-war years was the seventh symphony, though on at least one occasion the third movement had to be omitted, presumably because the orchestra could not master its tricky cross-rhythms in one rehearsal. Two benefit concerts for the violinist Franz Clement are intriguing, since they feature two works that have not survived. In December 1817 his concert included a work described as a 'Fantasy and Variations on a Theme (A major) by L. v. Beethoven (the principal theme of his Fantasy with Choir, already mentioned several times in these pages) composed and played by the concert giver', and in March 1819 another benefit concert included a further set of variations for violin and orchestra by Clement based on 'a new theme by Beethoven . . . simple and intimate, new and expressive'.[9]

The Vienna *Allgemeine musikalische Zeitung* commented interestingly in December 1818 that Beethoven's piano music was not especially well known in the city; music by new virtuosos such as Hummel and Moscheles had captured the imagination of the public while composers such as Anton Diabelli, Abbé Gelinek and Josef Wilde provided ample drawing-room fodder. There is, moreover, a clear sense in the pages of the journal that the uncompromising aspect of Beethoven's creativity is something to cherish, part of the image of someone who stood apart from the generality of musical life. Equally apparent in the journal, as it attempts to promote as well as reflect the musical life of Vienna, is the sense that Beethoven is now a Viennese composer. The journal notes with pride his popularity at the Philharmonic Society concerts in London in 1819 ('His colossal, original inventions seem particularly acceptable to the poetic contemporary spirit of the English nation') and reprints Neefe's evaluation of Beethoven's talents given in the *Magazin der Musik* in 1783, remarking how right this prophecy had turned out to be.[10] At a charity concert in January 1819 for the Widows and Orphans Institute of the Legal Faculty of the University, Beethoven made a rare public appearance, directing his seventh symphony with such energy and feeling that it was greeted with shouts of bravo and with tears of joy. 'He who has not experienced Beethoven's symphony under his direction, cannot comprehend fully this major instrumental work of our time . . . Praise him and us! We name him *ours*, *Europe's* greatest composer, and Vienna recognizes thankfully what it possesses in him.'[11] Although Beethoven had lived for nearly thirty years in Vienna, he remained self-consciously, even deliberately, an outsider, somebody who readily voiced his criticism of his adopted city; he would probably have regarded this act of possession with indifference.

Of much more interest to Beethoven were the articles in the Vienna *Allgemeine musikalische Zeitung* that dealt with old rather than contemporary music. During the first two years of the journal he could have read articles on musical instruments in the Middle Ages, Chinese music, Palestrina, music at the Austrian court in the reign of Karl VI, and on the codexes of music by Josquin and Obrecht held in the national library. Instead of the customary fare of short piano pieces, songs or piano reductions of popular operatic arias, the printed music supplements sometimes presented extracts from this older repertoire: a canon by Lully, Allegri's Miserere and the Kyrie from Josquin's Messe Gaudeamus.

A couple of months after the charity concert featuring the seventh symphony that prompted the outburst of veneration in the *Allgemeine musikalische Zeitung*, Beethoven was asked to contribute to a more overtly patriotic project. Anton Diabelli had been an employee at Steiner's firm, where his duties included proof-reading and, occasionally, preparing keyboard arrangements of instrumental and vocal music. Steiner also published much of Diabelli's own piano music, composed by the yard with the minimum of effort. Together with Pietro Cappi, Diabelli went on to form a new publishing company designed to exploit the unending demand for piano music in Vienna. A new, eye-catching venture was proposed. Rather than a set of variations by one composer, Diabelli planned a huge set written by several Viennese and Austrian composers, the whole to be issued under the title *Väterlandischer Künstlerverein (Patriotic Society of Artists)*. The composers, who were probably commissioned on an *ad hoc* basis over a number of years rather than simultaneously according to a predetermined plan, eventually numbered fifty-one, including Beethoven, Czerny, Förster, Abbé Gelinek, Hummel, Kalkbrenner, a boy wonder named Franz Liszt, Moscheles, Mozart (the son), Archduke Rudolph, Schubert and Maximilian Stadler. The chosen theme for the set of variations was a sixteen-bar waltz by Diabelli and the variations were to be printed in alphabetical order by composer. There is no reason to suppose that Beethoven regarded the project with disdain; after all he himself had always been willing to compose routine *Gebrauchsmusik* for money. But he was captivated by the potential of Diabelli's theme, a robust grid capable of supporting an enormous range of decoration and elaboration. Rather than the requested one variation, Beethoven embarked on his own set of variations, whose audacity is made apparent immediately: after Diabelli's waltz Beethoven's first variation transforms the theme into a march! His endless imagination ultimately yielded a set of thirty-three variations plus a coda which Diabelli, to his credit, published in 1824 as the first volume of his project; the other fifty composers appeared in a second volume.

The 'Hammerklavier' sonata and the 'Diabelli' variations were two compositions that far outstretched the accepted norms of, respectively, sonata and variations, while still firmly respecting their principles. Beethoven's new confidence as a composer in 1819, after a period of dormant activity, was soon to reveal itself in a third large-scale work, a mass.

In January 1819 the archbishop of Olmütz died. Archduke Rudolph had always had the right to succeed to this position. Eight years earlier he had declined the opportunity, presumably because he was too young, but now at the age of thirty-one he felt confident enough to accept the position. He was elected in March 1819, made a cardinal in June and the official ceremonies were set in motion for March 1820. Archduke Rudolph was the only one of the three patrons supplying Beethoven with his annual stipend who was still alive. With this notable appointment, Beethoven might well have entertained the idea that his own status would change too, from a financial protégé of an archduke to a full-blown Kapellmeister. Olmütz had always enjoyed an active musical life, sometimes reported in the Viennese *Allgemeine musikalische Zeitung*. Set in the undulating countryside of Moravia, it was only 110 miles from Vienna; unless he chose otherwise, Rudolph was not obliged to spend more than six to eight weeks a year in the town, enabling him to maintain full contact with life in Vienna, an arrangement that would have appealed to Beethoven too.

Beethoven wrote a seven-page letter to Archduke Rudolph in early March. It was not a formal letter of congratulation, rather a discursive and friendly one, typical of many sent by the composer to his patron and pupil:[12]

> I was not at home on the day when Y[our] I[mperial] H[ighness] graciously sent me a message; and immediately afterwards I caught a violent cold. Hence while lying in bed I am paying my respects in writing to Y.I.H. – However numerous may be the congratulations which have been pouring in to you, my most gracious lord, yet I know only too well that this new honour will not be accepted without *some sacrifices on the part of Y.I.H.* When I remember, however, what an enlarged sphere of activity is going thereby to be opened to you and to your fine and noble activities, I too cannot but add my congratulations to the many others which Y.I.H. must have received. There is hardly any good thing which can be achieved – without a sacrifice; and it is precisely the nobler and better man who seems to be destined for this more than other human beings, no doubt in order that his virtue may be put to the test.

Rudolph, too, had been unwell and Beethoven expresses the hope that he is now fully recovered. He then congratulates Rudolph on a major composition, recently completed, a set of variations on Beethoven's song 'O Hoffnung', draws attention to a copy of the first two movements of the 'Hammerklavier' sonata he was enclosing (it was eventually dedicated to the archduke) and tetchily protests at being summoned – presumably by a messenger – to appear in the archduke's apartments. Then, very casually, as if it had just occurred to him, Beethoven writes:

> The day on which a High Mass composed by me will be performed during the ceremonies solemnized for Your Imperial Highness will be the most glorious day of my life; and God will enlighten me so that my poor talents may contribute to the glorification of that solemn day.

By the following month Beethoven had begun serious work on this new mass intended for the enthronement of his principal benefactor, pupil and friend. He became consumed by the idea, set aside the 'Diabelli' variations for the time being, and worked assiduously on the composition. There was plenty of time before the official ceremonies. A typical mass for a major commemorative occasion, that is a 'missa longa' or a 'missa solemnis', could be expected to take about two months to compose, as in the case of each of Haydn's six late masses and Beethoven's own Mass in C. But it soon became clear that this new mass was going to be a work that was to outgrow any liturgical service, however grand. Several times, indeed habitually, Beethoven was to describe the mass as his greatest composition. It certainly reflected his intellectual preoccupations: a work that was firmly built on tradition but was ambitious in scope; a work that contained the widest contrasts imaginable within an inexorably unfolding and cumulative structure; and a work that enabled him to reflect his interest in religious vocal music from the renaissance to the present day.

In May 1819 Beethoven moved to Mödling for the summer. He rented rooms in the garden wing of a house in the main street. Karl was now at a new school in Vienna and, apart from occasional visits back to the city to attend to the welfare of the boy and, more irksome, to keep Johanna at bay, it was a highly productive and fulfilling summer. Refreshed by the rugged landscape of Mödling, with its rocky valleys and precarious vineyards, and totally absorbed in the composition of the Kyrie and Gloria of the mass, Beethoven stayed until the middle of October.

7   Towards a public comeback

As Beethoven continued work on the first two movements of the mass he still hoped to complete it in time for the liturgical ceremonies in Olmütz in March 1820. He also maintained the hope that the new archbishop would be in a position to employ a Kapellmeister. Although neither desire was to be realized, personal relations between Rudolph and Beethoven remained cordial, based on an affection that easily overcame frustrations and disappointments. Rudolph left Vienna on 6 March for the ceremonies in Olmütz. He was formally welcomed into the city on 8 March and enthroned as the archbishop in the Metropolitan church the next day. The music for the ceremony was suitably lavish, the orchestra alone numbering eighty-four players. Hummel's mass in B♭ was the main work, the Te Deum was provided by Joseph Preindl, successor to Albrechtsberger as Kapellmeister of St Stephen's, Vienna, and the 'splendid' offertory was by the 'immortal' Joseph Haydn, probably his 'Insanae et vanae curae'.[1]

Beethoven spent another summer at Mödling, renting rooms in a house in the main street once again, but paying extra for a balcony that overlooked the garden. Work continued on the mass, also on new compositions for the piano, the E major sonata (op. 109) and a collection of bagatelles (op. 119). It was not as relaxing as the previous summer, Beethoven complaining that he had to make the three-hour journey back to Vienna on several occasions to give composition lessons to Rudolph and to visit Karl at his school.

12 Archduke Rudolph

The immensity of the challenge that the composition of the mass posed – or rather which Beethoven forced it to pose – was the principal reason why progress was measured, but a severe bout of ill health also sapped his energies. He always maintained that the deafness and associated tinnitus were worse in the winter months; now it was aggravated by other stubborn conditions. The corset that he wore to mitigate a chronic stomach condition was no longer effective, he was increasingly prone to chest infections and he began to suffer from jaundice. Stoicism in the face of social isolation and ill health suggest an other-worldly, even saintly existence. Yet this was only one aspect of his life, as the composer pointed out in a letter to Peters, the Leipzig publisher: 'the artist is not allowed to be Jupiter's guest in Olympus every day; unfortunately vulgar humanity only too often drags him down against his will from those ethereal heights'.[2] Beethoven may have preferred to view himself as above the common fray but he was perfectly capable of acting out of 'vulgar humanity', often using his friend Jupiter as justification for the most dastardly behaviour.

For over twenty years Beethoven had been a wily negotiator with publishers. Arranging the publication of the Missa Solemnis in the early 1820s saw him at his most prevaricating, dissembling and ruthless. As early as the time of its would-be first performance Beethoven had approached Simrock about publication and agreed a fee of 100 louis d'or. No doubt because of their established friendship, warmly exemplified in Beethoven's indication that he hoped to travel to Bonn in the summer of 1821, Simrock forwarded this money in advance via the Brentano family, now living in Frankfurt. The composer kept on promising delivery of the mass and, then, in November, in response to a casual enquiry from Schlesinger, a publisher in Berlin, Beethoven sold the work for a second time, for the same price. Until the following summer both publishers were under the impression that the work was theirs. In June 1822 a third firm, Peters, was offered the mass for an increased sum of money, Beethoven enjoining the publisher to keep the discussions a secret. One publisher who had not been approached was Steiner of Vienna. Although the catalogues of that firm did include masses for use in country churches, a work of the size of the Missa Solemnis would have been a major risk for Steiner. In any case 'Generalissimo' and 'Lieutenant General' (Beethoven and Steiner) had fallen out. The composer was in long-term financial debt to Steiner but stated that he was unable to repay the money, concealing the fact that he had sufficient money in the form of bank shares while, at the same time, deflecting Steiner's repeated requests by complaining about the delay in the publication of the three overtures, *The Ruins of Athens*, *Namensfeier* and *King Stephen*. In the increasingly international world of music publishing, Steiner met Peters in a trade fair in Leipzig where they exchanged views on their mutual client: Peters also discovered that Schlesinger was being offered the mass. Beethoven's response to the disintegration of this elaborate web of deceit was to spin more threads. While brazenly denying that Schlesinger had shown interest and contending that he was the unfair victim of gossip, he approached yet another publisher, Artaria. The intrigue was to continue for two more years, with equally devious negotiations with Diabelli (Vienna), Probst (Leipzig) and Schott (Mainz). Finally, in December 1824 the last-named was entrusted with publication.

Begun in 1819, the mass was not completed until 1823, a four-year period that included also the composition of the 'Diabelli' variations and the last three piano sonatas. As a creative artist Beethoven was totally engrossed in the questing musical language of these works, a language that placed the capabilities of the performer and the predilections of the listener aside in favour of the integrity of the compositional process. In these works he was able to explore to the ultimate degree his duty to his art, a mission first set in his formative years in Bonn by Neefe. Deafness and social isolation played their part in this new artistic detachment. Some of the leading figures in Beethoven's musical life, such as Lobkowitz and Kinsky, had died, others such as Zmeskall were chronically ill, and many had left the city, including the Erdödy family, Gleichenstein and Schuppanzigh. For three years from 1819 Beethoven did not take part in a public concert in Vienna, while the hectic social world of private concerts in aristocratic homes that had featured in his early career no longer welcomed him. As the conversation books reveal Beethoven had a number of new and faithful friends, the editor of the *Wiener Zeitung* Carl Bernard, the pianist Joseph Czerny, the printer and publisher Tobias Haslinger, and the composer and writer Friedrich August Kanne. He particularly valued the services of his faithful copyist, Wenzel Schlemmer, while

Archduke Rudolph continued to fulfil his role as the most liberal of patrons, rewarded in this period with the dedication of the C minor sonata (op. 111) as well as the Missa Solemnis.

Taking this rather focused view of Beethoven's life and output it is easy to see how the 'third period' image of the composer was manufactured during the nineteenth century: a forgotten, lonely figure who produced unconventional and intractable music. But this view is far too restricted, ignoring the fact that Beethoven was never a forgotten figure in Vienna in this period. Indeed, his continuing popularity led to his re-emergence as a public figure after the completion of the Missa Solemnis.

From tentative beginnings the Gesellschaft der Musikfreunde was now beginning to emerge as a major force in Vienna's musical life: a library had been founded, based on the purchase of material from the lexicographer Ernst Ludwig Gerber, and later generously supplemented by material donated by Archduke Rudolph; a conservatoire for the training of musicians was starting to exert an influence; and public concerts sponsored by the Gesellschaft were a regular occurrence. There were usually four per year and Beethoven's music was well represented. In 1820 performances of the third, fifth and sixth symphonies were given, plus a chorus from *Christus am Oelberge*; in 1821 the fourth and seventh symphonies were given; and in 1822 the *Egmont* overture, the first and fifth symphonies and the chorus *Meeresstille und glückliche Fahrt* were presented. In due course the society hoped to present a new oratorio, already commissioned, from Beethoven. The concerts sponsored by the Gesellschaft were meant to elevate the tone of public concert life in Vienna, standing apart from the continuing tradition of the unambitious, sometimes trivial content of benefit concerts; typically, programmes placed major orchestral and choral works alongside works for a single instrument and orchestra, and operatic arias.

The organization was joined in 1819 by a second major force, the Concerts Spirituels, organized by Franz Xaver Gebauer (1784–1822). He was in charge of music at the Augustinerkirche, where he had revitalized standards after years of decline. Held at first in the assembly room of the Mehlgrube on the Neuer Markt, the Concerts Spirituels then moved to the so-called Landständischer Saal, a few minutes away in the Herrengasse. The concerts were held between four and six in the evening and consisted of the playing through of music without prior rehearsal, rather than a formal concert. Liturgical music from the repertory of the Augustinerkirche was played alongside symphonies, with the aim of raising the wider status of religious music and of the Viennese symphonic tradition. Presumably because the choral items were linked to the repertory of the Augustinerkirche, the censor did not object to liturgical texts being presented in secular surroundings which, in any case, were not the overtly secular ones of a theatre. In the first season the following works by Beethoven were performed: symphonies nos. 1, 2, 3, 4, 6, the Mass in C and *Meeresstille und glückliche Fahrt* (two performances). During the next season, 1820–1, Beethoven was represented by symphonies nos. 5, 7, 8 and *Christus am Oelberge*. This amounted to the most systematic presentation of Beethoven's symphonies since the short-lived Liebhaber Concerte of 1807–8.

A survey of the programmes presented between 1819 and 1821 by these two organizations, the Gesellschaft der Musikfreunde and the Concerts Spirituels, gives a revealing picture of the formation of public taste in Vienna. Music by fifty-two composers was given, but three dominate: Beethoven was top of the list with twenty-one performances, Mozart received eighteen and Haydn fifteen performances. The next most frequently performed composers were Abbé Vogler and Ignaz Mosel, with eight performances each. From the time of Beethoven's first symphonies nearly twenty years earlier, commentators had often linked his name with those of Haydn and Mozart. Now in a period, paradoxically, when he was not writing symphonies, the notion of a Viennese Classical School was being institutionalized by the leading organizations in the city. While the Gesellschaft had a self-proclaimed agenda to create a tradition that was Austrian, the Concerts Spirituels gave this emerging tradition another defining characteristic. Because its programmes presented sacred music that included the works of older composers such as Hasse, Jommelli and Martini as well as modern works, its symphonic repertoire soon acquired the same patina of stability, respectability and a sense of belonging to a hallowed tradition. For many composers of symphonies in the nineteenth century the triumvirate of Haydn, Mozart and Beethoven, especially the last, was to prove as intimidating as it was stimulating and, even today, musical life in Vienna is burdened by an accumulated tradition in a way that is not apparent in Berlin, London and Paris. In the repertoire of c. 1820 there is already a feeling that repeated performances of symphonies by Haydn, Mozart and Beethoven were stifling new symphonic talent. The concerts of the Gesellschaft and the Concerts Spirituels did present symphonies by other living composers, such as Krommer, Ries and Spohr, but rather than promoting the new, both organizations seemed more concerned with manufacturing a heritage.

In the autumn of 1820 Friedrich August Kanne wrote an extended article in the Viennese *Allgemeine musikalische Zeitung* with the polemical title: 'What is to be feared in the present taste in music'.[3] The journal, like the Gesellschaft and the Concerts Spirituels, had always striven to improve the quality of musical life in Vienna. Despite its forceful title and frequently rhetorical tone the article does not blame individual composers but draws attention to the difficulties faced by new composers of symphonies, church music, sonatas and quartets in comparison with composers of opera:

> But the symphony. Who will reward the composer...?
> The Missa Solemnis. Where are the spiritual institutions that will promote this branch of art? And where is the seat of judgment that will criticize the theatrical style in church music...?
> ... the sonata and the quartet are abandoned. The first lives only in North Germany and England... Through the pressure of the times the quartet has fallen almost entirely into decay...

Kanne ends his survey with an eccentric battle cry: 'What is the greatest bulwark against the destruction of music? Counterpoint!'

Broad-brush as they are, Beethoven would have sympathized with these sentiments, and they may well have arisen from conversations with the composer. They constituted a virtual manifesto for the composer in the last seven years of his life: he was currently writing sonatas and a missa solemnis, and was to complete a ninth symphony and five new quartets, all of which show an acute interest in counterpoint.

Beethoven was in regular contact with the Gesellschaft and the Concerts Spirituels. A commitment to compose an oratorio for the Gesellschaft was cemented in July 1819 by an advance payment of 400 gulden. Carl Joseph Bernard was preparing a libretto entitled *Der Sieg des Kreuzes*, based on the legend of the apparition of the cross that inspired Constantine the Great to victory against his enemy, Maxentius. But Beethoven's dissatisfaction with the first draft combined with Bernard's leisurely speed of working meant that the libretto was still unfinished four years later.

In March 1820, two-thirds of the way through the first season of the Concerts Spirituels, Gebauer paid a visit to Beethoven. His part of the conversation was written down in a pocketbook supplied by Beethoven and the composer's replies are easily conjectured.[4] Gebauer comments politely that everyone wishes that Beethoven would organize a concert of his music, since he must have so much that is new. Beethoven probably replied that he found the whole business of organizing concerts wearisome; Gebauer offers to undertake the running costs and other responsibilities. Beethoven mentions that he is supposed to be writing a work for the Gesellschaft (the oratorio), and enquires after the content of the next concert to be given by the Concerts Spirituels. Gebauer replies that the concert, to be held on the following day, will consist of a symphony by Haydn and a new mass with full orchestra specially composed for the society by Friedrich Schneider of Leipzig. Beethoven's interest in the Concerts Spirituels is evident and Gebauer paints an enthusiastic picture of concerts that feature forty-eight singers, a full orchestra (as in the theatre, he writes) and vocal music up to a full hour. He repeats his offer to organize a concert on Beethoven's behalf before the conversation moves on to his work at the Augustinerkirche. To the question 'What are you writing now?' Beethoven presumably replied 'A mass'. Gebauer's final written remark is a list of works in manuscript he wants to borrow: 'The chorus and the scores of Nos. 5 and 6'. The chorus was *Meeresstille und glückliche Fahrt*, performed twice in the next few weeks; the sixth symphony was performed at the last concert of the season and the fifth symphony in the following autumn.

As the conversation implies and the programmes of the Concerts Spirituels prove, Gebauer was interested in promoting Beethoven's music, and there is more than a hint that he is anxious to present new music by the composer. There is some intriguing circumstantial evidence that suggests that two completed movements from the Missa Solemnis were given at the first concert of the 1821–2 season of the Concerts Spirituels.

The concert was held in the Landständischer Saal on Thursday 25 October 1821. It included a symphony by Haydn, choral music by Beethoven and a Te Deum by Seyfried. Unusually, the local *Allgemeine musikalische Zeitung* gave a report on the concert:[5]

> A *Missa Solemnis* by Beethoven followed. The imposing, fantastic compositional power of this master emerges from the deeply felt harmonious choruses, and so tenderly do the sorrowful calls of *Eleison* stir the heart; the daring eagle flight of the composer praises just as powerfully in the exultant *Gloria*. Heartfelt and soulful are the solo passages that emerge from the frenzied large multitudes, and the heart yields itself joyfully to their thrilling impression.
>
> If Beethoven's daring genius occasionally presents its images in too sharp a light, or if some of the features are too strongly characterized, then he repeatedly shows the ability to appease the excited mood of the listener. Undeniably the impression of this great work is hugely exalted and powerful. The precision of the orchestra was well evident here too. The solo parts were sung by Mademoiselles Kamper and Weiss, and Herren Seipelt and Rauscher; they were generally well executed.

It could be argued that the term 'missa solemnis' in the report was being used in the generic sense, and that the work concerned was the Mass in C of 1807. But several factors suggest otherwise. The earlier work was usually referred to as a mass ('Missa', 'Messa' 'die Messe'), never a 'missa solemnis'; moreover, it is unlikely that the *Allgemeine musikalische Zeitung* would have reported in such obviously enthusiastic terms on a work that had been performed by the Concerts Spirituels in 1820. While there is nothing in the description of the Kyrie and Gloria that could not be made to apply to those movements in the C major mass, the vividness of the author's response, as well as his reservations about the exaggerated contrasts of the work, suggest that it is the Missa Solemnis that is being assessed. The description of the repeated calls of 'eleison' are particularly suited to the closing pages of the first movement of the new mass; likewise the extravagant characterization of the Gloria rings true.

What is known about the progress of the Missa Solemnis supports the view that the Kyrie and Gloria were played at this concert. By the end of 1821 Beethoven had essentially finished these two movements and had embarked on sustained work on the remaining movements. An autograph score of the Kyrie was prepared, in which amendments were later made; this score has survived. No autograph score of the Gloria exists but it is likely that one was prepared at this time. Beethoven would have been attracted by the idea of a 'practice-rehearsal' of the two completed movements; it was precisely the kind of arrangement he had profited from earlier in his career when, courtesy of Prince Lobkowitz and Archduke Rudolph, several major works were played in private before being presented to the public for the first time.

As Beethoven neared the completion of the Missa Solemnis in the summer of 1822 his thoughts turned to future large-scale projects. His immediate task was the completion of the 'Diabelli' variations, accomplished during the following winter. For the past seven years Beethoven had been detached from everyday musical life, a period of little productivity being followed by several unprecedentedly ambi-

13 Opening bars of Missa Solemnis from the autograph score (1821–4)

tious works. From 1822 through to May 1824, when he presented two concerts of his music, there is increasing evidence of Beethoven's wish to become, once more, a visible public figure in Vienna. His correspondence with friends and acquaintances in London had been dormant for a couple of years. Ferdinand Ries had sent him a score of an ambitious symphony in E♭, dedicated to his former teacher, which, however, never reached him. In July 1822 Beethoven wrote to Ries mentioning this fact and enlisting his assistance for two plans: finding a publisher in London for two of his piano sonatas (op. 110 and op. 111) and asking the Philharmonic Society whether it would be interested in commissioning a new symphony. Ries took the latter query to the directors of the society who approved a fee of £50. Beethoven had already started work on the symphony and readily accepted the offer:

I am delighted to accept the offer to write a new symphony for the Philharmonic Society. Even though the fee to be paid by the English cannot be compared with the fees paid by other nations, yet I would compose even without a fee for the leading artists of Europe, were I not still that poor Beethoven. If only I were in London, how many works would I compose for the Philharmonic Society! For, thank God, Beethoven can compose – but I admit, that is all he is able to do in this world. If God will only restore my health, which has improved at any rate, then I shall be able to comply with all the offers from all the countries of Europe, nay, even of North America; and in that case I might yet make a success of my life.[6]

The mention of North America was not an exaggeration. Beethoven had received a request from the Handel and Haydn Society of Boston for a new oratorio on a biblical text, a request the composer turned down, no doubt because he was already committed, albeit half-heartedly, to writing an oratorio for the Gesellschaft der Musikfreunde.

Less curious was the request for some new music for the opening of the Josephstadt Theatre in Vienna in October 1822. An old acquaintance of the composer, Carl Friedrich Hensler, had taken over the directorship of a new theatre in the Josephstadt, a western suburb of the city. A brand new text, *The Consecration of the House*, was fitted to music from *The Ruins of Athens*, to which Beethoven added an overture and a chorus, all arranged and composed in a matter of a few weeks in readiness for the official opening. Not since the days of the Congress of Vienna had Beethoven written music so quickly. A few weeks later, for a surprise serenade on Hensler's nameday (3 November), Beethoven provided a *Gratulations-Menuett*, written for full orchestra; after a fanfare to draw the attention of the assembled company, Hensler is treated to a swaggeringly deferential minuet, showing that Beethoven could still flatter and amuse when the mood took him. The friendship with Hensel probably prompted a third occasional work, a setting for three solo voices, chorus and an ensemble of clarinets, horns, violas and cellos of a text by Friedrich von Matthisson, 'Opferlied'; it was performed in Pressburg at a benefit concert for the tenor Wilhelm Weber.

For about a year Beethoven had envisaged composing some new quartets, his first for ten years, and possibly some quintets too. The final incentive came from the capital of imperial Russia, St Petersburg. Prince Nikolaus Borisowitsch Galitzin was a twenty-eight-year-old amateur cellist active in the promotion of musical life in St Petersburg. Writing in French to 'Monsieur Louis van Bethoven a Viennes' he explained:

> As much a passionate amateur in music as a great admirer of your talent, I take the liberty of writing to you to ask if you would consent to compose one, two or three new quartets, for which I would be pleased to pay you for the trouble what you judge appropriate. I shall accept the dedication with gratitude. Please let me know to which banker I ought to direct the sum that you wish to have. The instrument that I study is the violoncello. I await your reply with the most eager impatience.[7]

Three quartets were eventually written for Galitzin, op. 127 in E♭, op. 130 in B♭ and op. 132 in A minor.

To complete this encouraging autumn, *Fidelio* was revived at the Kärntnertortheater on 3 November, the first performance for three years. Beethoven's residual hearing had been sufficient for him to direct the music at the Josephstadt Theatre but after an embarrassing rehearsal of the opera he was persuaded to pass over the direction to Michael Umlauf. A total of seven performances were given during the 1822–3 season. The success of the music for *The Consecration of the House* and of *Fidelio* reactivated Beethoven's appetite for writing opera. A young law graduate from the university in Vienna named Johann Chrysostomus Sporschil prepared a new libretto for him designed to utilize music from *The Consecration of the House: The Apotheosis in the temple of Jupiter Ammon.* Sporschil later prepared an outline for a three-act opera, *Vladimir the Great.* Neither project came to anything.

The year 1822 also saw a period of increased stability in Beethoven's personal life. His health had improved considerably during the winter; Karl was now a youth of sixteen, a conscientious student at school in Vienna, and old enough to act as Beethoven's occasional secretary, writing in English and French as well as German; and there were signs of a limited reconciliation between Beethoven and Karl's mother. Beethoven also became much closer to his younger brother, Johann van Beethoven. Johann had amassed a small fortune as an apothecary in Linz and now lived in rented accommodation in Vienna in the winter and on a large estate at Gneixendorf, a village on the Danube near Krems, in the summer. To save money Beethoven proposed that they should share accommodation in Vienna, a more pressing consideration for Ludwig than Johann. But Johann's wife was another sister-in-law he disliked, regarding her as unsuitable because she had an illegitimate child before marrying Johann. Ludwig wrote a letter to Johann proposing the arrangement; his new found magnanimity did not, however, prevent him from reminding Johann of his dislike:

> Peace, let us have peace. God grant that the most natural bond, the bond between brothers, may not again be broken in an unnatural way. In any case, my life will certainly not last very much longer. I repeat that I have nothing against your wife, although her behaviour to me on a few occasions has greatly shocked me.[8]

Beethoven's proposal was not accepted, though the brothers did live in adjacent buildings during the following winter. Ludwig made use of Johann's business experience, giving him responsibility for many of his affairs, but a combination of Johann's lack of musical knowledge and Ludwig's inveterate meddling ensured that the relationship never became an established one. Instead a new figure in Beethoven's life, Anton Schindler, was to assume the role of secretary-cum-agent.

Born in 1795, Schindler had trained initially as a lawyer but his ability as a violinist soon led him to pursue a career as a player, becoming leader of the orchestra at the new Josephstadt Theatre. Beethoven may have known him for several years but the friendship was cemented probably during the rehearsals and performances of *The Consecration of the House*. Schindler was first and foremost an enthusiast, keen to be associated with a great figure; he was also something of a gossip who liked to lord his favoured status. Beethoven soon had a nickname for him: Papageno.

Beethoven did suffer one disappointment during this period. On 18 November 1822 the Imperial and Royal Court Composer, Anton Teyber, died at the age of sixty-six. He had been Archduke Rudolph's first teacher and had pursued a rather nondescript career at the court, composing mainly church music. Beethoven wrote a letter to Count Moriz von Dietrichstein, who was in charge of the court theatres, putting his own name forward as a candidate for the post. Given his close connection with one member of the Imperial and Royal court and his recent completion of a mass, Beethoven may well have thought himself a strong candidate to succeed and, after years of yearning for such a position, it would finally have provided him with status and security. Times, however, had changed. A century earlier the Habsburg court had been a major patron of music in the city, but during the lifetimes of Gluck, Mozart and Beethoven its direct sponsorship of opera and church music had declined greatly. Emperor Franz was certainly interested in music, especially church music, but this interest did not extend to employing composers.

Beethoven's ambitions to be a Kapellmeister were once again thwarted when the court decided that the post itself would be abolished.

Beethoven knew that Emperor Franz's taste in church music was a rather old-fashioned one, and he borrowed a score from the court library of a mass by Reutter, Haydn's teacher in the 1740s and Franz's favourite church composer. He began sketching a mass in C♯ minor and talked about writing yet another. One useful consequence of this genuine interest in writing further masses was that he was able to inform two of the publishers who had been promised the Missa Solemnis, Simrock (Bonn) and Peters (Leipzig), that he would, of course, be sending them a mass but had not yet determined which one. In reality not even the Missa Solemnis was available because Beethoven had already decided to sell it in quite a different way for the time being.

In January 1823 he had sounded out Georg August Griesinger, the diplomat and writer on music, about the feasibility of selling manuscript copies of the work to all the leading courts in Europe. As often, Beethoven's motives were a mixture of high-minded idealism and opportunism. He habitually referred to the mass as his greatest work and he was very conscious of his status as Europe's greatest living composer (he had just received one small indication of this, honorary membership of the Royal Swedish Academy of Music); now royal and aristocratic patrons throughout Europe were to be given an opportunity to demonstrate their esteem. At the same time and on a more mundane level Beethoven hoped that these exclusive sales would yield more income than commercial publication. Two or three encouraging precedents may have figured in the minds of Beethoven, Griesinger and others. First, there was the impressive list of subscribers that had been compiled for the official launch of Beethoven's career thirty years earlier, the publication of the op. 1 piano trios. Secondly – a particularly appropriate parallel – Haydn had distributed his greatest work, The Creation, in a handsome printed volume whose costs were underwritten by over 400 subscribers from throughout Europe. Thirdly, in 1814 Beethoven and Treitschke had offered manuscript copies of *Fidelio* to at least ten opera houses in central Europe, with considerable success. Griesinger's response must have been encouraging, since Beethoven and Schindler embarked on a concerted campaign to sell the work, one that preoccupied the composer in the first few months of 1823 and was still producing replies a year later.

Beethoven purchased a calendar for the new year that contained a list of all the foreign embassies and legations in Vienna. Based on this list, the first tranche of letters was sent out towards the end of January. They were directed to the Viennese representatives of the rulers of Bavaria, Mecklenburg, Prussia, Saxe-Weimar, Saxony and Württemberg. Written in Schindler's hand and signed by Beethoven, the following addressed to the Prussian embassy is typical:

> The undersigned cherishes the wish to send his latest work, which he regards as the most successful product of his mind, to the Most Exalted Court of Berlin. It is a grand Solemn Mass for solo voices with choruses and complete orchestra in score, which can also be used as a grand oratorio.
>
> He therefore requests that the High Embassy of His Majesty the King of Prussia might graciously condescend to procure for him the necessary permission of your most Exalted Court.
>
> Since the copying of the score, however, entails a considerable expense, the undersigned does not think it excessive if a fee of 50 ducats in gold were fixed for it.
>
> The work in question, moreover, will not be published in the meantime.[9]

The suggestion that the work could be performed as a 'grand oratorio' was included in all the letters, and was meant to encourage the increasingly common practice throughout Europe, especially Protestant Europe, of performing masses and other liturgical music as concert works; in truth, the Missa Solemnis was far beyond the capabilities of most church forces. Beethoven's assurance that the work would 'not be published in the meantime' was sincerely meant at the time, but it was also vague enough to allow him to publish at a later stage.

In February and March a second tranche of letters was sent directly to most of the European courts, including Denmark, England, France, Hessen-Darmstadt, Nassau, Russia, Spain, Sweden and Tuscany. A few individuals like Prince Nicolaus Esterházy and Archbishop Rudnay (primate of Hungary) were targeted too, as were some institutions like the Cäcilien-Verein in Frankfurt and the Gewandhaus in Leipzig. The third and final element in the plan was to send letters to individuals such as Cherubini (Paris), Goethe (Weimar), Spohr (Cassel) and Zelter (Berlin), urging them to persuade their respective patrons to subscribe. A few positive responses began to be received, which then involved Beethoven in further administrative work. His trusted copyist Wenzel Schlemmer provided a fresh manuscript score in each case, usually minus one or two pages of the Gloria to prevent performances not authorized in advance by the composer; Beethoven then checked the score before it was despatched.

If this time-consuming exercise had produced maximum results, Beethoven would have sold some two dozen copies of the score. The actual response was a modest ten subscribers which, nevertheless, in monetary terms yielded a respectable profit of 165 gulden on each copy. The response of the Bavarian court must have been typical of many. It informed Beethoven that it would not subscribe for two reasons: first, because the court already had so many masses by famous composers sitting on shelves, many unperformed, and, secondly, because the asking price of fifty ducats for the score would have to be supplemented by a further outlay in order to have parts prepared for any actual performance. However, the court authorities assured Beethoven that if the work was eventually published they would consider buying it. Prince Nicolaus Esterházy, whose response to the Mass in C had so dismayed the composer two decades earlier, was more blunt: he had no plans to extend his collection of church music and so rejected the offer. Beethoven's caustic comment to Schindler was that the patronage of the Esterházy prince 'can only be got out of him through women', a reference to Nicolaus's notorious lifestyle.

Beethoven was certain of a beneficent response from Archduke Rudolph. He was presented with his copy on 19 March, just over five years since the day when the composer had first intimated the project to him, and just over four years after the ceremonies at Olmütz. Beethoven promised the archduke that he would add a gradual, an offertory and a setting of 'Tantum ergo' so that, on paper at least, the archduke could imagine a complete musical service. Alas, none of these additional movements materialized.

Beethoven's buoyant mood in the first four months of 1823 was enhanced by the news that 'Falstaff' – Ignaz Schuppanzigh – was returning to Vienna after an absence of seven years in St Petersburg. Beethoven greeted him with an excitably comic canon in five parts: 'Little Falstaff, let's see you.' Schuppanzigh immediately re-entered the mainstream of musical life in Vienna. During the next twelve months he organized several subscription concerts devoted to the chamber music of Haydn, Mozart and Beethoven, plus the occasional work by Georg Onslow and Franz Weiss. Seven different quartets by Beethoven were given, from op. 18, op. 59 and op. 74, plus the Eb trio (op. 3), the G major trio (op. 9 no. 1), the C major quintet and the septet. These performances, expertly led by Schuppanzigh, no doubt encouraged Beethoven to fulfil the commission from Galitzin for new quartets, though for the time being other projects were given first priority.

Beethoven's symphony for the Philharmonic Society of London had been promised for the 1823 concert season, as always a hopelessly unrealistic deadline since the composer normally required the long summer months, ideally in the countryside, to work in a sustained manner on a major work. By April 1823 the first movement was beginning to take shape, but ideas for the remaining movements were in a rudimentary state. At the end of April he wrote a prevaricating letter to Ries. His excuse may not represent the whole truth but many teachers of composition would vouch for the genuineness of the remarks:

14 Drawing of Beethoven by Stephan Decker (1824)

The Cardinal's stay in Vienna for about four weeks, during which period I had to give him every day a lesson lasting two and a half, and sometimes three hours, has robbed me of a great deal of time. For after such lessons one is hardly able on the following day to think and, still less, to compose.[10]

The first part of the summer was spent in Hetzendorf, to the south of the city beyond Schönbrunn palace, where Beethoven's creativity was disturbed by continuing correspondence with Schindler concerning subscriptions to the Missa Solemnis, uncongenial rooms, some poor weather and an irritating new affliction, sore eyes.

Nevertheless, good progress was made on the symphony; as he wrote to Schindler, 'The weather is bad. But even if I am alone, I am never *alone*.'[11] Perhaps because of the weather and the inevitable decline in general health that now seemed to accompany intense creativity, Beethoven moved in August to Baden, where he was able to take the cure and indulge in long walks. By the time the composer returned to Vienna in the last week of October the symphony was virtually complete.

In duration the ninth symphony is only a few minutes shorter than the mass, but it had taken much less time and effort to compose. Its stunning inclusion of voices in the finale has tended to obscure its more conservative features, ones that help to explain the comparative fluency with which it was composed. It retained the conventional four-movement structure that had served Beethoven in seven of his previous symphonies; there are no hints that he even contemplated alternative structures such as are found in the last three piano sonatas, the late quartets and the mass. Together with the emotional journey from minor key to major key, anguish to joy, this familiar approach suggests an eagerness to court the public acclaim enjoyed by earlier works. Even the text for the last movement, lines from Schiller's 'An die Freude', represents the ardour of a previous age. The 'joy' theme is a variant of the theme used in the Choral Fantasy, and there are several procedural parallels between that work and the finale of the symphony. Beethoven himself frequently drew a parallel between the symphony and the Choral Fantasy, an indication of how he thought the work might be understood. The nineteenth and twentieth centuries were to take the view that the inclusion of voices was a radical step forward in the evolution of the symphony and were to construct a sometimes highly polemical debate about the legitimacy of voices in the hitherto abstract world of the symphony. Such a debate would have struck Beethoven and his public as rather peculiar. In a city that had openly enthused about the many pieces Beethoven had written for the Congress of Vienna and knew the incidental music to *Egmont*, *The Ruins of Athens*, *Leonore Prohaska* and, most recently, *The Consecration of the House*, the mixing of orchestral and vocal movements in the ninth symphony would not have presented an aesthetic dilemma. For Beethoven, there is some evidence that he regarded this very accessibility as a problem, undermining the carefully planned resolution of tension that the final movement achieves. On more than one occasion he told Czerny that he had committed a blunder and wanted to write a new, purely instrumental movement.

A new opera was extensively discussed during the summer and autumn, but here Beethoven's misgivings got the better of him and the project never materialized. Dietrichstein had recommended that he approach Franz Grillparzer (1791–1872), rapidly establishing himself as the leading literary figure in Austria. At first nervous about collaborating with the composer, Grillparzer produced a libretto based on a Bohemian legend, *Drahomira*, before he completed a draft based on the French story of the water sprite Melusine. He visited Beethoven in Hetzendorf to discuss revisions to the text, negotiations were begun in the autumn with the management of the court theatres about a commission, and the local *Allgemeine musikalische Zeitung* made the potential collaboration public. For some unknown reason Beethoven's interest petered out in the last few months of 1824, and not a note of the opera survives.

Meanwhile, aware that Beethoven had completed a mass and a symphony, and that he was contemplating an opera, the Gesellschaft der Musikfreunde became anxious about the oratorio he had long promised them and for which he had been paid a fee. On behalf of the society its vice-president, Raphael Georg Kiesewetter, wrote a firm but polite letter to Beethoven, pointing out that the society understood that Bernard had delivered his libretto in October 1823 and requesting an indication of when the work would be available. In his reply Beethoven stated that the text was fundamentally unsuitable and would have to be rewritten before he could contemplate setting it; however, he was anxious to maintain cordial relations and thanked the society for the offer, already mooted, of assistance with any future concert that he might be planning. Finally, with an audacity bordering on the brazen, he attempted to substitute the Missa Solemnis for the promised oratorio:

> For to tell the truth the grand Mass is more in the style of an oratorio and was really intended for the Society. I shall be particularly pleased if people discern in my action my unselfishness and at the same time my zeal to serve the Society, in whose charitable activities in the cause of art I shall always take the greatest interest.[12]

Since the autumn Beethoven, Schindler and the increasingly involved Karl had been thinking of a concert to present the ninth symphony. From February through to May 1824 Beethoven's energies were primarily directed towards organizing this concert. It was his first benefit concert for ten years and it was like old times. Venues, dates, performers and programme were all in a constant state of flux, the parts had to be prepared, aggrieved performers placated and the censor satisfied. As these preparations began Beethoven was presented with a petition urging him to present his recent works to the anxious Viennese public. The tone and content of this letter were designed to appeal to Beethoven's high-mindedness, reflecting the familiar outlook that his works were the epitome of educated musical taste and that he represented Austrian artistic endeavour at its most laudable:

> Out of the wide circle of reverent admirers that surrounds your genius in this your second native city, a small number of disciples and lovers of art approach you today to express long-felt wishes, and timidly to proffer a long-suppressed request. . .
> Above all, the wishes of those of our countrymen who venerate art are those that we desire to express here; for although Beethoven's name and his creations belong to all contemporaneous humanity and every country that opens a sensitive heart to art, it is Austria that is best entitled to claim him as her own. Among her inhabitants, appreciation for the great and immortal works that Mozart and Haydn created for all time within the lap of their home has not died, and [these inhabitants] are conscious with joyous pride that the sacred triad, in which these names and yours glow as the symbol

of the highest within the spiritual realm of tones, sprang from the soil of the fatherland. . .

Do not withhold any longer from the popular enjoyment, do not keep any longer from the oppressed sense of that which is great and perfect, the performance of the latest masterworks of your hand. We know that a grand sacred composition has joined the first one in which you immortalized the emotions of the soul, penetrated and transfigured by the power of faith and superterrestrial light. We know that a new flower grows in the garland of your glorious, still unequalled symphonies. For years, ever since the thunders of the *Victory at Vittoria* ceased to reverberate, we have waited and hoped to see you distribute new gifts from the fulness of your riches to the circle of your friends. Do not disappoint the general expectations any longer! Heighten the effect of your newest creations by giving us the joy of becoming first acquainted with them through you yourself! Do not allow these, your latest offspring, to appear some day, perhaps as foreigners in their place of birth, perhaps introduced by persons who are also strangers to you and your spirit! Appear soon among your friends, your admirers, your venerators! This is our first and foremost prayer . . .[13]

Thirty people signed the letter, representing a cross-section of friends, patrons, publishers, administrators and fellow musicians; amongst their number were Artaria, Carl Czerny, Diabelli, Dietrichstein, Prince Eduard Lichnowsky (son of Carl), Pálffy, Abbé Stadler, Steiner and Zmeskall. The letter was later published in two journals: the *Allgemeine Theaterzeitung Wien* and the *Wiener Allgemeine musikalische Zeitung* ('Wiener' had recently been added to the title).

During this period Beethoven's music was by no means absent from Viennese concerts in general. February and March saw the latest of Schuppanzigh's chamber music concerts containing several works by Beethoven; the Concerts Spirituels, by accident or design, promoted the music of 'the sacred triad', Haydn, Mozart and Beethoven, in four successive concerts, one devoted to each composer and the fourth to all three; Beethoven was represented by performances of the Pastoral Symphony, the Credo from the Mass in C, the *Coriolan* overture, two numbers from *Christus am Oelberge*, the Agnus Dei from the Mass in C and the *Egmont* overture. A concert in the Kärntnertortheater on Easter Sunday included the overture to *Fidelio*, while the first of the summer concerts at the Augarten on 1 May included a performance of the fifth symphony. For the writers of the petition the presentation of Beethoven's newest works was designed to capitalize on a continuing performance tradition rather than to impose a completely new and alien one.

Beethoven's friends had set up an unofficial committee to organize the concert: Schindler, Moritz Lichnowsky, Schuppanzigh and Beethoven, plus the eager Karl. Four venues were considered: the composer's favourite Theater an der Wien, the Kärntnertortheater, the Landständischer Saal (the home of the Concerts Spirituels) and the Redoutensaal. At one stage Beethoven felt that arrangements were being made behind his back and peremptorily cancelled the concert. Eventually, it was agreed that there would be two concerts, the first at the Kärntnertortheater on Friday 7 May, the second just over a fortnight later on Sunday 23 May at the Redoutensaal. Vocal and orchestral forces from the theatre were to be supplemented by players and singers provided by the Gesellschaft der Musikfreunde. At first Beethoven wanted the concert to include the overture *The Consecration of the House*, the whole of the Missa Solemnis as well as the ninth symphony. Preliminary rehearsals convinced him that only three movements of the mass should be given, the Kyrie, Credo and Agnus Dei. The first concert was a highly emotional occasion – one report stated that the contralto Caroline Unger, aged only twenty-one, had to direct the deaf composer's attention to the sight of clapping hands and waving hats and handkerchiefs – though the financial profit was less than Beethoven had hoped. Johann van Beethoven, who resented Schindler's influence on Ludwig, fuelled his brother's insecurity by suggesting that Schindler had cheated him. A celebratory meal at an inn in the Prater was spoilt by a row between Beethoven and Schindler. Subsequently, Beethoven sent him a letter in which he seems to be withdrawing any accusation of theft while at the same time wounding him with a brutal display of egotism:

> I do not accuse you of having done anything wicked in connection with the concert. But stupidity and arbitrary behaviour have ruined many an undertaking. Moreover I have on the whole a certain fear of you, a fear lest some day through your action a great misfortune may befall me. Stopped up sluices often overflow quite suddenly; and that day in the Prater I was convinced that in many ways you had hurt me very deeply – In any case I would much rather try to repay frequently with a small gift the services you render me, than *have you at my table*. For I confess that your presence irritates me in so many ways. . .
>
> In no circumstances would I care to entrust my welfare to you, because you never reflect but act quite arbitrarily. I have found you out once already in a way that *was unfavourable to you*; and so have *other people too* – I must declare that the purity of my character does not permit me to reward your kindnesses to me with friendship alone, although, of course I am willing to serve you in any matter concerned with your welfare.[14]

With considerable justification Schindler might have regarded these sentiments as grossly hypocritical coming from someone who a few days earlier had triumphantly proclaimed 'Alle Menschen werden Brüder' ('All humanity shall be brothers'). In truth, it was typical of the paradox, formed of idealism and reality, that Beethoven himself saw at the heart of his art as well as his life. As a musician he wanted to compose only the greatest of music, but was obliged also to compose for money; as an individual he wished to maintain the highest ethical and moral standards but continually fell short. Schindler disappeared from Beethoven's life for nearly three years.

For the second concert, in the hope of increasing the box office, the Credo and Agnus Dei were omitted in favour of a vocal trio 'Tremate, empi, tremate' (a good example of Beethoven the populist) and an aria from Rossini's *Tancredi*, 'Di tanti palpiti'. The chosen date of 23 May was, however, very late in the social season and the starting time,

12.30, discouraged attendance on what turned out to be a sunny day; the concert made a loss.

In artistic terms the concerts were a success, a perfect demonstration of those qualities that leaders of Viennese musical opinion sought in their champion. To complete this deification the *Wiener Allgemeine musikalische Zeitung* offered a new engraving of Beethoven (based on the drawing reproduced on p. 163) and devoted three successive issues to a detailed and reasoned appraisal of the concerts, an essay of some 5,500 words and by far the largest review in the history of the journal.

8 Facing death

Beethoven's first choice of residence for the summer following the two concerts was Penzing, a few minutes away from the main entrance to Schönbrunn palace. His first-floor apartment overlooked the river Wien and after a while he began to complain that people crossing an adjacent footbridge were staring into his rooms. Increasingly disgruntled, he moved in mid July to Baden, to complete seclusion, a hermitage in the garden of a castle, where he stayed until the end of October. From there he wrote to his lawyer, Johann Baptist Bach:

> My heartfelt thanks to you for recommending this house, where I
> am really well looked after – I must remind you of my will which
> concerns Karl. For I have the idea that some day I shall have a stroke,
> like my very worthy grandfather whom I somewhat resemble. Karl is
> now and will ever be sole heir to the property which I possess at the
> moment and which may be found after my death. But since one must
> bequeath something to relatives as well, even if one has nothing at
> all in common with them, my worthy *brother* is to have my French
> pianoforte from *Paris*.[1]

Three quartets had been promised for Prince Galitzin in St Petersburg and Beethoven was working assiduously on the first of these, in E♭ major (op. 127). String quartets were to occupy his creative energies for the last three years of his life, eventually reaching a total of five plus a substitute finale for the B♭ quartet (op. 130). He had not written quartets for over ten years and the welcome opportunity to return to a genre that always challenged his creativity is evident in the total absorption with which he composed them. Referring to the quartets, Beethoven told Holz that 'Art demands of us that we should not stand still.' All preconceptions are laid aside as the composer probes anew formal principles (local and large-scale), texture, emotional balance and instrumentation; the works have an intellectual beauty that is in turn challenging, elusive, strident and otherworldly.

Given the nature of these late quartets and the occasional melancholy indication of mortality, as in Beethoven's letter to Bach, it would be easy to paint a picture of the composer's last three years as one of isolation and resignation, an inevitable reaction to the public comeback evident in the two concerts in May. But this would be too neat, and misleading. The tension between the progressive artist and the successful composer that had governed Beethoven's life for nearly a quarter of a century continues. He craved recognition and, more basically, as he repeatedly wrote to friends and potential publishers, he needed to compose in order to live. Beethoven believed there was a public for the late quartets in the same way as there patently was for a waltz in E♭ for piano (WoO 84) that was published by Müller in December 1824 as part of a miscellaneous collection of forty small piano pieces by a variety of composers. Until the last three months of his life Beethoven's health was no better or worse than at any time in the previous fifteen years; it sometimes caused him to stop working, as in the middle of the A minor quartet, but there was always a determination to overcome illness. It was in this spirit that he wrote to Schott in the middle of September 1824:

> I am staying at Baden on account of my health or, rather, on account of my ill health. But I am feeling better already. Apollo and the muses are not yet going to let me be handed over to Death, for I still owe them so much; and before my departure for the Elysian fields I must leave behind me what the Eternal Spirit has infused into my soul and bids me complete. Why, I feel as if I had hardly composed more than a few notes. I wish you every success in your efforts on behalf of art. For, after all, only art and science give us intimations and hopes of a higher life – I will write again very soon and at greater length.[2]

Although Beethoven was disappointed with the financial results of the two concerts in May his inevitable castigation of Viennese taste was both intemperate and unfair, ignoring the esteem in which he was held. With the notable exception of concertos, music from earlier in the composer's career continued to be played in concerts and the fact that Beethoven constantly challenged his audience suited the ambitious, self-improving agenda of many of the musical institutions in Vienna, the *Wiener Allgemeine musikalische Zeitung*, the Gesellschaft der Musikfreunde, the Concerts Spirituels and the subscription concerts of chamber music organized by Schuppanzigh. Intellectually, therefore, Beethoven was not an isolated figure in Vienna in the last few years of his life. Twenty and thirty years earlier Lobkowitz and Lichnowsky had sustained this intellectual leadership; in post-war Austria it had passed to urban institutions. As he worked on the challenges of the late quartets Beethoven knew that this elite stratum in musical Vienna would help to promote the works: Schuppanzigh and his colleagues duly performed the quartets; Mathias Artaria published one of them, op. 130; and when Artaria suggested that a new finale be substituted for op. 130 and that the original one (the 'Grosse Fuge') be published separately, also arranged as a piano duet, Beethoven readily agreed. As he worked on the last quartets Beethoven sketched two orchestral works, an overture featuring the motif B–A–C–H (B is German for B♭, H is B♮) and a tenth symphony in E♭. Occasionally Beethoven and his friends talked of organizing concerts devoted to his music, and Schuppanzigh and Johann Andreas Streicher were only two figures who promised to include works by Beethoven in their own benefit concerts. Given time, Beethoven might even have fulfilled his commitment to the Gesellschaft der Musikfreunde – the story of Saul captured his interest for a while – and there could have been a new opera too.

In this continuing story of hopes and ambitions, plans thwarted and plans realized, one supportive element disappears. For several years Rudolph's lessons with Beethoven had been fitted in during his visits to Vienna. His duties at Olmütz apparently left him little time for composition and his new interest in painting – portraits, historical topics, animals, flowers and landscapes – seems to have taken over. He stopped composing towards the end of 1824 and lessons with Beethoven came to an end too. Teacher and pupil, would-be Kapellmeister and patron, never forgot their association, however. Beethoven was to honour his most musically sophisticated patron with the dedication of the 'Grosse Fuge'; while Rudolph, after the composer's death, carefully copied out in his own hand the many tributes and notices of death that appeared in the German press.

In 1824 Prince Galitzin was a figure whose patronage seemed to promise much. Not only had he commissioned three quartets, but his subscription to a manuscript copy of the Missa Solemnis had led to the first complete performance of that work, on 7 April 1824, a few weeks before the partial performance in Vienna. The prince purchased manuscript copies of the ninth symphony and the overture *The Consecration of the House* too, and hoped to arrange a second performance of the mass for the benefit of flood victims in St Petersburg. His enthusiasm prompted an eruption of opportunism from Beethoven: perhaps Galitzin could arrange for the mass to be dedicated to the Emperor of Russia (it was eventually dedicated to its begetter, Archduke Rudolph); indeed 'perhaps so munificent a monarch as the Emperor of Russia might even disburse a yearly pension for me, in return for which I would first carry out His Majesty's commissions with all speed'.[3] Nothing came of these grandiose schemes and the relationship between the prince and Beethoven cooled when Galitzin delayed payment for the quartets.

Schott of Mainz was Beethoven's main publisher in the last few years of his life, issuing the Missa Solemnis (with a list of patrons who had previously subscribed to manuscript copies), the ninth symphony, the six bagatelles for piano (op. 126) and the E♭ quartet (op. 127). Together with Breitkopf & Härtel, Schlesinger and Simrock, the firm ensured that a substantial quantity of Beethoven's music was easily available in the German states. His popularity in urban Germany was fast moving towards idolatry. In August 1824 Hans Georg Nägeli wrote to the composer:

In six South German cities (Frankfurt, Darmstadt, Mainz, Karlsruhe, Stuttgart and Tübingen), I have given Lectures on Music, in which you are historically and critically portrayed as the artistic hero of the new century. For a long time you have had many admirers there, as well as in all of culturally educated Europe. Nevertheless, I may claim to have raised the appreciation for your unique high art to a *more conscious level of recognition*.[4]

Beethoven would have taken further pleasure in a letter he received the following June from Ferdinand Ries, now living in Germany. He reported on the hugely successful performance of the ninth symphony at the Lower Rhenish Music Festival in Aachen, though he tactfully did not mention that the scherzo and parts of the slow movement had to be omitted because of their difficulty.

The reception of Beethoven's music in France had always been more intermittent, partly because the country was culturally isolated during the Napoleonic wars and, more specifically, because the composer had never succeeded in his ambition to secure a French publisher for his music alongside German and English publishers. While much of Europe was enthusiastically embracing Beethoven's music, concert life in Paris was still dominated by the music of Haydn, even in the 1820s. Sporadic performances apart, Beethoven's symphonies did not make a sustained impact in Paris until after the composer's death, when the young and impressionable Berlioz was only one of many people bowled over by them. Piano music and chamber music had fared better, usually available through imported editions, especially from Simrock (Bonn). Schlesinger of Berlin, who had published Beethoven's last three piano sonatas, had an office in Paris run by the son, Moritz, now Maurice. Following a visit to the composer in Baden in 1825 Maurice Schlesinger became the authorized publisher of two of the later quartets, op. 132 in A minor and op. 135 in F.

In London, and Britain generally, enthusiasm for Beethoven's music was reaching new heights. British concert life was occasionally reported in the Viennese *Allgemeine musikalische Zeitung*, Beethoven continued to receive direct reports from musicians such as Moscheles who lived in London, and the 1820s saw a steady stream of British visitors to Vienna: Sandra Burney Payne, Johann Schultz, Johann Strumpff and Sir George Smart. Beethoven had promised the Philharmonic Society the ninth symphony and the performance was finally set for the 1825 season. The previous December Charles Neate wrote to the composer on behalf of the society offering him 300 guineas for a visit from mid February to late June, plus a benefit concert which, the composer was assured, would earn him at least £500; for these sums Beethoven was expected to direct performances of his own music, including the ninth symphony, and compose a new symphony and a new concerto. Like many Austrians of the time Beethoven was a committed anglophile and had long wished to travel to London. Once again, however, he declined, partly because of chronic indecision about what might be advantageous to his career (he constantly complained about his plight in Vienna but at least he understood it), and partly because of the new works that were expected from him. The non-appearance of Beethoven only fuelled public curiosity about the composer; music journals and books fed this curiosity with reminiscences and tittle-tattle so that, even in his absence, he became a celebrity. For instance in 1825 the English musician and author Thomas Busby published three volumes entitled *Concert Room and Orchestra Anecdotes of Music and Musicians Ancient and Modern*. Under the heading 'Beethoven's Eccentricity' the following is recounted:

> Beethoven's neglected person, wild appearance, strong and prominent features, widely energetic eye, and broad bull-like brow, overshadowed with his uncut, uncombed hair, together with his not very conciliatory disposition, bespeak a character somewhat consistent with the following specimen of his demeanour. Not long since, in a certain cellar [an obvious mistranslation of *Keller*] in Vienna, where he was in the habit of spending his evenings, in a particular corner, by himself, drinking wine, eating red herrings, and reading the newspapers, a person took a seat near him, with whose countenance he was by no means pleased. After looking steadfastly at the stranger, he spat on the floor, as if he had seen a toad; then

glanced at the newspaper, then again at the intruder, and spat again; his disordered hair gradually bristled into more shaggy ferocity, till he closed the alternation of spitting and staring, by suddenly rising from the chair, and loudly exclaiming, as he rushed out of the room, 'What a scoundrelly phiz!'

Beethoven's health was especially troublesome in the early summer of 1825; he felt weak, his digestion was poor and he was spitting blood. He had returned to the hermitage in Baden but, initially at least, the cold weather only exacerbated his discomfort. His relationship with his 'dear son', Karl, was deteriorating rapidly. A year before Karl had taken an enthusiastic part in the preparation for the two public concerts but since then the boy, now a young man of eighteen, had become increasingly independent. Much to Beethoven's disappointment he had indicated that he wanted to enter the army. Karl's later transference from studying philology at the university to business studies at the polytechnic was also a disappointment, made worse when Karl's enthusiasm for this course meant that he saw less of his 'father'. They squabbled about everything and anything: laundry bills, whether Karl was really studying or wasting time playing billiards, the suitability of friends and, inevitably, whether he was seeing too much of his mother. Beethoven's love was now smotheringly possessive rather than caring and when questioned it turned to callousness:

Spoilt as you are it would not do you any harm to cultivate *at last simplicity and truth*. For my heart has suffered too much from your deceitful behaviour to me; and it is hard to forget it. Even if I were willing to pull the whole burden like a yoked ox and without murmuring, yet your behaviour, if it is directed against others in the same way, can never attract to you people who will love you – God is my witness that my sole dream is to get away completely from you and from that wretched brother and that horrible family who have been thrust upon me. May God grant my wishes. For I *can* no longer trust *you* –

Unfortunately your father
or, better still, not your father.[5]

Beethoven's dealing with the Schuppanzigh quartet led to a close friendship with the second violinist, Karl Holz. In his mid twenties, Holz was a minor official in local government and only a part-time musician. His easy-going, conscientious nature appealed to Beethoven and he soon assumed the position of unofficial assistant and secretary. Like others before him, Holz became the willing butt of Beethoven's affectionate teasing; his name (Holz = wood) caused him to be called 'mahogany', 'chip' and 'cupboard'. This new friendship coincided with an improvement in Beethoven's health towards the end of the summer of 1825 that encouraged renewed work on the A minor quartet. By the end of his stay in Baden he had nearly completed a third quartet, in B♭ (op. 130). He returned to Vienna to take up residence in a spacious four-room apartment (plus rooms for the servants) in the Schwarzspanierhaus, a handsome building with a broad view across the open space known as the Glacis towards the city walls and the Schottentor. It was to be his last home, and, coincidentally, it was only a few minutes walk away from the rooms he had occupied when he first moved to Vienna in 1792. He was delighted to renew acquaintanceship with an old friend, Stephan Breuning (author of the first revision of *Leonore*), who lived near by. It was here that Beethoven began work on a tenth symphony and the B–A–C–H overture, before setting them aside in favour of the C♯ minor quartet.

Content in this spacious apartment, Beethoven hoped that Karl would visit him more frequently, but the relationship, rather than improving, went into free fall. Instead of moving to the country in the summer of 1826 the composer decided to stay in Vienna, partly so that he could keep a watchful eye on Karl. Unable to break the emotional stranglehold that his 'father' exerted, Karl began to contemplate suicide. At the end of July he bought a pistol which was fortuitously discovered by his landlord and confiscated. He pawned a watch and bought a second pistol. On 6 August he drove to Baden, walked up the wooded Hellenthal, a favourite walk of the composer and one which no doubt had fond memories for Karl too, and climbed up to the ruins of an old fortress, the Rauhenstein. Luckily his nerve or his ability failed him as he pointed the pistol to his head; the first bullet missed and the second passed through the flesh and grazed the bone. A passing teamster found him lying on the ground and drove him back to Vienna to his mother's house, and then went to inform Beethoven. The following day Karl was taken into the Allgemeines Krankenhaus, where he remained for six weeks.

During these weeks Beethoven, with the firm but tactful counselling of Holz and Breuning, deliberated how Karl should be rehabilitated. While Beethoven's views were largely negative – he did not want Karl to return to his mother and he disapproved of the proposed career in the army – Holz and Breuning did their best to accommodate Karl's views and persuade Beethoven of their efficacy. Eventually, it was agreed that Karl would return to Beethoven, but that a period of convalescence in the autumn should be spent at Johann van Beethoven's country estate in Gneixendorf. From there he was to join the army, a regiment based in Iglau (Jihlava) in Moravia.

Johann van Beethoven's estate was on a high rugged plateau covered with vineyards with intermittent views of the Danube; Beethoven wrote to Schott that the area reminded him a little of his native Rhineland. Other letters written from Gneixendorf show that he continued to work, if without much enthusiasm, and to contemplate future projects. Occasionally his spirits were raised as when he heard the news that Holz was besotted with a girlfriend, eliciting the remark that 'ecstasy of love' had caused the 'wood' to catch fire, but there was an increasing world-weariness; the relationship with Karl was cordial rather than loving and, as ever, Johann and his wife irritated him. With some difficulty he completed his last quartet, op. 135, towards the end of October. His next project was a string quintet in C. As had been his custom for over ten years, he prepared a new, homemade pocket sketchbook. Three large sheets of manuscript paper were each folded in half three times, the edges cut, and one side crudely stitched together to form a book of twenty-four leaves. Only six leaves were to be used.

On 1 December Beethoven and Karl started their return journey to Vienna, staying overnight in a cold and draughty tavern. The composer became seriously ill, took to his bed on reaching the Schwarzspanierhaus and the doctors were summoned. Dropsy was diagnosed, signifying fluid retention caused by heart, liver or kidney disease, singly or in combination; a modern diagnosis would be oedema. To relieve the pain large measures of fluid were drained from the abdominal cavity on four occasions between December and February.

Karl left, as planned, to join his regiment on 2 January. On the following day Beethoven confirmed in a letter to Bach that Karl was to be his sole heir: 'May God preserve you – A thousand thanks for the love and friendship you have shown me.'[6] Many faithful friends visited the bed-ridden composer in the last three months of his life. Gleichenstein called; Pasqualati brought favourite small dishes and some champagne; Diabelli gave him a picture of Haydn's birthplace in Rohrau; Schindler resumed his role as unofficial secretary following the marriage of Karl Holz; and the Breuning family were especially solicitous. There was a touching exchange of letters with the Wegeler family, now living in Koblenz. Franz suggested that they should meet in Carlsbad, take the cure for three weeks 'and then a little journey through part of southern Germany and finally the happiness and youthful reminiscences upon being in our homeland and the caring circle of my family . . .' In a postscript Eleonore Wegeler (Lorchen), Beethoven's first love in Bonn, was even more concerned, though, unlike her husband, she hid her affection behind the polite 'Sie' form: 'Why then should the journey to a spa precede it? Come here first and see what influence the happiness of being in your homeland will have upon you.'[7] Two letters were received from Karl, reporting on his progress in the army and ending with affectionate greetings; their content suggests that he was being shielded from the seriousness of Beethoven's illness. He remained in the army for five years, then married and led a contented and comfortable life until his death in 1858.

Beethoven himself occasionally rallied, his creative faculties stimulated by reading the large folio volumes of *The Works of Handel, In Score, Correct, Uniform, and Complete*, recently received as a gift from London. It was to London and the Philharmonic Society that he sent his only direct plea for support. Writing to Sir George Smart and Moscheles he suggested that the society should organize a benefit concert on his behalf. Convinced by the urgency of the situation, the society immediately dispatched £100 without waiting to organize a concert. On 17 March a Viennese bank official named Sebastian Rau wrote to Moscheles acknowledging receipt of the gift:

> I drove to him at once, to convince myself of his condition and to tell him of the assistance at hand. It was heartrending to see him, how he clasped his hands and almost dissolved in tears of joy and gratitude. How rewarding, what a blessing it would have been for you, you magnanimous people, if you could have been witness to this highly touching scene!
>
> I found poor Beethoven in the saddest state, more like a skeleton than a living being. The dropsy had seized him to such an extent that he had already had to be tapped 4 or 5 times. For his medical treatment he is in the hands of Dr Malfatti, and thus is well cared for. Malfatti gives him little hope. It cannot be determined how long his present condition can still last, or whether he can be saved at all.[8]

A few days later Beethoven received Holy Communion. On Saturday 24 March a consignment of wine and herbal wine from Schott arrived to which Beethoven's alleged comment was 'Pity, pity – too late'. He lapsed into a coma, never to regain consciousness. Two days later, on Monday 26 March, he died in the late afternoon.

News of the death spread quickly. Rosenbaum, whose diaries had described many events in Beethoven's Vienna, including the two French invasions, some of the composer's concerts and the premiere of *Leonore*, wrote simply:

> Monday 26th. Freezing. Frequent snow, north wind. Towards 4 o' clock it darkened. Snow blizzards. Thunder and lightning. Nature in revolt. Three terrific thunderclaps followed. Death of Ludwig van Beethoven in the evening towards 6 o' clock from dropsy in his 56th year. He is no more. His name lives in glorious light.[9]

Einladung

zu

Ludwig van Beethoven's

Leichenbegängnisse,

welches am 29. März um 3 Uhr Nachmittags Statt finden wird.

Man versammelt sich in der Wohnung des Verstorbenen im Schwarzspanier-Hause Nr. 200, am Glacis vor dem Schottenthore.

Der Zug begibt sich von da nach der Dreyfaltigkeits-Kirche bey den p. p. Minoriten in der Alsergasse.

Die musikalische Welt erlitt den unersetzlichen Verlust des berühmten Tondichters am 26. März 1827 Abends gegen 6 Uhr. Beethoven starb an den Folgen der Wassersucht, im 56. Jahre seines Alters, nach empfangenen heil. Sacramenten.

Der Tag der Exequien wird nachträglich bekannt gemacht von

L. van Beethoven's

Verehrern und Freunden.

(Diese Karte wird in Tob. Haslinger's Musikalienhandlung vertheilt.)

15 Invitation card to Beethoven's funeral (1827)

Breuning and Schindler made the arrangements for the funeral for which an invitation card was printed and distributed from Steiner's music shop. At three o' clock on Thursday 29 March the mourners gathered at the Schwarzspanierhaus. The weather was kind as the cortege, surrounded by torchbearers, made its way through the crowded Glacis to the Minoritenkirche in the Alsergasse. Following the service, the cortege moved to the Friedhof, the parish cemetery in Währing, for the burial. At the graveside an actor declaimed a funeral oration by Grillparzer:[10]

let not your hearts be troubled! You have not lost him, you have won him. No living man enters the halls of the immortals. Not until the body has perished, do their portals unclose. He whom you mourn stands from now onward among the great of all ages, inviolate for ever. Return homeward therefore, in sorrow, yet resigned! And should you ever in times to come feel the overpowering might of his creations like an onrushing storm, when your mounting ecstasy overflows in the midst of a generation yet unborn, then remember this hour, and think, we were there, when they buried him, and when he died, we wept.

Beethoven's musical life was over. The musical legend had already begun.

1 The young courtier

1 E. Anderson (trans. and ed.), *The Letters of Beethoven*, 3 vols. (London, 1961), vol. I, pp. 57–8. Throughout this biography the dating and content of Beethoven's correspondence have been checked against the recently completed German edition of the letters; all amendments have been tacitly made. S. Brandenburg (ed.), *Ludwig van Beethoven. Briefwechsel Gesamtausgabe*, 7 vols. (Munich, 1996–8).

2 Beethoven to Neefe, some time between October 1792 and October 1793; Anderson (trans. and ed.), *The Letters of Beethoven*, vol. I, p. 9.

3 C. P. E. Bach, *Essay on the True Art of Playing Keyboard Instruments*, trans. and ed. W. J. Mitchell (London, 1949), p. 152, p. 150.

4 Quoted in L. Schiedermair, *Der junge Beethoven* (Leipzig, 1925), p. 153.

5 The entire report is given in ibid., pp. 73–82.

6 Ibid., pp. 57–9.

7 Mozart to his father, 23 January 1782; E. Anderson (trans. and ed.), *The Letters of Mozart and His Family*, 2 vols. (London, 1966), vol. II, pp. 794–5.

8 Letter of 15 September 1787; E. Anderson (trans. and ed.), *The Letters of Beethoven*, vol. I, pp. 3–4.

9 *Remembering Beethoven. The Biographical Notes of Franz Wegeler and Ferdinand Ries* (London, 1988), pp. 14–16.

10 Junker's report is quoted in full in Schiedermair, *Der junge Beethoven*, pp. 85–90.

11 An English translation of the fifteen entries is given in T. Albrecht (ed. and trans.), *Letters to Beethoven and Other Correspondence*, 3 vols. (Lincoln, Nebraska, 1996), vol. I, pp. 15–29.

2 A new career in Vienna

1 For a transcription and commentary see D. von Busch-Weise, 'Beethovens Jugendtagebuch', *Studien zur Musikwissenschaft* 25 (1962), pp. 68–88.

2 H. C. Robbins Landon, *Haydn: Chronicle and Works. Haydn in England* (London, 1976), p. 233.

3 Anderson (trans. and ed.), *The Letters of Beethoven*, vol. I, p. 12.

4 Landon, *Haydn in England*, p. 233.

5 Letter of 2 November 1793; Anderson (trans. and ed.), *The Letters of Beethoven*, vol. I, pp. 14–15.

6 Ibid., p. 16.

7 Ibid., p. 18.

8 S. Novello (trans.), J. C. [sic] *Albrechtsberger's Collected Writings on Thorough-Bass, Harmony, and Composition, for Self-Instruction* (London, 1855), p. 238.

9 *Jahrbuch der Tonkunst von Wien und Prag*, facsimile edn by O. Biba, (Munich, 1976), p. 77.

10 Letter of 19 February 1796; Anderson (trans. and ed.), *The Letters of Beethoven*, vol. I, pp. 22–3.

11 *Jahrbuch der Tonkunst von Wien und Prag*, pp. 7–8.

12 Letter possibly written in August or September 1796; Anderson (trans. and ed.), *The Letters of Beethoven*, vol. I, pp. 25–6.

13 Ibid., p. 24.

14 *Allgemeine musikalische Zeitung* 1 (1798–9), cols. 523–6; translation partly from E. Forbes (rev. and ed.), *Thayer's Life of Beethoven* (Princeton, New Jersey, 1967), p. 205.

15 Letter probably written in 1795; Anderson (trans. and ed.), *The Letters of Beethoven*, vol. I, p. 22.

16 Ibid., p. 41.

17 *Allgemeine musikalische Zeitung* 3 (1800–1), cols. 41–51; translation (amended) from Forbes (rev. and ed.), *Thayer's Life of Beethoven*, p. 255.

3 Cursing his creator and his existence

1 Anderson (trans. and ed.), *The Letters of Beethoven*, vol. 1, pp. 57–62.
2 Beethoven to Wegeler, 16 November 1801; ibid., p. 67.
3 Beethoven to Countess Susanna Guicciardi (Giulietta's mother), 23 January 1802; A. Tyson, 'Beethoven to the Countess Susanna Guicciardi: A New Letter' in *Beethoven Studies* [1], ed. A. Tyson (London, 1974), pp. 2–6.
4 Anderson (trans. and ed.), *The Letters of Beethoven*, vol. 111, p. 1435.
5 Information from *The Times*, January–May 1801.
6 Translation from B. Cooper (ed.), *The Beethoven Compendium* (London, 1991), pp. 170–1.
7 *Allgemeine musikalische Zeitung* 29 (1827), cols. 705–10.
8 From *Neuestes Sittengemählde von Wien* (Vienna, 1801) quoted in H. Tietze (ed.), *Das vormärzliche Wien in Wort und Bild* (Vienna, 1925), p. 19.
9 Letter of 23 November 1802; Albrecht (ed. and trans.), *Letters to Beethoven and Other Correspondence*, vol. 1, p. 84.
10 B. Cooper, 'Beethoven's Oratorio and the Heiligenstadt Testament', *Beethoven Newsletter* 10 (1995), pp. 19–24.
11 See H. C. Robbins Landon, *Beethoven. A Documentary Study* (London, 1970), pp. 147–8.
12 Ibid., p. 147.

4 Drama and symphony

1 Anderson (trans. and ed.), *The Letters of Beethoven*, vol. 1, pp. 88–9.
2 Ibid., pp. 105–6.
3 O. Biba (ed.), '*Eben komme ich von Haydn . . .*'. *Georg August Griesingers Korrespondenz mit Joseph Haydns Verleger Breitkopf & Härtel 1799–1819* (Zurich, 1987), pp. 212–17.
4 Letter written some time in May 1805; Anderson (trans. and ed.), *The Letters of Beethoven*, vol. 1, p. 138.
5 *Remembering Beethoven*, pp. 88–9.
6 Letter written some time in May–June 1804; Anderson (trans. and ed.), *The Letters of Beethoven*, vol. 1, p. 108.
7 Deym's letter from early 1805; Albrecht (ed. and trans.), *Letters to Beethoven and Other Correspondence*, vol. 1, pp. 160–1. Beethoven's letter

from before the end of March 1805; Anderson (trans. and ed.), *The Letters of Beethoven*, vol. I, pp. 131–2.

8 Albrecht (ed. and trans.), *Letters to Beethoven and Other Correspondence*, vol. I, p. 169.

9 Diary extracts from E. Radant (ed.), 'The Diaries of Joseph Carl Rosenbaum 1770–1829', *Haydn Yearbook* 5 (1968), pp. 125–9.

10 Quoted in S. Musulin, *Vienna in the Age of Metternich* (London, 1975), pp. 64–5.

11 Anderson (trans. and ed.), *The Letters of Beethoven*, vol. I, p. 149.

12 Brandenburg (ed.), *Ludwig van Beethoven. Briefwechsel Gesamtausgabe*, vol. I, p. 290.

13 Anderson (trans. and ed.), *The Letters of Beethoven*, vol. I, p. 174.

14 T. Albrecht (ed. and trans.), *Letters to Beethoven and Other Correspondence*, vol. I, p. 121.

15 Brandenburg (ed.), *Ludwig van Beethoven. Briefwechsel Gesamtausgabe*, vol. I, p. 323.

16 Anderson (trans. and ed.), *The Letters of Beethoven*, vol. III, pp. 1444–6.

17 Quoted in O. Biba, 'Beethoven und die "Liebhaber-Concerte" in Wien im Winter 1807/08' in *Beiträge '76–78: Beethoven Kolloquium 1977. Dokumentation und Aufführungspraxis*, ed. R. Klein (Kassel, 1978), pp. 82–93.

18 J. F. Reichardt, *Vertraute Briefe geschrieben auf einer Reise nach Wien und den Österreichischen Staaten zu Ende des Jahres 1808 und zu Anfang 1809*, ed. G. Gugitz, 2 vols. (Munich, 1915), vol. I, pp. 205–8.

5 Patrons and patriotism

1 Contract between Beethoven and Archduke Rudolph, Prince Lobkowitz and Prince Kinsky, 1 March 1809; Albrecht (ed. and trans.), *Letters to Beethoven and Other Correspondence*, vol. I, pp. 205–6.

2 Reichardt, *Vertraute Briefe*, vol. II, pp. 148–9.

3 Radant (ed.), 'The Diaries of Joseph Carl Rosenbaum', pp. 147–8.

4 Letter of 26 July 1809; Anderson (trans. and ed.), *The Letters of Beethoven*, vol. I, p. 234.

5 Quoted in Tietze (ed.), *Das vormärzliche Wien*, p. 32.

6 Letter of 20 April 1813; Anderson (trans. and ed.), *The Letters of Beethoven*, vol. I, p. 343.

7 M. Solomon, *Beethoven* (New York, 1977), pp. 158–89; S. Lund, 'Beethoven: A True "Fleshy Father"?', *Beethoven Newsletter* 3 (1988), pp. 1, 8–11, 25, 36–40.

8 See M. Solomon, 'Beethoven's Tagebuch of 1812–1818' in *Beethoven Studies 3*, ed. A. Tyson (Cambridge, 1982), pp. 193–288.

9 Letter of 27 May 1813; Anderson (trans. and ed.), *The Letters of Beethoven*, vol. I, p. 420.

10 Forbes (rev. and ed.), *Thayer's Life of Beethoven*, p. 494.

11 Ibid., p. 537.

12 Letter of 9 August 1812; Anderson (trans. and ed.), *The Letters of Beethoven*, vol. I, p. 384.

13 *Allgemeine musikalische Zeitung* 16 (1814), cols. 70–1.

14 Letter of early March 1814; Anderson (trans. and ed.), *The Letters of Beethoven*, vol. I, p. 454.

15 Quoted in G. Gruber (ed.), *Vom Barock zum Vormärz*, vol. II of *Musikgeschichte Österreichs*, 2nd. edn (Vienna, 1995), p. 306.

16 Quoted in Brandenburg (ed.), *Ludwig van Beethoven. Briefwechsel*, vol. III, p. 77.

6 Empires of the mind

1 Letter to Sir George Smart, London, c. 7 October 1816; Anderson (trans. and ed.), *The Letters of Beethoven*, vol. II, p. 606.

2 Letter, autumn 1814; ibid., p. 474.

3 See Solomon, 'Beethoven's Tagebuch of 1812–1818', pp. 193–288.

4 Letter of 23 July 1817; Anderson (trans. and ed.), *The Letters of Beethoven*, vol. II, p. 691.

5 Forbes (rev. and ed.), *Thayer's Life of Beethoven*, p. 625.

6 See M.-E. Tellenbach, 'Psychoanalysis and the Histocritical Method: On Maynard Solomon's Image of Beethoven (Part 1)', *Beethoven Newsletter* 8–9 (1993–4), pp. 88–9.

7 Letter of 14 November 1816: Anderson (trans. and ed.), *The Letters of Beethoven*, vol. II, pp. 612–13.

8 Albrecht (ed. and trans.), *Letters to Beethoven and Other Correspondence*, vol. II, p. 121.

9 [Wiener] *Allgemeine musikalische Zeitung* 2 (1818), cols. 5–6; 3 (1819), cols. 234–5.

10 Ibid., 3 (1819), col. 586; 4 (1820), col. 126.

11 Ibid., 3 (1819), cols. 45–6.

12 Anderson (trans. and ed.), *The Letters of Beethoven*, vol. II, pp. 813–15.

7 Towards a public comeback

1 Report in the [Wiener] *Allgemeine musikalische Zeitung* 3 (1819), col. 196.

2 Letter of 5 June 1822; Anderson (trans. and ed.), *The Letters of Beethoven*, vol. II, p. 948.

3 [Wiener] *Allgemeine musikalische Zeitung* 4 (1820), cols. 725–32, 737–41, 745–9, 753–7 and 761–4.

4 *Ludwig van Beethovens Konversationshefte*, 10 vols. (Leipzig, 1972–93), vol. I, pp. 342–3.

5 [Wiener] *Allgemeine musikalische Zeitung* 5 (1821), cols. 705–7.

6 Letter of 20 December 1822; Anderson (trans. and ed.), *The Letters of Beethoven*, vol. II, pp. 978–9.

7 Letter of 9 November 1822; Albrecht (ed. and trans.), *Letters to Beethoven and Other Correspondence*, vol. II, p. 228.

8 Letter of early May 1822; Anderson (trans. and ed.), *The Letters of Beethoven*, vol. II, pp. 946–7.

9 Letter of 23 January 1823; Albrecht (ed. and trans.), *Letters to Beethoven and Other Correspondence*, vol. II, p. 235.

10 Letter of 25 April 1823; Anderson (trans. and ed.), *The Letters of Beethoven*, vol. III, p. 1026.

11 Letter written some time between 3 and 27 June 1823; ibid., p. 1052.

12 Letter from Beethoven to Kiesewetter, 23 January 1824; ibid., pp. 1105–6.

13 Albrecht (ed. and trans.), *Letters to Beethoven and Other Correspondence*, vol. III, pp. 4–6.

14 Letter of 13 May 1824; Anderson (trans. and ed.), *The Letters of Beethoven*, vol. III, pp. 1124–5.

8 Facing death

1 Letter of 1 August 1824; Anderson (trans. and ed.), *The Letters of Beethoven*, vol. III, pp. 1134–5.

2 Letter of 17 September: ibid., p. 1141.

3 Letter to Galitzin, 26 May 1824; ibid., p. 1129.

4 Letter of 3 August 1824; Albrecht (ed. and trans.), *Letters to Beethoven and Other Correspondence*, vol. III, p. 49.

5 Letter from Beethoven to Karl, 31 May 1825; Anderson (trans. and ed.), *The Letters of Beethoven*, vol. III, p. 1202.

6 Ibid., p. 1329.

7 Letter of 1 February 1827; Albrecht (ed. and trans.), *Letters to Beethoven and Other Correspondence*, vol. III, p. 178.

8 Ibid., p. 196.

9 From the manuscript of the diary in the Österreichische Nationalbibliothek; kindly forwarded by Else Radant Landon.

10 Forbes (rev. and ed.), *Thayer's Life of Beethoven*, p. 1058.

General literature

Thayer's multi-volume biography of Beethoven in German first appeared over a hundred years ago, and remains the standard source. The most recent edition in English was prepared by Elliot Forbes and published under the title *Thayer's Life of Beethoven* (rev edn, 1967). Of the many one-volume biographies the one by Maynard Solomon is unfailingly stimulating: *Beethoven* (New York, 1977). *The Beethoven Compendium* (ed. B. Cooper; London, 1991) is an invaluable and very accessible reference volume with comprehensive lists of the composer's output, short essays on aspects of his life and music, plus an ample bibliography. H. C. Robbins Landon's *Beethoven. A Documentary Study* (London, 1970) is a lavishly produced volume containing illustrations, many in colour, of Beethoven, his patrons, his acquaintances, his music and his physical environment, together with a generous selection of extracts from contemporary and posthumous memoirs. For an up-to-date 'life and works' volume readers would be well advised to wait for Barry Cooper's book in the Master Musicians series due in 1999. *The Beethoven Newsletter*, produced by the Ira F. Brilliant Center for Beethoven Studies at San José University, California, is a model of its kind: authoritative and attractively presented. The centre also has a web site: http://www.music.sjsu.edu/beethoven/home_page.html

Specialized literature

Although Emily Anderson's translation and edition of Beethoven's letters is still indispensable (*The Letters of Beethoven*, 3 vols., London,

1961), it should be used in conjunction with the recently completed German edition of Beethoven's correspondence edited by Sieghard Brandenburg, *Ludwig van Beethoven. Briefwechsel Gesamtausgabe*, 7 vols. (Munich, 1996–8). Also of fundamental value is an English translation of letters addressed to Beethoven plus those of the composer discovered since Anderson prepared her edition: Theodore Albrecht (ed. and trans.), *Letters to Beethoven and Other Correspondence*, 3 vols. (Lincoln, Nebraska, 1996). Beethoven's conversation books are available in ten volumes, *Ludwig van Beethovens Konversationshefte* (Leipzig, 1972–93).

Ludwig Schiedermair's volume on Beethoven in Bonn remains a standard work, *Der junge Beethoven* (Leipzig, 1925). It is usefully supplemented by S. Brandenburg's essay 'Beethovens politische Erfahrungen in Bonn' in H. Lühning and S. Brandenburg, *Beethoven. Zwischen Revolution und Restauration* (Bonn, 1989), pp. 3–50, and Max Braubach's biography of Maximilian Franz (*Maria Theresias jüngster Sohn Max Franz*, Vienna, 1961). Rudolf Klein's *Beethovenstätten in Österreich* (Vienna, 1970) is a fascinating volume devoted to buildings in Vienna and its environs – apartments, theatres, inns etc. – associated with the composer. Julie Moore has written authoritatively on the complex issue of Beethoven's finances and the Austrian economy in general. Her essay, 'Beethoven and Inflation' is to be found in *Beethoven Forum* 1, ed. C. Reynolds, L. Lockwood and J. Webster (Lincoln, Nebraska, 1992); for further documentation see her doctoral thesis, 'Beethoven and Musical Economics' (University of Illinois, Urbana-Champaign, 1987). Two books are useful guides to concert life in Vienna in the period: Eduard Hanslick, *Geschichte des Concertwesens in Wien*, 2nd edn (Vienna, 1897) and Mary Sue Morrow, *Concert Life in Haydn's Vienna: Aspects of a Developing Musical and Social Institution* (Stuyvesant, New York, 1989). For a history of the theatre (including opera houses) see Franz Hadamowsky, *Wien. Theater Geschichte von den Anfängen bis zum Ende des ersten Weltkriegs*, special edn (Vienna, 1994). An interesting essay by the same author on censorship in Austria between 1751 and 1848 ('Ein Jahrhundert Literatur- und Theaterzensure in Österreich') can be found on pages 289–306 of the first volume of *Die österreichische Literatur. Ihr Profil an der Wende vom 18. zum 19. Jahrhundert (1750–1830)*, ed. H. Zeman (Graz, 1979).

Three valuable essays on Prince Lobkowitz as a patron of music are included in S. Brandenburg and M. Gutièrrez-Denhoff (eds.), *Beethoven*

und Böhmen. Beiträge zu Biographie und Wirkungsgeschichte Beethovens
(Bonn, 1988): Jaroslav Marek, 'Franz Joseph Maximilian Lobkowitz.
Musikfreund und Kunstmäzen', pp. 147–202; Tomislav Volek and
Jaroslav Macek, 'Beethoven und Fürst Lobkowitz', pp. 203–17; and Jana
Fojíková and Tomislav Volek, 'Die Beethoveniana der Lobkowitz-
Musiksammlung und ihre Kopisten', pp. 219–58. The volume also
contains an essay on the composer's visits to various Bohemian spas:
Sigrid Bresch, 'Beethovens Reisen zu den böhmischen Bädern in den
Jahren 1811 und 1812', pp. 311–45. The life and music of Beethoven's
other major patron, Archduke Rudolph, is covered in Susan Kagan,
Archduke Rudolph, Beethoven's Patron, Pupil, and Friend (Stuyvesant, New
York, 1988). For an account of music in Vienna immediately before and
during the Congress of Vienna see Michael Ladenburger, 'Der Wiener
Kongreß im Spiegel der Musik' in H. Lühning and S. Brandenburg,
Beethoven. Zwischen Revolution und Restauration, pp. 275–306. Dr Thomas
G. Palferman provides a useful summary of the composer's medical
history and final illness in 'Beethoven's Medical History; Themes and
Variations', Beethoven Newsletter 7 (1992), pp. 2–9.

Aachen 40, 175
Albinoni, Tomaso Giovanni 109
Albrechtsberger, Carl Friedrich 36
Albrechtsberger, Johann Georg 5, 30,
    35–6, 38, 40, 44, 47, 78, 108, 144
Allegri, Gregorio 36, 109, 140
Allgemeine musikalische Zeitung 48–9,
    54, 61, 68, 77, 119, 138
Allgemeine Theaterzeitung Wien 167
Amenda, Karl 58, 59, 65, 72
America 155
Amsterdam 5, 6
André 62, 72
Anfossi, Pasquale 6
Antibes 125
Apponyi, Count Anton Georg 43, 123
Arnim, Achim von 116
Artaria 16, 32, 42, 44, 60, 61, 62, 63,
    135, 147, 167, 173
Asplmayr, Franz 55
Attwood, Thomas 17
Auernhammer, Josepha 49
Augsburg 2, 18
Austerlitz 90
Austrian Netherlands 2, 39–40
Averdonk, Johanna Helena 5, 20
Averdonk, Severin Anton 20

Bach, Carl Philipp Emanuel 9–10
Bach, Johann Baptist 171, 172, 180
Bach, Johann Sebastian 8–9, 36, 37,
    61, 69, 74, 109

Bach, Wilhelm Friedemann 109
Baden (state) 90
Baden (town) 106, 114, 164, 171, 172,
    175, 177, 178
Bamberg 2
Basel 2
Bause, Johann Friedrich 7
Bavaria 2, 88, 90, 160, 161
Beethoven, Caspar Anton Carl van
    (brother) 4, 29, 38, 49, 63, 65,
    67–8, 131–2, 133
Beethoven, Johann van (father) 3–5,
    6, 8, 14, 29, 72, 103, 106
Beethoven, Johanna van (sister-in-
    law) 131–3, 143, 177, 179
Beethoven, Karl Franz van (nephew)
    126, 131–4, 143, 144, 157, 166,
    168, 171, 177, 178–9, 180
Beethoven, Ludwig van (grandfather)
    3–4, 5, 171, 178–9, 180
Beethoven, Ludwig van
    appearance 28, 53, 59, 90, 112, 121,
        173, 176
    deafness 57–9, 64–7, 86, 112, 115,
        126, 130–1, 145
    education 4–5, 8–10, 12, 17, 28–31,
        35–6
    finance 28–9, 33–4, 60, 73, 80,
        82–3, 96, 103, 110–12, 124,
        146–7, 168, 170
    health 18, 56–9, 95, 112, 114–15,
        126, 129–30, 142, 145–6, 163–4

love of nature 64, 114, 128–9, 164
personality 11, 19, 23, 39, 50,
  59–60, 65, 68–9, 92, 113–14, 116,
  130–1, 135, 137–8, 146, 169,
  176–7
as pianist 12, 23, 36, 44–5, 46,
  47–9, 100, 104
relationship with women 19, 59,
  85–6, 112–13
religious belief 10–11, 67, 129
as teacher 10, 59, 64, 107–8, 144,
  163, 173–4
WORKS (completed)
'Adelaide' (op. 46) 51, 125
'Ah perfido' (op. 65) 46, 99, 100
'An die Hoffnung' (op. 35) 85
Bagatelles (op. 119) 144
Bagatelles (op. 126) 174
Canon: 'Falstafferel, lass' ich dich
  sehen' (WoO 184) 162
Cantata on the accession of
  Leopold II (WoO 88) 21
Cantata on the death of Joseph II
  (WoO 87) 20–1
Cello Sonatas (op. 5) 46
Cello Sonatas (op. 102) 126
Choral Fantasy (op. 80) 79, 94, 139,
  164
Christus am Oelberge (op. 85) 71–3,
  77, 80, 126, 136, 138, 148, 149,
  168
Consecration of the House (op. 124)
  156, 157, 158, 164–5, 168 174
Coriolan (op. 62) 93, 97, 98, 99,
  100–1, 168
Der glorreiche Augenblick (op. 136)
  123, 135
Egmont (op. 84) 69, 115, 131, 138,
  148, 164, 168
Fidelio (op. 72) 69, 120–2, 123, 124,
  126, 135, 136, 156–7, 160, 168
Folksong settings 119, 127, 135, 136
'Für Elise' (WoO 59) 112
'Germania' (WoO 94) 120
Gratulations-Menuett (WoO 3) 156
'Grosse Fuge' (op. 133) 173, 174
Horn Sonata (op. 17) 44, 56, 60

'Ihr weisen Gründer' (WoO 95) 123
King Stephen (op. 117) 135, 136, 147
'Kriegslied der Oesterreicher'
  (WoO 122) 75
Leonore (op. 72) 86–91, 93, 96, 97,
  98, 120–2, 178, 181
Leonore Prohaska (WoO 96) 164
Marches for piano duet (op. 45) 82
Mass in C (op. 86) 94–5, 99, 100,
  136, 143, 149, 153, 161, 167, 168
Meeresstille und glückliche Fahrt (op.
  112) 148, 149, 152
Missa Solemnis (op. 123) 44,
  142–8, 152–4, 159–61, 162, 163,
  164, 165, 166–70, 174
Namensfeier (op. 115) 135, 136, 147
'Opferlied' (op. 121b) 156
Piano Concerto in E♭ (WoO 4) 21
Piano Concerto No. 1 (op. 15) 45,
  53–4, 98, 108
Piano Concerto No. 2 (op. 19) 21,
  45, 61, 78
Piano Concerto No. 3 (op. 37) 52,
  64, 69, 71, 78, 98, 108
Piano Concerto No. 4 (op. 58) 78,
  92, 93, 98, 99, 100, 108
Piano Concerto No. 5 (op. 73)
  ('Emperor') 94, 107, 108, 115,
  127, 138
Piano Quartets (WoO 36) 21
Piano Sonata in C minor (op. 13)
  (Sonate pathétique) 61
Piano Sonatas (op. 14) 56
Piano Sonata in B♭ (op. 22) 61
Piano Sonatas (op. 31) 62, 84
Piano Sonata in C (op. 53)
  ('Waldstein'), 81, 82, 83
Piano Sonata in F (op. 54) 83
Piano Sonata in F minor (op. 57)
  ('Appassionata') 83
Piano Sonata in E♭ (op. 81a) ('Les
  Adieux') 94, 107, 108
Piano Sonata in B♭ (op. 106)
  ('Hammerklavier') 126, 128, 137,
  140, 142
Piano Sonata in E (op. 109) 144,
  147, 151, 164, 175

Beethoven, Ludwig van (cont.)
Piano Sonata in Ab (op. 110) 147,
  151, 155, 174, 175
Piano Sonata in C minor (op. 111)
  147, 148, 151, 155, 164, 175
Piano Trios (op. 1) 38, 42–4, 45, 54,
  80, 159
Piano Trios (op. 70) 104
Piano Trio in Bb (op. 97)
  ('Archduke') 128, 135, 136
Prometheus (op. 43) 55–6, 72, 75, 98,
  119, 138
Quartets (op. 18) 51, 80, 162
Quartets (op. 59) ('Razumovsky')
  162
Quartet in Eb (op. 74) ('Harp') 107,
  162
Quartet in F minor (op. 95)
  ('Quartetto serioso') 128, 135
Quartet in Eb (op. 127) 151, 156, 164,
  171–2, 173, 174
Quartet in Bb (op. 130) 151, 156, 164,
  171–2, 173, 178
Quartet in C# minor (op. 131) 151,
  164, 171–2, 173, 178
Quartet in A minor (op. 132) 151,
  156, 164, 171–2, 173, 175, 178
Quartet in F (op. 135) 151, 164,
  171–2, 173, 175, 179
Quintet for piano and wind (op. 16)
  44, 46
Quintet in C (op. 29) 62, 162
Ritterballett (WoO 1) 20
The Ruins of Athens (op. 113) 120, 135,
  136, 147, 156, 164
Septet (op. 20) 52, 61, 63, 83, 162
Songs (op. 52) 82
Songs (op. 75) 115
Songs (op. 83) 115
String Trio in Eb (op. 3) 162
String Trios (op. 9) 80, 162
Symphony No. 1 (op. 21) 44, 51–2,
  54, 61, 71, 73, 80, 98, 148, 149
Symphony No. 2 (op. 36) 55, 64, 69,
  71, 73, 75, 77, 78, 92, 98, 119, 149
Symphony No. 3 (op. 55) (Eroica

Symphony) 74–6, 77, 78, 79, 80,
  81, 83, 84, 91, 93, 98, 107, 148,
  149
Symphony No. 4 (op. 60) 78, 92, 93,
  98, 138, 148, 149, 168
Symphony No. 5 (op. 67) 98–100,
  148, 149
Symphony No. 6 (op. 68) (Pastoral
  Symphony) 81, 98–100, 148, 149,
  156, 167
Symphony No. 7 (op. 92) 117, 119,
  120, 123, 124, 135, 136, 138, 139,
  148, 149
Symphony No. 8 (op. 93) 117, 120,
  135, 138, 149
Symphony No. 9 (op. 125)
  ('Choral') 69, 137, 151, 155, 162,
  164–5, 166–70, 174, 175, 176
'Tremate, empi, tremate' (op. 116)
  120, 135, 169
Triple Concerto (op. 56) 80, 83, 84,
  98, 138
Variations in Eb (op. 35)
  ('Prometheus', 'Eroica') 62, 74,
  75
Variations in F (op. 34) 62
Variations on 'God save the King'
  (WoO 78) 60, 118
Variations on a march by Dressler
  (WoO 63), 12
Variations on 'Rule, Britannia'
  (WoO 79) 60, 118
Variations on 'Se vuol ballare'
  (WoO 40) 32–3, 36, 42
Variations on a theme by Righini
  (WoO 65) 31–2
Variations on 'Tändeln und
  Scherzen' (WoO 76) 61
Variations on a waltz by Diabelli
  (op. 120) 137, 140–1, 143, 147,
  153
Violin Concerto in D (op. 61) 78,
  94, 98
Violin Sonata in A (op. 47) 74–5
Violin Sonata in G (op. 96) 135, 136
Waltz in Eb (WoO 84) 172

Wellington's Victory ('Battle
   Symphony') (op. 91) 118–20, 123,
   135, 167
Wind octet (op. 103) 33
Wind quintet (Hess 19) 33
WORKS (incomplete and
   contemplated)
The Apotheosis in the temple of Jupiter
   Ammon 157
Der Sieg des Kreuzes 151, 155, 165
Die schöne Melusine 165
Drahomira 165
Mass in A 82
Mass in C♯ minor 159
Oboe Concerto in F (Hess 12) 21, 33
'Östreich über alles' 105
Overture on B-A-C-H 173, 178
Piano Concerto in D (Hess 15) 127
Piano Trio in F minor 127
Polyhymnia oder die Macht der Töne 79
Quintet in C (WoO 62) 179
Romulus und Remus 126
Saul 173
Vestas Feuer (Hess 115) 77–8
Violin Concerto in C (WoO 5) 21
Vladimir the Great 157
Symphony in C 51–2
Symphony in C minor (Hess 298)
   22
Symphony in D minor 82
Symphony in E♭ ('No. 10') 173, 178
'Tantum ergo' 162
Beethoven (née Keverich), Maria
   Magdalena (mother) 4, 17–19
Beethoven, Nicolaus Johann (brother)
   4, 29, 46, 65, 67–8, 157–8, 168,
   171, 177, 179
Beldersbuch, Baron Kaspar Anton
   von 13
Berlin 5, 36, 37, 46, 115, 146, 150, 161,
   175
Berlioz, Hector 175
Bernadotte, Jean-Baptist 88
Bernard, Carl Joseph 147, 151, 165
Birchall, Robert 136
Blumenthal 91

Boccherini, Luigi 46
Bohemia 20, 80, 111, 114–16
Bolla, Maria 45
Bonaparte, Jerome 99, 102
Bonn 28, 30, 34, 38–41, 43, 49, 56, 57,
   64, 82, 94, 103, 146, 147, 159,
   175, 180
   Gymnasium 4
   Lesegesellschaft 20
   Tirocinium 4
Boston 155
Bouilly, Jean-Nicolas 79, 88
Braun, Baron Peter von 56, 70
Braun, Baroness Josephine 56
Breitkopf & Härtel 48, 61–2, 69, 74,
   75, 82, 83, 84–5, 95, 106, 117, 174
Brentano, Antonie 112–13, 115, 116,
   146
Brentano, Bettina 115, 116
Brentano, Franz 115, 116, 146
Breuning, Christoph von 25–6
Breuning, Stephan von 90, 120,
   178–9, 180, 183
Bridgetower, George Polgreen 74
Browne, Count Johann Georg 43, 44
Browne, Countess Anna Margarete 44
Brunsvick, Countess Anna 85, 86
Brunsvick, Count Franz 85
Brunsvick, Countess Therese 85
Brussels 36
Budapest 47, 60
Bureau des Arts et d'Industrie 60, 78,
   83, 94, 135
Busby, Thomas 176–7

Cäcilien-Verein 161
Caldara, Antonio 5, 36
Cambini, Giuseppe Maria 6
Campo Formio, Peace of 75
Cappi, Pietro 140
Carissimi, Giacomo 36
Carlsbad (Karlovy Vary) 115–16, 180
Cartellieri, Anton
   Gioas, rè di Giuda 45
Cassel 102–3, 161
Castlereagh, Robert Stewart 123

Catherine of Württemberg, Princess
102
Charpentier, Marc-Antoine 109
Chemische Druckerey 134
Chemnitz 7
Cherubini, Luigi 80, 92, 109, 118, 161
  Anacreon 107
  Eliza 76
  Faniska 90
  La prisonnière 76
  Les deux journées 76
  Lodoïska 76, 118
Cibulka 32
Cimarosa, Domenico 6
Clary, Josephine de 46
Clemens August, Elector 2
Clement, Franz 42, 47, 91–2, 107,
  138–9
Clementi, Muzio 45, 83–5, 93–4, 136
Collin, Heinrich 97, 105
Cologne 2, 14, 40
Concerts Spirituels 148–50, 151–3,
  167–8, 173
Congress of Vienna 122–5, 128, 134,
  136, 156, 164
Cooper, Barry 72
Cramer, Carl Friedrich 11
Crevelt, Johann Friedrich 26
Czerny, Carl 10, 46, 64, 107, 117, 133,
  140, 165, 167
Czerny, Joseph 147

Danube 57–8, 88, 106, 157, 179
Darmstadt 175
Daube, Johann Friedrich 109
Decker, Stephan 163
Deym, Count Joseph 74, 85
Deym (née Brunsvick), Countess
  Josephine 85–6
Diabelli, Anton 122, 139, 140–1, 147,
  167, 180
Die gute Nachricht 120, 121
Dietrichstein, Count Moriz von 97,
  158, 165, 167
Die wiedergefundene Tochter Otto des II.
  Kaisers der Deutschen 55

Dittersdorf, Carl Ditters von 32, 109
  Doktor und Apotheker 15
Dresden 7, 37, 46, 88
Duport, Jean-Louis 46
Dussek, Franz 109
Dussek, Josepha 42, 46

Eder 60
Edinburgh 84, 127
Eeden, Aegidius van den 5, 7
Eichner, Ernst 6
Eisenberg (Jezeří) 80
Eisenstadt 29, 31, 94
Elba 125
Engel, Johann Jakob 7
Erdödy, Count Peter 43, 147
Erdödy, Countess Anna Maria 104,
  147
Esterházy, Prince Anton 29
Esterházy, Princess Marie
  Hermenegild 94
Esterházy, Prince Nicolaus (II) 43,
  94–5, 161–2
Eybler, Joseph 32, 35, 47

Förster, Emanuel Aloys 51, 138, 140
France 2, 14, 175
Frank, Peter 56, 59
Frankfurt 146, 161, 175
Franz II (I), Emperor 38, 38, 90, 107,
  122, 158–9
Franzensbad (Františkovy) 115
French Revolution 24–5
Friedrich Wilhelm II, King 46, 99
Fries, Count Moritz Johann Christian
  62, 74
Fuchs, Johann Nepomuk 94
Fuss, Johann 126
Fux, Johann Joseph 36
  Gradus ad Parnassum 30, 35, 108

Galitzin, Prince Nikolaus
  Borisowitsch 156, 162, 171, 174
Galuppi, Baldassare 6
Galvani, Luigi 59
Gassmann, Florian Leopold 5, 109

Gebauer, Franz Xaver 148, 151–2
Gelinek, Abbé Joseph 139, 140
Gerber, Ernst Ludwig 148
Gesellschaft der Associierten 37, 93
Gesellschaft der Musikfreunde 78,
    126–7, 148, 149–50, 151, 155,
    165–6, 168, 173
Gewandhaus (Leipzig) 161
Giannattasio (family) 132
Gleichenstein, Baron Ignaz 103, 112,
    113, 147, 180
Gluck, Christoph Willibald 55, 158
Gneixendorf 157, 179
Goethe, Johann Wolfgang von 115–17,
    161
Goldoni, Carlo 6
Gossec, François-Joseph 6
Götz, Johann Michael 31
Grassalkovicz, Prince Anton 43
Grätz (Hradec u Opavy) 37, 92
Graun, Carl Heinrich 109
Grétry, André-Ernest-Modeste 6
    Richard Cœur-de-Lion 44
Griesinger, Georg August 48–9, 54,
    61–2, 79, 159
Grillparzer, Franz 165, 183
Grimm, Jacob 102
Grossmann, Georg Friedrich
    Wilhelm 6, 7, 8
Guglielmi, Pietro
    L'inganno amoroso 18
Guicciardi, Countess Giulietta 59,
    74
Gyrowetz, Adalbert 120

Hagen, Johann August 32
Haibel, Jakob
    Le nozze disturbate 44
Hamburg 7, 11
Hanau, Battle of 119
Handel, George Frideric 36, 37, 109,
    180–1
    Alexander's Feast 37
    The Choice of Hercules 37
    Judas Maccabaeus 37
    Messiah 107, 127

Ode for St Cecilia's Day 77, 92
    Samson 127
    Timotheus 118, 127
    Hanzmann 5
Häring 47
Härtel, Gottfried Christoph 61
Harrach, Count Karl Leonhard 43
Haslinger, Tobias 135, 147
Hasse, Johann Adolf 150
Haydn, Joseph 3, 5, 6, 7, 16, 17, 19, 21,
    23–4, 26–7, 29–36, 38, 40, 41,
    44, 45, 46, 47, 51–2, 61, 62, 63,
    69, 78, 79, 83, 94, 96, 101, 103,
    106, 108, 109, 138, 149–50, 151,
    152, 159, 162, 166, 167, 175, 180
    The Creation 53, 54, 72, 79, 98
    'Gott erhalte Franz den Kaiser' 75,
    122
    'Insanae et vanae curae' 144
    Quartets (op. 20) 50
    Quartets (op. 71 and op. 74) 31
    The Seasons 72, 79, 118
    Six late masses 94, 143
    Symphonies Nos. 93–8   23, 31
    Symphony No. 99   31
    Symphony No. 100 ('Military') 118
    Symphony No. 101 ('Clock') 31
    Variations in F minor 31
Haydn, Michael 16, 109
Heiligenstadt 64, 76, 114
Heiligenstadt Testament 65–9, 72, 12
Hellenthal 178
Hensler, Carl Friedrich 155–6
Herder, Johann Gottfried 25, 113
Hetzendorf 163, 165
Hiller, Johann Adam 7, 8
Hoffmeister, Franz Anton 54, 60–1,
    62, 63, 82, 135
Holland 2, 5
Holy Roman Empire 2–3, 13
Holz, Karl 178, 179, 180
Holzbauer, Ignaz 6
    Günther von Schwarzburg 6
Homer
    The Iliad 114, 129
Hummel (publisher) 5

Hummel, Joseph Nepomuk 35, 94,
120, 139, 140
Die Rückfahrt des Kaisers 122
Mass in B♭ 144
Iglau (Jihlava) 179
Italy 90, 114
Jahrbuch der Tonkunst von Wien und Prag
41, 47, 60
Jommelli, Niccolò 150
Jones, Sir William 129
Joseph II, Emperor 17, 20, 25, 55, 78
Josquin des Pres 140
Messe Gaudeamus 140
Junker, Carl Ludwig 22
Just, Johann August 32

Kalkbrenner, Frédéric 140
Kamper 152
Kanka, Johann Nepomuk 128
Kanne, Friedrich August 120, 147, 150
Kant, Immanuel
*Allgemeine Naturgeschichte und Theorie
des Himmels* 129
Karl VI, Emperor 140
Karlsruhe 175
Kiesewetter, Raphael Georg 165
Killitschky, Josephine 100
Kinsky, Prince Ferdinand Johann
Nepomuk 95, 103, 107, 110–11,
124, 147
Kinsky, Princess Maria Charlotte 111,
125
Kirnberger, Johann Philipp 36
Die Kunst des reinen Satzes 108
Klengel, Alexander 84
Koblenz 180
Koch, Willibald 5
Kolowrat-Liebsteinsky, Count Franz
Anton 111
Kozeluch, Leopold 16, 47, 56, 109
Kraft, Nicolaus 104, 123
Kreibig 47
Krems 157
Krommer, Franz 150
Kurzbeck, Magdalene 49

Landon, Else Radant 190
Lassus, Orlande de 36
Leipzig 7, 37, 46, 48, 54, 60–1, 82,
117, 147, 151, 159, 161
Leo, Leonardo 109
Leopold I, Emperor 107
Leopold II, Emperor 21, 25, 37, 55, 76
Lessing, Gotthold Ephraim 6
Lichnowsky, Prince Carl 37, 42–4, 45,
46, 49, 60, 64, 67, 72–3, 80, 92,
173
Lichnowsky, Prince Eduard Maria
167
Lichnowsky, Count Moritz 74, 168
Liebhaber Concerte 97–8, 149
Liechtenstein, Prince Johann Joseph
43
Linz 157
Liszt, Franz 140
Liverpool 136
Lobkowitz, Prince Franz Joseph
Maximilian 43, 74, 80–2, 92, 93,
97, 99, 103, 107, 110–12, 124, 147,
153
London 17, 21, 23–4, 25, 27, 29, 31,
34–5, 36, 41, 52, 63, 74, 83–4,
107, 118, 128, 136–7, 139, 150,
155, 162, 173, 176–6, 181
King's Theatre, Haymarket 63
Longford, Earl of 43
Loudon, Marshal 85
Louis XIV 2
Louis XVI 38
Lucchesi, Andreas 3, 7, 12, 14
Lully, Jean-Baptiste 140

Maelzel, Johann Nepomuk 117–19
Magazin der Musik 11–13, 139
Mainz 2, 147, 174, 175
Malfatti, Joseph Baptist 113, 114, 181
Malfatti, Therese 112, 113, 114
Mannheim 3, 5, 7, 12, 31
Maria Theresia, Empress 13
Marie Antoinette 38
Marie Therese, Empress 88
Martín y Soler, Vicente
Das Liebesfest in Catalonien 76

Die Insel der Liebe 76
L'arbore di Diana 15
Martini, Padre 150
Mastiaux, Johann Gottfried von 6–7,
  12, 23
Matthisson, Friedrich von 51, 156
Mattioli, Gaetano 12
Maximilian Franz, Archduke and
  Elector 2, 13–17, 19, 22, 23, 25,
  28, 29, 33–5, 38, 43, 49, 54, 107
Maximilan Friedrich, Elector 2, 13
Méhul, Etienne-Nicolas 54, 92
  Héléna 76
  Le trésor supposé 76
  L'irato 76
  Une folie 76
Melk 35
Metastasio, Pietro 77
Metternich, Clemens Wenzel 13, 123
Metternich-Winneburg, Franz Georg
  13
Meyer, Sebastian 79
Mödling 143, 144
Molière, Jean-Baptiste 6
Mollo, Tranquillo 60
Monsigny, Pierre-Alexandre 6
Moscheles, Ignaz 118, 139, 140, 175,
  181
Mosel, Ignaz 149
Mozart, Constanze 45, 61
Mozart, Franz Xaver Wolfgang 140
Mozart, Leopold 4
Mozart, Wolfgang Amadeus 3, 5,
  12–13, 19, 22, 23, 24, 26, 30, 32,
  37, 40, 41, 45, 51, 52, 53, 56, 61,
  69, 85, 92, 97–8, 101, 107, 109,
  120, 138, 149–50, 158, 162, 166,
  167
  Die Entführung aus dem Serail 6, 8, 76
  Die Maurerfreude 42
  Don Giovanni 15, 17–18, 22
  Idomeneo 131
  Il rè pastore 16
  La clemenza di Tito 45
  The Magic Flute 69, 76
  Le nozze di Figaro 15, 32
  Quintet in C (K515) 17

Müller, Wenzel 47
Münster 25
Musikalische Korrespondenz 22–3

Nägeli, Hans Georg 62, 82, 84, 174
Napoleon 76, 89, 98, 99, 102, 106,
  120, 125
Napoleonic wars 76, 88–90, 98,
  105–7, 108, 110, 118–20, 126, 175,
  181
Neate, Charles 136–7, 176
Neefe, Christian Gottlob 7–13, 14, 16,
  19, 20, 23, 50, 139, 147
  Adelheit von Veltheim 8
Neidl, Johann Joseph 53
Niemetschek, Franz Xaver Peter 109

Oberdöbling 76
Ober-Glogau (Głogówek) 92
Obrecht, Jacob 140
Odescalchi, Countess Anna Luise
  Barbara 44, 74
Oeser, Adam Friedrich 7
Offenbach 62
Olmütz (Olomouc) 107, 141, 144, 162,
  173
Onslow, André Georges Louis 162
Oppersdorff, Count Franz Joachim
  92, 98

Pachelbel, Johann 109
Paer, Ferdinando 88
  Camilla 104
Paisiello, Giovanni
  Il barbiere di Siviglia 15
  Il rè Teodoro 15, 22
  La molinara 44
  Le gare generose 18
Palestrina, Giovanni Pierluigi da 36,
  109, 140
Pálffy, Count Ferdinand 126, 167
Paradies, Therese 47
Paris 6, 36, 41, 76, 84, 94, 120, 122,
  125, 150, 161, 175
Partzel 32
Pasqualati, Baron Johann Baptist 180
Payne, Sandra Burney 176

Pensing 171
Pergen, Count Johann Anton 39
Peri, Jacopo 36
Peters 146–7, 159
Philharmonic Society (London) 136,
 137, 139, 155, 162, 176, 181
Philidor, François-André Danican 6
Piccinni, Niccolò 6
Pichl, Wenzel 109
Pleyel, Ignaz 22, 30, 32, 94, 109
Ployer, Babette 17
Polledro, Giovanni Battista 115
Potsdam 37
Poussin 117
Prague 46, 47, 80, 88, 114, 128
Preindl, Joseph 144
Pressburg (Bratislava) 47, 156
Probst, Heinrich Adalbert 147
Prussia 2, 14, 160
Punto, Wenzel 60

Rameau, Jean-Philippe 109
Raphael 117
Rau, Sebastian 181
Raudnitz (Roudnice) 80
Rauhenstein 179
Rauscher 152
Razumovsky, Count Andreas 43, 92,
 123
Recke, Elisa von der 115
Reichardt, Johann Friedrich 99–101,
 104–5
 Bradamante 104
Regensburg 118
Reutter, Georg 5, 159
Ries, Ferdinand 64, 84, 102, 136, 137,
 150, 155, 162, 175
Ries, Franz Anton 22, 64
Righini, Vicenzo 22, 31
Ritter, Peter 32
Rochlitz, Johann Friedrich 77
Rode, Jacques-Pierre Joseph 91
Rohrau 180
Romberg, Bernard Heinrich 138
Rosenbaum, Johann Carl 89, 95, 105,
 181

Rosetti, Antonio 16, 32
Rossini, Gioachino
 Elisabetta, regina d'Inghliterra 138
 Il barbiere di Siviglia 138
 L'italiana in Algeri 138
 Otello 138
 Tancredi 138, 169
Royal Swedish Academy of Music 159
Rudnay, Archbishop Alexander 161
Rudolph, Archduke Johann Joseph
 Rainer 103, 105, 107–10, 114, 117,
 128, 140, 141–5, 148, 153, 158,
 162, 163, 173–4
 Variations on 'O Hoffnung' 142
 Violin Sonata in F minor 108
Russia 156

Salieri, Antonio 30, 40, 47, 78, 109
 Axur, re d'Ormus 15
 Der Tyroler Landsturm 75
 Falstaff 44
 La grotta di Trofonio 15
Salomon, Johann Peter 21, 23–4, 25,
 63, 136
Salzburg 2, 16
Saurau, Count Franz Joseph 39
Schaden, Baron Joseph Wilhelm 18
Schikaneder, Emanuel 69, 70, 75,
 76–7
Schiller, Friedrich von 6
 'An die Freude' 164
Schindler, Anton 158, 160, 161, 163–4,
 166, 168–9, 180, 183
Schlemmer, Wenzel 147, 161
Schlesinger, Adolf 146–7, 174, 175
Schlesinger, Moritz 175
Schmidt, Johann Adam 59, 64, 95
Schneider, Friedrich 151
Schönfeld, Count Johann van 48
Schönfeld, Therese 74
Schott 147, 172, 174, 179, 181
Schubert, Franz 140
Schultz, Johann Reinhold 176
Schuppanzigh (father) 29
Schuppanzigh, Ignaz 29, 85, 101, 104,
 147, 162, 167, 168, 173, 178

Schwarzenberg, Prince Joseph
    Johann Nepomuk 41
Schwarzenberg, Princess Caroline
    Iris 43
Sebald, Amalie 115
Seipelt 152
Seyfried, Ignaz 35, 70, 97, 109, 152
    Zum goldenen Löwen 90
Shakespeare, William 6
Siegen 2
Simrock, Nicolaus 1, 15–16, 22, 42,
    82, 94, 146, 159, 174, 175
Smart, Sir George 128, 136–7, 176, 181
Solomon, Maynard 112
Sonnleithner, Christoph 78
Sonnleithner, Joseph 78–9, 83, 87–8,
    90, 120, 122
Speyer 22
Spielmann, Baron Anton 97
Spohr, Louis 150, 161
Sporschil, Johann Chrysostomus 157
Stackelberg, Baron Christoph 86
Stadler, Anton 56
Stadler, Maximilian 74, 140, 167
    Die Befreyung von Jerusalem 127, 138
Stamitz, Johann 6
Starzer, Joseph 55
Steibelt, Daniel 45, 54
Steiner, Sigmund Anton 134–5, 136,
    138, 140, 146–7, 167, 183
Steffan, Joseph Anton 109
St Petersburg 156, 162, 171, 174
Strauss, Joseph 91
Streicher, Johann Andreas 48, 173
Strumpff, Johann 176
Stuttgart 3, 48, 175
Süssmayr, Franz Xaver
    Moses 71, 72
    Solomon II 44
Swieten, Gottfried van 36–7, 43, 54,
    78, 93

Talleyrand, Charles Maurice 123
Teplitz (Teplice) 114–16
Teyber, Anton 107, 158
Thomson, George 84–5, 119, 127, 136

Thun, Count Franz Joseph 43
Thun, Countess Maria Wilhelmine 44
Tiedge, Christoph August 115
Tomasini, Luigi 29
Tonkünstler-Societät 42, 45, 52
Traeg, Johann 31, 60
Trauttmansdorff, Prince Ferdinand
    97
Treitschke, Georg Friedrich 121–2,
    126, 160
Trier 2
Troyes 117
Tübingen 48, 175
Tuma, Franz 5
Türk, Daniel Gottlieb
    Kürze Anweisung zum Generalbass 108

Umlauf, Michael 157
Unger, Caroline 168

Vanhal, Johann Baptist 6, 32
Varena, Joseph Ignaz 115
Varnhagen, Karl August 115
Vering, Gerhard von 56, 59
Vienna 1, 14–17, 23–4
    Allgemeines Krankenhaus 179
    Alsergasse 28, 132, 183
    Augarten 54, 74, 168
    Augustinerkirche 148, 149, 152
    Burgtheater 42, 45, 52, 54, 55–6,
        71, 72, 79, 93, 105
    Carmelite Church 35
    Freihaus 69
    Glacis 69, 178, 183
    Graben 105
    Gumpendorf 105
    Herrengasse 149
    Hofburg 80, 108
    Hofkapelle 47
    Hungarian Chancellery 50
    Josephplatz 89
    Josephstadt 155, 157, 158
    Kärntnerstrasse 50
    Kärntnertortheater 42, 71, 79, 80,
        90, 93, 117, 120, 122, 156, 168
    Laimgrube 62, 89

Vienna (cont.)
  Landständischer Saal 149, 152,
    168
  Landstrasse 17, 132
  Lobkowitz palace 80, 93, 104–5
  Mehlgrube 97, 149
  Minoritenkirche 183
  Neuer Markt 97, 149
  Paternostergassel 134
  Polytechnic 177
  Prater 168–9
  Redoutensaal 45, 93, 120, 123, 168
  Schauflergasse 37
  Schönbrunn palace 89, 106, 171
  Schottenkirche 47
  Schottentor 178
  Schwarzspanierhaus 178, 180, 183
  St Marx hospital 123
  St Stephen's 35, 144
  Theater an der Wien 69–72, 74, 76,
    79–80, 87, 89–91, 93, 98–101,
    106–7, 117, 168
  Theater auf der Wieden 69
  University 97, 117, 139, 177
  Währing 183
  Wasserkunstbastei 29
  Winter Riding School 89
  'Zum weissen Schwann' 50, 84
Viganò, Salvatore 55
Viotti, Giovanni Battista 80
Vittoria, Battle of 118
Vivaldi, Antonio 109
Vogler, Abbé Georg Joseph 23, 70–1,
    109, 149
  The Evocation of the midnight sun in
    Lapland 79
  The Praise of Harmony 79
Voltaire (François Marie Arouet) 6

Waldstein, Count Ferdinand Ernst 17,
    20, 23, 24, 26–7, 37
Warsaw 36
Waterloo, Battle of 125
Weber, Carl Maria von 30
Weber, Edmund von 30
Weber, Fritz von 30

Weber, Wilhelm 156
Wegeler (née Breuning), Eleonore
    Brigitte (Lorchen) 19, 25, 32, 36,
    37, 49, 180
Wegeler, Franz Gerhard 1, 19, 49–50,
    56–9, 60, 68, 72, 180
Weigl, Joseph 35, 56, 97, 105, 120
  Die Weihe der Zukunft 122
  'Österreich über alles' 105
Weimar 161
Weiss 152
Weiss, Franz 162
Weitersfeld 134
Wellington, Duke of 118
Werner, Gregor 30
Westphalia 99, 102–3
Wetzlar, Baron Raimund 74
(Wiener) Allgemeine musikalische Zeitung
    138–40, 141, 150, 152–3, 165,
    167, 170, 173, 175
Wiener Zeitung 31, 45, 62, 131
Wild, Franz 125
Wilde, Josef 139
Wineberger, Paul Anton 22
Winter, Peter
  Das Labyrinth 76
  Das unterbrochene Opferfest 44
Wölfl, Joseph 49
Wranitzky, Anton 30
Wranitzky, Paul 52, 56
  Das Waldmädchen 44, 56
  'Grande sinfonie caractéristique
    pour la paix avec la République
    française' 175
Württemberg 90, 160
Würzburg 2

Zarlino, Gioseffo 109
Zelter, Carl Friedrich 115, 116, 161
Zensen 5
Zielinska, Countess Henriette 95
Zimmermann, Anton 109
Zmeskall von Domanovecz, Nikolaus
    Paul 50, 85, 128, 130, 135, 147,
    167
Zurich 62, 82, 84